Making the World Safe for Dictatorship

Making the World Safe for Dictatorship

ALEXANDER DUKALSKIS

OXFORD

UNIVERSITY PRESS

OXFORD
UNIVERSITY PRESS

Oxford University Press is a department of the University of Oxford. It furthers
the University's objective of excellence in research, scholarship, and education
by publishing worldwide. Oxford is a registered trade mark of Oxford University
Press in the UK and certain other countries.

Published in the United States of America by Oxford University Press
198 Madison Avenue, New York, NY 10016, United States of America.

Library of Congress Cataloging-in-Publication Data
Names: Dukalskis, Alexander, author.
Title: Making the world safe for dictatorship / Alexander Dukalskis.
Description: New York, N.Y. : Oxford University Press, 2021. |
Includes bibliographical references. |
Identifiers: LCCN 2020051765 (print) | LCCN 2020051766 (ebook) |
ISBN 9780197520130 (hardback) | ISBN 9780197520161 (oso) | ISBN 9780197520147 (updf) |
ISBN 9780197520154 (epub)
Subjects: LCSH: Authoritarianism—Public relations. |
Authoritarianism—Press coverage. | Mass media and propaganda. |
Mass media and public opinion.
Classification: LCC JC480 .D85 2021 (print) | LCC JC480 (ebook) |
DDC 320.53—dc23
LC record available at https://lccn.loc.gov/2020051765
LC ebook record available at https://lccn.loc.gov/2020051766

DOI: 10.1093/oso/9780197520130.001.0001

1 3 5 7 9 8 6 4 2

Printed by Integrated Books International, United States of America

Contents

Contents

Acknowledgments

Books take a long time to research and write, so some people mentioned here may not even remember that they helped me. But I remember and I am grateful to them for their time, generosity, and intellect. As is customary, all errors and shortcomings are my own and no one mentioned in the following should be held responsible for them.

Many people provided feedback on draft chapters, working papers, and/ or conference papers that ultimately comprised this book. I'd like to thank (in alphabetical order): Fiona Adamson, Julia Bader, Darren Byler, Marie-Eve Desrosiers, Julia Grauvogel, Kingsley Edney, Sandra Fahy, Saipira Furstenberg, Johannes Gerschewski, Seva Gunitsky, John Heathershaw, Edward Howell, Seraphine Maerz, Maria Repnikova, Andy Storey, Oisín Tansey, Ben Tonra, Ernesto Verdeja, Christian von Soest, and Yaqiu Wang. Participants in the 2019 European Consortium for Political Research Joint Sessions workshop "Authoritarianism Beyond the State" provided insights and comments that improved the project. Colleagues at UCD provided helpful comments when I presented this project there in February 2020. Two anonymous reviewers for OUP read the manuscript closely and provided useful suggestions. Many thanks to Angela Chnapko at OUP for seeing value in the project and shepherding it through to completion.

Several people helped facilitate my fieldwork in Japan. I owe Markus Bell a particularly deep debt of gratitude for introducing me to colleagues and contacts and explaining Chongryon and the Korean community in Japan to me. Apichai Shipper, Kanae Doi, and several others were generous with their time and trust. Ryo Watanuki provided excellent research assistance. And, of course, I am truly appreciative of the people who agreed to be interviewed to help me understand Chongryon.

For research in China, I will not identify names, but if you are reading this and recognize yourself in the pages that follow, please know that I am grateful for your time and generosity.

Several people helped this project by contributing excellent research assistance. Eman Abboud, Junhyoung Lee, and Redmond Scales were instrumental in constructing the Authoritarian Actions Abroad Database. Emily

Weinstein, Mathieu Doogan, Emir Yazici, and Artur Holavin all contributed by searching non-English media for new cases and verifying details of existing ones. Junhyoung Lee and Redmond Scales helped to gather FARA filings, track down North Korean friendship groups, and organize references. Many thanks to all of you. Thanks also to Amanda Bell for constructing the index.

This project was assisted with funding from Enterprise Ireland (project CS20192051) and UCD's Output-Based Research Support Scheme.

Finally, I would like to thank my wife Laura and our son Felix. As the child of two academics, Felix is getting used to us talking about grants, articles, books, teaching, administrative duties, and the other particulars of academic life. One photograph that sticks in my mind from the period spent writing this book is one of Felix (then two and a half years old) looking directly into my eyes and plugging his ears as I explain to the family in apparently excruciating detail the finer points of North Korea's foreign relations with Japan. Thanks to you both—to Laura for listening and to Felix for reminding me that I had better work on presenting things in a more compelling way.

About the Companion Website

A companion website housing the following appendices referenced in the book can be found at https://alexdukalskis.wordpress.com/data/

Appendix 1. Authoritarian Actions Abroad Database

1

Introduction

Making the World Safe for Dictatorship

In March 2018, Saudi women's rights activist Loujain al-Hathloul was detained by authorities in the United Arab Emirates, where she had been living. She was abducted and deported back to Saudi Arabia, where she was arrested, tortured, and threatened (Michaelson 2019). She had been an important figure advocating for an end to Saudi Arabia's ban on female driving and its system of male guardianship, which stipulates that women must have the consent of a male guardian to undertake a range of legal and administrative activities (Human Rights Watch 2016). Al-Hathloul was not the only critic of the Saudi government to be targeted outside the kingdom's borders, as the well-known murder of journalist Jamal Khashoggi in Turkey and several other cases illustrate (Graham-Harrison 2018b). These actions came in the context of Mohammad bin Salman's rise to the top of Saudi politics and his determination to remake the kingdom's image. Activists and critics—even those residing abroad—were to be silenced, lest they call into question the crown prince's preferred political narrative.

In Kazakhstan's 2011 presidential election, the incumbent Nursultan Nazarbayev won, with over 95% of the vote. Nazarbayev had already been president for two decades and the outcome of this election was never in serious doubt. Shortly after that election, the Kazakh government contracted with former United Kingdom prime minister Tony Blair and a host of other foreign public relations (PR) and consulting specialists (Corporate Europe Observatory 2015). Blair spoke up publicly for Kazakhstan on several occasions, particularly if the country's human rights record came in for criticism. He especially liked to frame Kazakhstan's progress in terms of development and stability (Silverstein 2012). The country's PR consultants produced YouTube videos highlighting Kazakhstan's development and organized and promoted international events in the country designed to bolster its prestige and present a positive image. Two PR firms apparently even changed

Making the World Safe for Dictatorship, Alexander Dukalskis, Oxford University Press (2021). © Oxford University Press.
DOI: 10.1093/oso/9780197520130.003.0001

Wikipedia entries to portray Kazakhstan's leaders and their actions in a more favorable light (Tynan 2012).

Russia's Internet Research Agency (RIRA) came to international prominence for its attempts to influence the 2016 United States presidential election. The organization is a "troll farm" in which paid internet commentators attempt to distort online conversations, in part by posting intentionally misleading or distracting content. This has been going on in the domestic politics of authoritarian states for quite some time (Gunitsky 2015). While the RIRA is primarily concerned with domestic opponents, it also attempts to influence international discourse about Russia and its rivals (Chen 2015; Pomerantsev 2019, 33–40). The posts are not so much meant to bolster Russia's image or extol the virtues of its leader Vladimir Putin—although they may do that, too—but rather to distract and distort public conversations so that criticisms of Russia are relativized or buried entirely (Haynes 2018). When Russia is implicated in something harmful, such as the shooting down of Malaysian Airlines Flight 17 over Ukrainian airspace in 2014, its internet troll farms help muddy the waters of public discourse abroad so that it is more difficult to focus on Russian culpability.

In November 2018, an assistant professor at University College Dublin received an email from the Chinese embassy in Ireland inviting him on a trip to China, along with about 10 other "Irish friends," including politicians, academics, business leaders, and journalists. The idea behind the trip was "to find the achievements since China's reform and opening-up 40 years ago, and also to experience the exchanges and cooperation between Chinese mainland and Taiwan Province." Details were still being determined, the message explained, but the embassy would cover all costs, including flights and accommodation. Here was a clear effort to show China in its most positive light to a local political scientist, with the unwritten implication that he would return to teaching at the local university, commenting in media, and carrying out research with that positive experience in mind. I did not accept the invitation.

What do all these episodes have in common? Despite their apparent differences, they are each a part of what this book calls "authoritarian image management." They reveal the diversity of tactics that authoritarian governments use to influence how they are perceived abroad. Authoritarian image management is about more than just telling a good story about the country, although that is certainly a big part of it, as the Kazakh example illustrates. It is also about cultivating specific individuals or groups to promote the government's perspectives, such as when the Chinese embassy invited me to visit China.

More than just advancing flattering information about the state, it also involves trying to censor or distract from bad news about the country abroad, as the RIRA and other similar entities attempt to do. Authoritarian image management additionally involves protecting the state's preferred image from criticism by silencing or undermining citizens critical of the government abroad, as the case of Loujain al-Hathloul illustrates. Authoritarian governments use these tactics in combination with one another to mitigate perceived threats to their security. While the tactics appear compartmentalized, thus allowing "respectable" PR firms and opinion leaders to distance themselves from torturers and murders, each tactic is an integral part of a single strategy. Autocrats try to make their world safe for dictatorship by disseminating positive messages and messengers and undermining critical messages and messengers.

Ever since Joseph Nye pioneered thinking about "soft power" in the early 1990s, observers have had a new language to understand the public relations efforts of states (Nye 1990). Tactics to enhance soft power, or the ability to achieve one's aims through attraction rather than coercion, have long been used by all states, including authoritarian ones (Nye 1990, 167). For example, the Soviet Union's early external propaganda apparatus featured carefully crafted trips for foreign visitors to show off Soviet achievements and ideology (David-Fox 2012). This sat alongside external propaganda containing material that sometimes resonated because it was accurate (such as stressing the United States' racial discrimination) or because it convincingly portrayed the Soviet experiment as exciting and successful. These strategies helped increase the attractiveness of the Soviet Union among a select group of Western observers and opinion leaders, particularly before Stalin's Great Terror in the late 1930s.

Concepts like soft power or public diplomacy, which entails engaging directly with foreign publics (Melissen 2005; Nye 2008), take us part of the way to understanding authoritarian image management. So do arguments that states "brand" themselves (van Ham 2002) or "frame" themselves (Jourde 2007) in particular ways to enhance their international appeal. But these concepts when applied to authoritarian states leave much to be desired. They leave out deception and the harsh—even occasionally murderous—realities of authoritarian image management.

Authoritarian states engage not only in anodyne public diplomacy, branding, or framing to influence their images; they also try to police the information environment into which they disseminate their messages. Dictatorships try to eliminate or refute criticisms of their rule in the international public sphere. From the state's perspective, the ideal international context would be one in which there are no serious criticisms of its political system, or prominent exiles trying to frustrate the state's latitude to do as it wishes. Sticking with the Soviet example, Moscow not only used various tactics associated with soft power and public diplomacy (in today's vocabulary), but also engaged in disinformation campaigns and sometimes threatened or even assassinated exiled critics of the government, the most famous of whom was Leon Trotsky, who met his end in Mexico City in 1940 at the hands of a Soviet agent wielding an ice pick.

Even in terms of communication alone, the softer concepts as applied to authoritarian states can seem naïve and incomplete. As the new concept of "sharp power" highlights, authoritarian states are not always transparent or honest about the information they produce, and sometimes they are trying to distract or discredit rather than persuade (Walker 2018; see also Michaelsen and Glasius 2018). For example, South Africa's Apartheid government undertook a multidimensional effort to burnish its image and deflect criticism around the world (Nixon 2016). This included familiar tools of soft power and public diplomacy, such as hiring PR firms, inviting key opinion leaders on "fact finding trips" to South Africa, buying advertising space in foreign publications, and hiring spokespeople to defend the government against criticism. But it also included efforts like funding think tanks abroad to produce positive research about South Africa without making funding sources clear. The Apartheid government's information ministry attempted to secretly purchase a major American newspaper while obscuring its ownership through layers of financial deception. The government and its foreign spokespeople worked to discredit anti-Apartheid activists as a part of a wider communist threat amid the polarization of the Cold War. The government's efforts moved beyond standard visions of soft power or public diplomacy and embraced tactics for which those concepts are ill-suited to explain.

The concept of authoritarian image management is meant to bring the full range of tactics that authoritarian states use to bolster or protect their images abroad into the same analytical frame. It can be defined as *comprising efforts by the state or its proxies to enhance or protect the legitimacy of the state's political system for audiences outside its borders.* This includes not only the classic strategies of external propaganda or public diplomacy, but also the extraterritorial censorship and repression meant to shape the international information environment relevant to that state's image. This book will argue that examples like the case of Loujain al-Hathloul, Kazakhstan's public relations blitz, the RIRA's foreign trolling, and my invitation to "learn" about China all reside in the same realm of comprehensibility and are options available to dictators looking to bolster their regime security by shaping their image abroad.

This book is about how authoritarian states try to cultivate a positive image of themselves abroad and attempt to protect that image from criticism. It is wide-ranging and exploratory in the sense that it discusses several cases of different sizes, political systems, and geographic locations, as well as providing cross-national data on different modalities of authoritarian image management. However, in a theoretical sense it is more tightly focused on arguing for the importance of authoritarian image management as a concept and providing tools to study it. The theoretical frameworks developed in this book can put the four vignettes presented at the outset of this book into the same analytical domain in ways that competing theories have difficulty doing.

So What, or Why Keep Reading?

Why should we care how authoritarian states try to make themselves look good abroad?[1] The most obvious answer is that it matters for the well-being and rights protections of citizens what type of political regime they inhabit. If the image management efforts of authoritarian states succeed, then it increases the likelihood that more people will live in authoritarian political systems in the future. It is already the case that more than roughly one out of every three people in the world lives in an authoritarian state (Freedom House 2019, 8), and it is worth understanding how that experience is being packaged and promoted abroad for clues about authoritarianism's appeal and power. This matters for understanding the resilience of authoritarian regimes globally. Scholars have made much progress in understanding the

---

[1] While recognizing that there are terminological and typological debates, this book will use the words like "dictatorship," "authoritarianism," and "autocracy" interchangeably to mean broadly nondemocratic political systems. Chapter 4 and Appendix 2 discuss in more detail the inclusion/exclusion criteria for cases.

international sources of authoritarian stability, and this book contributes to that tradition.

Political science scholars will benefit from having new conceptual tools to analyze the foreign policies of authoritarian states. The book will help us connect concepts like authoritarian soft power or public diplomacy to concepts like extraterritorial repression. It will also help us understand how authoritarian states influence global norms and international public discourse. The conventional wisdom for much of the 1990s and the first decade of the 2000s held that authoritarian states mimicked the norms of democracy to legitimize their rule. This entailed encouraging foreign audiences to view the state as democratic. So long as authoritarian states conform on paper to the norms of democracy, then the challenge to democratic norms is less severe. At least the rules of the game are acknowledged, even if in practice they are violated using the "menu of manipulation" (Schedler 2002) or the "autocratic menu of innovation" (Morgenbesser 2020a).

However, given the global rise of China as an unapologetically authoritarian state, the normative terrain is rapidly changing. There is no authoritarian alliance trying to make a world of dictatorships, but China is so big, politically important, and globally ambitious that political spillovers are almost unavoidable. Understanding how the international normative environment enables China's political vision, and how aggressively Beijing attempts to defend that vision, is necessary in order to grasp the political dynamics of the twenty-first century. China is not the only case analyzed in this book, but it is so important that two chapters are devoted to understanding various aspects of its authoritarian image management.

Finally, as the book's conclusion will elaborate upon, the targets of authoritarian image management efforts should care about this research. Authoritarian states try to influence policymakers, manipulate the work of journalists, and convince broader publics that their authoritarian political systems are not that bad after all. Knowing the lengths to which authoritarian regimes go in their attempts to make the world safe for dictatorship will help inform the ways in which information is produced and consumed.

Clarifying Concepts and Definitions

As the vignettes at the outset of this chapter indicate, authoritarian image management is a multidimensional concept that includes numerous kinds of behaviors. It can best be understood as an analytical framework that brings multiple related concepts into the same realm of analysis. Chapter 3 will address these issues in more detail, but at the outset it useful to clarify that authoritarian image management efforts may include state-driven soft power and public diplomacy initiatives, foreign-facing propaganda, the cultivation of key opinion leaders overseas, extraterritorial or other types of censorship that aim to control bad news about the state abroad, and/or repression of particularly threatening messengers of critical ideas abroad. To move beyond the often-siloed analytical categories of soft power, public diplomacy, extraterritorial repression, foreign influence, and so on, an umbrella concept helps bring these activities into the same sphere of concern. Many authoritarian states do all these things to burnish and police their image abroad, so it seems unsatisfactory to examine them in isolation from one another. Doing so misses the forest for the trees. It also obscures connections between methods and the ways in which they can bolster or undermine one another.

However, as an umbrella concept, one might object that authoritarian image management risks including so much that it undermines its analytical utility. Put more bluntly, one might ask what kinds of actions do *not* count as authoritarian image management? Although there are unavoidable gray areas, the basic requirement for an action to be defined as such is that it must concern the international sphere and must relate primarily to protecting or enhancing the state's preferred political image, narrative, or perceived unassailability abroad.

Some examples may clarify the point. Authoritarian image management excludes domestic repression of citizens but includes what the state says abroad about its repression. It excludes official promotion or branding that is purely about tourism, or promoting a product or company that does not directly relate to the politics of the state. It includes repressing citizens abroad who are critical of the state or have the potential to undermine its image by virtue of their identity. But it excludes trying to arrest or repress non-political criminals abroad, fighting a rebel group in a neighboring state, assassinating a violent terrorist or rebel leader or organized crime leader abroad, or gathering intelligence on any of these. It includes trying to lobby or flatter a foreign decision-maker or opinion shaper so that s/he views the state more positively, but it excludes cases in which an opinion leader views that state positively on his/her own terms without influence by the state. It includes external media outlets owned and/or editorially controlled by the state, but excludes media outlets editorially independent of the government.

It includes a government trying to coerce a foreign company to adopt or renounce a political stance under threat of losing market access, but it excludes that same government denying market access to a company for a host of other non-political or regulatory reasons. Obviously, there are borderline areas and cases in all these domains, but at their root, authoritarian image management activities should be state-directed and connected to enhancing a dictatorship's image or protecting it from criticism abroad.

Clarifications and Caveats

All research efforts are limited in what they can explain. It is worthwhile to be transparent about these so that the reader knows what to expect. For this book, three clarifications should be acknowledged at the outset.

First, the book does not address the image management efforts of democracies. This is not to say that democratic states do not care about their images; far from it. Democracies engage in public diplomacy, hire public relations firms, and are worried if they have a negative image abroad. Particularly during the Cold War, for example, the United States undertook a multidimensional effort to make its political system look positive to foreign audiences (Parker 2016). The practices and innovations of authoritarian states designed to erode accountability often find counterparts in democratic states (Glasius 2018a; Morgenbesser 2020a). However, as Chapter 2 will make clear, in today's world, authoritarian states have extra incentives to engage in image management. Rhetorically at least, democracy is still a preferred global norm, and so the case for authoritarian norms is a defensive one at minimum and an insurgent one at most. Making the world safe for dictatorship is an existential endeavor for leaders of authoritarian regimes.

Furthermore, the tactics of authoritarian regimes are likely to differ. Most contemporary democracies are more restrained in what they can and will do in this realm. For example, with a few notable exceptions, today's democracies generally do not threaten or assassinate their exiled critics. This is primarily because they have fewer exiles to begin with, but also because citizens in democratic states can generally already criticize their governments without fear of reprisal. Free speech protections in consolidated democracies mean that governments have less control over the type of information that can be reported about them in the global public sphere. The point here is not that democracies are perfect or that they do not try to manipulate their image, but rather that the dynamics of image management differ between democracies and non-democracies. The latter is interesting and important enough to deserve its own book.

Second, a persistent question is how effective the methods of authoritarian image management are. It is difficult to answer this question in the vocabulary of causal effect size. This book does not approach the question with the aim to understand whether the world is x% safer or less safe for dictatorship. Rather, it focuses on process. As Chapter 3 will explain, there are clear causal mechanisms that undergird the various tactics of authoritarian image management. This means that "success" needs to be thought of as context-dependent given the tactic in question. From a big-picture perspective, one could construct global measurements and use proxy data to test the success of authoritarian image management. However, the topic would first benefit from more conceptual development and exploration of causal mechanisms.

Third, studying authoritarian regimes necessarily entails data limitations. They are secretive by nature, and so scholars of dictatorship often must find creative ways to gather the data they need to substantiate arguments. Obscuring information is a feature of authoritarian systems, not a bug. Overcoming the challenge is made more severe when studying the actions that authoritarian states have special incentive to hide. Some dimensions of authoritarian image management fit this precise category. Extraterritorial repression, for example, or covertly influencing a key decision-maker, are actions that are usually not designed to be public. This challenge is inherent, which means that it is undoubtedly the case that the data in this book are incomplete. It is hoped that this limitation is mitigated by bringing different kinds of data from different angles to the question. Indeed, because authoritarian image management is characterized by diverse tactics, multidimensional data are necessary to begin to understand it. At various points, the book uses interviews conducted by the author, a cross-national events database built from public media and nongovernmental organization (NGO) sources, corporate documents registered with the US federal government, primary government documents and speeches by political leaders of authoritarian states, analysis of foreign-facing propaganda, media frequency analysis, and process tracing using secondary sources. The aim is to foster a well-rounded understanding of authoritarian image management, however imperfect the data may be.

Chapter Preview

The remainder of this book is organized in eight subsequent chapters. Chapter 2 builds the theoretical foundation to understand authoritarian image management. Scholarship on authoritarian legitimation and on autocracy promotion both suggest that authoritarian image management is important to analyze. The bulk of the chapter addresses the motivations to engage in authoritarian image management and argues, drawing on Owen (2010), that authoritarian states do so for both internal security (to bolster their domestic rule) and external security (to help build a friendlier international environment for their policies). In doing so, it argues that authoritarian states in the post–Cold War era have special incentives to manage their image abroad given the predominance of democracy as an international norm.

How exactly do authoritarian states manage their image abroad, and what are the causal chains linking their activities to their desired outcomes of internal/external security? Chapter 3 proposes four sets of mechanisms to explain how authoritarian image management is meant to have tangible effects for states. The framework categorizes specific methods (i.e., external propaganda or silencing exiles) into higher-order groupings of mechanisms organized by their form and intended audience. The idea is to create a framework that can facilitate case study and comparative causal analysis across a range of contexts. The framework captures the sorts of activities described in the four vignettes presented at the outset of this book, tracing out their intended causal processes.

Chapter 4 takes a "big picture" view by presenting cross-national data on two empirical manifestations of authoritarian image management. First, using filings with the US Department of Justice, it presents descriptive information on the scope of publicly available lobbying and public relations outlays by authoritarian states in the United States. Second, it presents the Authoritarian Actions Abroad Database (AAAD), which documents publicly available cases in which authoritarian states coerce their exiled critics and citizens. There are nearly 1,200 instances presented between 1991 and 2019 in the AAAD, ranging from vague threats to assassinations. The data presented are descriptive and can assist other researchers in (1) selecting cases for analysis, and (2) situating detailed analysis in a larger universe of processes and institutions. This chapter is a first step in coming to terms with the magnitude of authoritarian image management.

As the largest and most powerful authoritarian state in today's world, China deserves a particularly close look and therefore will be discussed in two chapters. Chapter 5 focuses on how Chinese authorities attempt to control the information that leaves China and enters the international media. The analysis draws on semi-structured interviews with current and former foreign correspondents in China. The interviews reveal the techniques that the government uses to try to limit negative news about China reaching global audiences. These include direct persuasion, restricting sites and/or persons from being investigated, surveillance, intimidation, and the specter of visa non-renewal. Examining how foreign correspondents are "managed" in China is important because controlling what information leaves China in independent outlets is foundational to China's other efforts at image management.

Chapter 6 turns to Beijing's more direct attempts to promote itself and protect its image abroad. The chapter discusses four main areas, each corresponding to one of the mechanisms developed in Chapter 3. It analyzes the Chinese government's ideological vision, its efforts to cultivate journalists from the developing world to tell China's story, its propaganda campaign in response to criticism of its repressive Xinjiang policies after 2014, and its targeting of exiles. Data are drawn from publicly available documents and speeches, global media frequency analysis, video from China's main external propaganda television station, interviews with journalists, and secondary literature.

Chapter 7 turns its attention to Rwanda. It was selected because, unlike China, it is a small regional power, but it has also developed a sustained and sophisticated authoritarian image management strategy. Rwanda's dependence on foreign aid from mostly democratic states means that the government has clear incentives to present itself as a democratic and technically competent government. Rwandan president Paul Kagame has ruled the country for more than two decades. During his time in power, Kagame has suppressed dissent and has warped the institutions of democracy. However, he has also gained praise on performance grounds, as there has not been a return to widespread political violence domestically, the economy has grown rapidly, and female rates of participation in the legislature are among the highest in the world. The Kagame government therefore has the material to tell a good story, and it has done so with vigor. This chapter covers the government's image management efforts abroad to be seen as a success story and as a regional leader. To protect this image, the government engages in obstructive techniques ranging from impugning the credibility of its critics, restricting access to academics and journalists, obscuring its role in supporting militias in neighboring Congo, and threatening or even assassinating critical dissidents abroad. The chapter uses secondary literature and publicly available documents to paint a picture of an authoritarian regime that pays close attention to how it is perceived abroad and has succeeded in mitigating pressure to democratize.

Chapter 8 focuses on North Korea (or the Democratic People's Republic of Korea, the DPRK). North Korea was chosen as a case for analysis because its image management is more limited in scope and aspiration than a globally ambitious great power like China and has had different outcomes than a regional power in a different context like Rwanda. North Korea is often seen as an anachronistic dictatorship—a relic from the Cold War. And yet, its political system has survived far longer than skeptical observers anticipated. North Korea became even more inward-looking as the global communist movement essentially vanished, but it has nonetheless maintained a carefully considered image management strategy. Analyzing it can illuminate how authoritarian image management can function as a strategy of relatively small, ideologically defensive states and thus help demonstrate the generalizability of the concept. After a historical overview, the chapter focuses on two aspects of the DPRK's authoritarian image management: its efforts to make North Korea appealing to the Korean minority in Japan, and its network of supportive "friendship" groups around the world. This approach gives a detailed look at authoritarian image management in both a specific context and more diffuse sense.

Finally, Chapter 9 offers concluding remarks. The study of authoritarian politics is usually—and understandably—focused on the domestic realm. It often incorporates international forces by considering how they act on domestic processes. This book reverses that optic by considering how authoritarian states shape the idea and image of authoritarian political systems abroad. The concluding chapter elaborates on the implications of this perspective, suggests productive lines of academic inquiry, and sketches some recommendations for citizens and policymakers.

2

The Motivations Behind Authoritarian Image Management

Nursultan Nazarbayev ruled Kazakhstan for 29 years as president from 1990 until 2019 and had been an elite politician in the communist government prior to that. Nazarbayev stepped down, taking a behind-the-scenes leadership role, and as of this writing he still visits with foreign leaders and exercises veto powers over some appointments to top positions (Lillis 2019). During his rule, Kazakhstan's human rights record was poor, with civil liberties restricted and activists or journalists who criticized the government's policies too vociferously targeted, harassed, and sometimes imprisoned (see list of cases at Frontline Defenders 2019).

However, Kazakhstan went to great lengths to convince the outside world that it was anything but authoritarian. It engaged in "transnational image making" (Schatz 2008). To appear democratic during the Nazarbayev period, the country held presidential elections at regular intervals, with Nazarbayev never winning less than 80% of the vote, and officially reaching over 97% in his last campaign. As mentioned at the outset of this book, to counter those who were unconvinced of Kazakhstan's democracy and development, it retained public relations firms to launder its image. This entailed creating glossy graphics and videos marking Kazakhstan as a post-Soviet success story and hosting international events like the World Expo (Corporate Europe Observatory 2015, 39–42). Of course, these efforts met challenges, as in the case of the Sacha Baron Cohen movie *Borat* that portrayed the country as absurdly backward, but authoritarian states can learn and adapt as they shape their image (Schatz 2008). Furthermore, beyond just spinning a positive image for international audiences, the government targeted critics abroad. It harassed, intimidated, and even attacked exiled regime critics in at least 10 foreign countries (according to the data presented in Chapter 4).

Making the World Safe for Dictatorship, Alexander Dukalskis, Oxford University Press (2021). © Oxford University Press.
DOI: 10.1093/oso/9780197520130.003.0002

Underpinning Kazakhstan's considerable soft power efforts lies hard coercion for some actors who insist on challenging the regime's image from abroad. Nazarbayev used a combination of various tactics to make the world safe for his dictatorship.

This example highlights how authoritarian states care not only about how foreign audiences view them, but also take active steps to try to manage their image abroad. Authoritarian states make intentional, strategic, and multifaceted efforts to improve how they are perceived outside their borders. While most of the state's rhetorical and symbolic power is directed toward its own population, efforts at external image control aim to bolster the status of the state among foreign audiences and to mitigate criticisms of it in international discourse. All states attempt to manage their image abroad to some degree, but authoritarian states in the post–Cold War era have special incentives to do so given the rhetorical predominance of democracy as an international norm.

As mentioned previously, authoritarian image management can be defined as comprising efforts by the state or its proxies to enhance or protect the legitimacy of the state's political system for audiences outside its borders. It encompasses not only "soft" promotional efforts by authoritarian states, but also the "hard" coercive methods designed to protect threats to their image. The Kazakhstan example reveals several of the motivations and tactics that drive authoritarian image management. Taking a wider view, this chapter builds a theoretical foundation to understand why authoritarian states engage in image management.

To do so, it is necessary to answer two questions. First, does it matter that autocracies do this? To address this question, the chapter discusses two strands of scholarship, one on authoritarian legitimation and the other on autocratic promotion, to help understand what is at stake in studying the external dimensions of autocratic information politics. Second, what motivates autocracies to influence their image for foreign audiences? Here concepts associated with the imposition of ideological systems are useful. States impose their ideologies on other states for both internal and external security, and while authoritarian image management is only a pale imitation of direct ideological imposition, a similar logic holds. Autocratic states pay attention to external image management to bolster their domestic rule and to help build a friendlier international environment for their policies and practices.

Authoritarian Legitimation and Autocratic Promotion

Two recent strands of research about authoritarian politics have enhanced our understanding of how autocracies work and relate to how and why they would internationalize their image management. The first concerns how authoritarian regimes legitimate or justify their rule domestically. The second pertains to the international dimensions of authoritarian rule. With a few notable exceptions (e.g., Holbig 2011; Hoffmann 2015; Del Sordi and Dalmasso 2018; Tsourapas 2020), they often operate in isolation from one another. This section will review each briefly before making the case that when combined they can tell us why it is important that authoritarian governments aim to manage their images abroad. The basic idea is that we know that authoritarian regimes try to justify their rule and repress criticisms domestically, sometimes by way of reference to international developments, and we know that they care about how the international environment bears upon their stability. Combined, this gives us good reason to believe that dictatorships care about how they are perceived abroad.

Authoritarian regimes maintain their power through three main pillars: repression, co-optation, and legitimation (Gerschewski 2013). Repression concerns the punishment or deterrence of behaviors deemed to be threatening to the government. Co-optation is a process of tying strategically relevant actors to the survival of the regime, often through institutions. Until not long ago, most modern research on authoritarian regimes focused on some combination of these two dimensions (see review articles of the field, e.g., Gandhi and Lust-Okar 2009; Magaloni and Kricheli 2010; Art 2012; Brancati 2014). However, students of authoritarian politics now pay sustained attention to the third pillar of authoritarian rule, namely, legitimation.

Legitimation pertains to the claims that a government makes to justify its rule. It can be distinguished from legitimacy insofar as the former are the efforts the government makes to secure the latter (Dukalskis and Gerschewski 2017). Legitimation claims can be made on diverse foundations, such as performance, procedure, ethnic or nationalist appeals, personalistic charisma of the ruler, utopian ideologies, and so on (Kailitz 2013; von Soest and Grauvogel 2017). The aim of legitimation efforts is to secure, at best, active belief in the regime's ideology or, at minimum, passive compliance among most of the population (Gerscehwski 2013). Various aspects of autocratic legitimation have been fruitfully examined in case studies of, for example, China (Holbig 2013), North Korea (Dukalskis and Hooker 2011;

Dukalskis and Lee 2020), Cuba (Schedler and Hoffmann 2016), Singapore (Morgenbesser 2017), Central Asian states (Schatz and Maltseva 2012; Omelicheva 2016; Maerz 2018), Arab states (Schlumberger and Bank 2001; Thyen and Gerschewski 2018), as well as in quantitative cross-national studies (Kailitz and Stockemer 2017; Dukalskis and Patane 2019).

However, domestically the legitimation claims of authoritarian governments are not allowed to compete on an even playing field with alternative ideas. Authoritarian governments more routinely censor political information than do their democratic counterparts (Stier 2015). They also restrict rights such as freedom of association or assembly that facilitate the ability of citizens to convene and articulate political critiques of the government (Bueno de Mesquita and Smith 2010; Møller and Skaaning 2013).

In other words, there is a darker side to the legitimation efforts of authoritarian regimes insofar as they engage in repression to protect their ideas from scrutiny. Authoritarian regimes censor information to bolster the appeal of their own ideological claims (Dukalskis 2017; Roberts 2018). They also physically target journalists who may report on human rights abuses or other information threatening to the regime, such as corruption (Ghodes and Carey 2017). Vocal critics of the government are often punished, sometimes severely.

Censorship and the targeting of journalists or vocal activists are of course not forms of legitimation. Rather, they are acts of repression (Davenport 2007). The repression can be thought of as "soft" in the case of censorship and "hard" in the case of physical intimidation or action against the carriers of threatening messages (Gerschewski 2013). Either way, these behaviors cannot be considered legitimation, but rather acts that shield the government's legitimation claims from scrutiny or criticism (Dukalskis 2017). Such acts are a form of "legitimation-protecting repression" insofar as they target carriers of information that threaten the state's dominant narrative. Of course, repression can backfire if the repression itself becomes a new source of grievance for the population (on repressive backfire generally, see Chenoweth et al. 2017). Each act of repression requires its own explanation, which then may stoke its own dissent and subsequent repression, which requires explanation, and so on (see Edel and Josua 2018; Dukalskis and Patane 2019; Josua 2020).

Legitimation to garner support and repression aiming to expunge competing messages do not always stay neatly contained within borders. During the Cold War, for example, the West and the Soviet bloc worked tirelessly to promote their own literature in the rival bloc and censor the literature supportive of the other (White 2019). Even in less Manichean times, legitimation messages can have external and internal audiences (Del Sordi and Dalmasso 2018), and authoritarian states have incentives to distract from or mitigate criticisms of their actions abroad (a theme addressed in the human rights "naming and shaming" literature; see, e.g., Hafner-Burton 2008; Hendrix and Wong 2013). Exiles who criticize authoritarian politics from abroad undermine the tidy legitimation narratives that authoritarian states provide (Michaelsen 2018). There are thus good reasons to theorize external authoritarian legitimation and the repression to which it relates (for an effort in this direction focusing on migration and exiles, see Tsourapas 2020).

Alongside advances in research on legitimation in authoritarian regimes has come a wave of scholarship on the international dimensions of authoritarian rule. Much of this research posits authoritarian resilience as the dependent variable by focusing on the ways that international factors such as multilateral sanctions, cross-border linkages, and human rights norms bear on the domestic processes of authoritarian regimes (e.g., Levitsky and Way 2006; Grauvogel and von Soest 2014; Escriba-Folch and Wright 2015). However, scholars have also begun to consider authoritarian politics as the independent variable by examining how, if at all, autocracies promote authoritarianism outside their borders (Tansey 2016a; for reviews, see Tansey 2016b; Yakouchyk 2019).

This "autocracy promotion" scholarship tries to understand how authoritarian powers—in particular, contemporary Russia and China, but also regional powers like Saudi Arabia—seek to export or bolster authoritarianism in other states (e.g., Bader, Grävingholt, and Kästner 2010; Burnell and Schlumberger 2010; Vanderhill 2013). Regionally this research often has a focus on Central Asia as the putative target of Russian or Chinese efforts to promote autocracy (e.g., Jackson 2010; Melnykovska, Plamper, and Schweickert 2012; Bader 2017). However, scholars have also examined historical cases in interwar Europe (Weyland 2017b), Latin American cases relating to Hugo Chavez's Venezuela (Vanderhill 2013; de la Torre 2017), consolidated democracies such as Australia as the target of authoritarian diffusion (Chou, Pan, and Poole 2017), and global cross-national studies of the influence of major authoritarian powers on the regime types of other states (Bader 2015; Brownlee 2017).

The emergent consensus of this research is that contemporary authoritarian powers generally do not intend to export their own models of autocratic governance in a direct fashion (Way 2015; von Soest 2015; Tansey 2016b; Bank 2017; Weyland 2017a; Yakouchyk 2019). Venezuela's regional relations under Chavez (de la Torre 2017) and Belarus as a target of Russian autocracy promotion in the mid-1990s are partial exceptions to this consensus (Way 2015, 697). In terms of the two major authoritarian powers, most argue that China and Russia promote their own interests abroad in ways that sometimes coincide with promoting or bolstering autocratic regimes but sometimes do not (Ambrosio 2010; Way 2015; Bank 2017). Rather, this argument goes, their interests are basically defensive since they do not feature universalist ideologies. As Weyland (2017a, 1245–1246) argues:

> non-democratic regimes that do not embody a novel ideological model are fundamentally on the defensive. Their basic, acute political interest is in self-preservation; they seek insulation from foreign pressures.

However, it is increasingly questionable whether Russia and China's ideologies are fundamentally defensive. Further, there are still some recent or contemporary autocracies, such as Saudi Arabia and Cuba, as well as historical cases, such as the Soviet Union, that feature active attempts to promote their political blueprint in other states. States with a specific ideological agenda to spread their regime type go beyond merely protecting their interests or bolstering allies and try to recreate the politics of other states in their own image (Gould-Davies 1999). As Tansey (2016a, 52, emphasis in original) observed with reference to the early Soviet Union, for example, "Stalin sought to create *communist regimes* rather than simply *compliant governments*" (on the Comintern, see Vatlin and Smith 2014). While most authoritarian foreign policy in today's world does not have the ideological zeal of the early Soviet Union, exceptions exist, and powerful states have expansive interests and visions.

At any rate, having one's authoritarian system regarded positively abroad brings clear benefits, as the following section will argue. Even accepting the premise that most contemporary autocracies are fundamentally defensive, international pressures such as the human rights movement, democratic diffusion, or politically threatening exiles prompt states to adopt tactics of authoritarian image management. Even if they do not intend to create a world of dictatorships, they still want to create a world safe for their own dictatorship.

Insights from these two strands of research—on authoritarian legitimation and on autocratic promotion—can fruitfully speak to one another. On the one hand, scholarship on autocratic legitimation, although sometimes addressing international sources of legitimacy (e.g., von Soest and Grauvogel 2017; Del Sordi and Dalmasso 2018), generally does not pay attention to how and when authoritarian states promote their legitimation messages abroad. On the other hand, the autocracy-promotion literature focuses on processes at the elite or government-to-government level and does not typically pay sustained attention to how authoritarian states try to make a friendlier ideational environment for themselves by shaping their image abroad. Taken together, the two literatures suggest that (1) autocracies legitimate their rule and protect it from criticism, and (2) they are interested in how political developments beyond their borders bear on the fate of, at minimum, their own authoritarian rule and, at maximum, authoritarian models more generally. It is therefore important to understand conceptually and empirically how these two impulses interact. The next section develops theoretical tools for understanding more specifically why an authoritarian state would have an interest in managing its image for foreign audiences.

Motivations for Authoritarian Image Management

To understand in more depth why authoritarian states bother with managing their image abroad and what they get in return, it is useful to think about why states impose or propagate ideologies abroad.[1] In his study of forcible regime promotion over a 500-year period, Owen (2010) provides an analytical starting point with his distinction between *internal security* and *external security* motivations for great powers to impose ideologies on foreign states. Although Owen's analysis is only about forcible regime imposition and not related components of it, like inducements or propaganda, his categories are applicable to the less extreme strategies of authoritarian image management under consideration here. A state managing and policing its image externally through messaging, extraterritorial censorship, and/or repression is using less elaborate and less direct tactics than a state imposing its ideas abroad by invasion. States prefer to avoid using force to advance

---

[1] There are long-running debates in political science and political theory about what counts as an *ideology*, but these will not be rehearsed here. Interested readers can consult Freeden (1996); Gerring (1997); Knight (2006); Jost (2006); Eagleton (2007, 28–31); and Maynard (2013). This book will use the term in a broad sense as a system of political ideas designed to help legitimate political power, which means that ideologies do not need to be static over time and may be adapted to changing circumstances (Dukalskis and Gerschewski 2020).

their ideologies because of the high costs involved (Owen 2010, 241) and so also use other forms of regime promotion. Indeed, Owen (2010, 14) himself notes that over time "non-forcible regime promotion . . . has probably been even more common" than the forcible type, but that it is difficult to measure and analyze. The general point is that regimes promote their political ideas and images abroad "to make their domestic and international environments friendlier" (Owen 2010, 252).

Internal security has to do with the desire to strengthen one's power domestically. Rulers have committed to their ideologies publicly and have organized their societies to be commensurate with them, and therefore would face high domestic audience costs by abandoning them (Owen 2010, 252). Therefore "sometimes they find it in their interests to promote their ideology, because their hold on power depends on the progress of their ideology abroad" (Owen 2010, 36). Showing that their domestic system is taken seriously abroad can make for an appealing message to a domestic audience eager to be a part of something larger. However, internal security has another side that calls for external action: discrediting or mitigating the impact of potentially threatening ideologies. When confronting a hostile ideology, "the government can degrade it by attacking it abroad as well as at home. By suppressing an enemy ideology abroad, it can remove a source of moral and perhaps material support for enemy ideologues at home" (Owen 2010, 4).

External security pertains to a government's interest in shaping the international sphere to its advantage. By imposing their ideology on other states, rulers are "attempting to transform their environment so as to make it friendlier to the regime and hence to themselves," and in so doing, they hope to "set the standards by which regimes are judged," thus making their own regime internationally legitimate (Owen 2010, 69). An external environment friendlier to a state's ideology is beneficial because it allows the state to pursue its foreign policy goals in a more enabling structure. As with internal security, there is both a promotional aspect (as states amplify their ideas abroad) and an obstructive aspect (as states undermine threatening ideas abroad) to external security. States wish to see the international environment reflect their domestic ideas, and this may entail undermining the ideologies of rival states. While Owen's framework is built around one state forcibly imposing an ideology on another state, I argue that the same motivations apply to states attempting to alter the international public sphere toward their preferred vision through authoritarian image management.

Thus far the discussion in this section has not been particular to authoritarian states, although for most of the historical period in Owen's study most regimes promoting their ideologies would be considered authoritarian by today's standards. Nonetheless, while democratic states have certainly promoted their political values abroad to varying degrees and with varying outcomes (e.g., Cox, Ikenberry, and Inoguchi 2000), authoritarian states also have incentives to promote their ideas externally. Jackson (2010, 114) encapsulates this point succinctly:

Just as Western democracies attempt to make the world secure for their ideas, values, and political practices, so do other states. All governments engage to some degree in advocacy to promote regimes similar to their own.

Indeed, in the contemporary moment at least three considerations suggest that autocracies have particularly strong incentives to pay attention to their images abroad. First, authoritarian regimes face challenges when it comes to securing domestic legitimacy. It is more difficult for them to base their domestic legitimacy on procedural grounds than their democratic counterparts. Sometimes they simulate compliance with democratic procedural legitimacy, but this can be a fragile foundation for non-democratic legitimacy insofar as it entails associated rights like freedom of the press or freedom of association. They cannot therefore take procedural legitimacy too seriously and therefore may appeal more actively to other legitimation grounds. Some may feature an international dimension, such as communism, or various forms of religious political thought, while others may be insular and particularistic, such as nationalism or the personal charisma of the leader.

Second, the post–Cold War normative order, however hypocritical it may often be (Finnemore 2009), has usually privileged the legitimacy of democracy (Ikenberry 2001; Allan, Vucetic, and Hopf 2018). This means that in the contemporary world, authoritarian regimes are norm-challengers who must more vigorously defend their legitimacy abroad since it deviates from widely accepted standards. This may change as China rises with an authoritarian political system and works to change international norms, but it is still in a challenger position in terms of normative power (Brazys and Dukalskis 2017; Pu 2019).

Third, democracy promotion is existentially threatening to authoritarian states and so they are compelled to respond (Whitehead 2014).

While powerful democracies prefer their neighborhoods to be democratic for instrumental and perhaps value-based reasons (Bader, Grävingholt, and Kästner 2010, 86), autocracies have existential fears if their region swings democratic. From the perspective of a powerful authoritarian state, preventing democracy in nearby or particularly salient countries "helps to safe-guard authoritarian powers' developmental and geostrategic interests as well as to prevent democracy at home—that is, to maximize the chances of authoritarian regime survival" (von Soest 2015, 629).

Given these broad incentives, it is useful to turn to more specific motivations for an authoritarian state to control and manage its image for foreign audiences. Owen's theoretical framework of internal/external security will be supplemented by subsequent literature to elaborate on why authoritarian states seek to craft friendlier ideational environments for their rule. Of course, there is never a perfect division between internal and external politics, and there is unavoidably a degree of overlap between motivations for internal and external security. Nevertheless, the dichotomy is useful as a conceptual organizing device.

Internal Security

Authoritarian regimes jealously guard their hold on power. The assumption in virtually every political science study on autocracy is that the leadership's most important objective is to remain in office. Without holding on to power, dictators cannot instrumentalize that power to achieve their other goals, whatever those may be. Part of retaining control domestically revolves around legitimating the regime to the population domestically, but there are two sides to understanding how external authoritarian image management can contribute to internal security: highlighting a positive image of the political system abroad and attacking foreign entities or ideas associated with domestic challengers.

First, authoritarian image management can boomerang back to the domestic audience and assist with the government's domestic legitimation efforts. In other words, "in their quest for domestic legitimacy, non-democratic regimes can ... seek 'legitimation from abroad'—that is, through activities on, or by way of reference to, the international stage" (Hoffmann 2015, 558). Authoritarian states pay attention to how they package and explain their foreign policies to domestic audiences for the purposes of maintaining domestic support (Weiss and Dafoe 2019). Drawing on

Beetham's classic formulation of political legitimacy as based on legality, justifiability, and consent, Holbig (2011) provides a framework for how external legitimation can reverberate back to the domestic sphere. In terms of legality, states can emphasize their active membership and participation in international organizations to demonstrate to the domestic audience that they are an accepted member of the international community. To bolster their justifiability, states can burnish their credentials in solving international problems and can show that their ideas are considered legitimate abroad. Consent can be shown internationally by mobilizing external recognition and praise and highlighting it to the domestic audience.

In the case of Fidel Castro's Cuba, for example, Hoffmann (2015, 563) writes about the leader's strategy of drawing on international legitimation, which relied on

symbolic gratifications derived when the island's leader acted as a heavyweight in international politics. As Castro wrestled with Kennedy and Khrushchev, any night watchman in a remote Cuban village could feel part of an epic global struggle. As Che Guevara became an icon of worldwide anti-imperial protest, any material shortcomings could be framed as a Che Guevara-inspired sacrifice in pursuit of higher goals. . . . Under Fidel Castro's tenure, symbolic participation in Cuba's global fame became the charismatic "currency" of the social contract Cuba's socialism offered to the population.

Actions like this show that the country's political system has appeal and respect abroad and is thus worthy of guiding domestic politics. This gives authoritarian regimes incentives to "try to improve international responses to specific political ideologies" or other belief systems upon which their rule is based in order to help "justify political rule at home" (Holbig 2011, 170). Kneuer and Demmelhuber (2016, 788–789) summarize the logic for why authoritarian regimes are eager to see their domestic ideas taken seriously abroad, particularly in their immediate region:

Autocratic regimes are interested in creating transnational networks in order to disseminate ideas. The transport of ideas, arguments, or ideational frames aims at synchronizing perceptions in the neighborhood and at providing a common ground for a regional or sub-regional identity. The construction of strong ideational bonds is considered by autocratic leaders as a means of generating the legitimacy they are usually lacking, but remains simultaneously vital.

Ideological dissemination may be due to a missionary zeal on the part of the autocratic state (Weyland 2017a, 2017b). However, even absent a prose-lytizing impulse born out of a deep belief in the rectitude of the ideology, a dictatorship still has domestic reasons to burnish its image and political ideas beyond its borders. The more the authorities are able to highlight that the state's worldview is legitimate abroad, the more material they have to dem-onstrate to a domestic audience that the leadership is guiding the state to in-ternational prestige and respect based on its domestic legitimating formula.

Second, there is a flip side to promoting a state's image abroad for internal security, namely, suppressing challenges to its legitimacy emanating from abroad. On a general level, this may involve externally facing media of the authoritarian state disseminating information designed to refute criticisms, "correct" the record, and/or question the credibility of challengers. This is bound up with processes of authoritarian "image crafting" designed to bol-ster the credibility of the dictator while undermining public criticisms in the host state (Cooley and Heathershaw 2017, 77–78). In doing so, autoc-racies can engage in lobbying, draw on networks of influential persons with connections to the foreign policy establishment of the host state, fund think tank activities, and retain public relations firms, among other tactics (Cooley and Heathershaw 2017, 77–78).

Beyond general image crafting to blunt criticisms circulating inter-nationally, authoritarian regimes actively target individuals, groups, or ideas that threaten their rule from abroad. They target messengers in ad-dition to messages. Focusing on messengers abroad is important because it undermines their ability to garner the funds and attention necessary to pursue their goals. The international advocacy sphere can be seen as a market, with groups that wish to challenge governments needing to pre-sent themselves and their goals as appealing and in line with the aims of funders who are able to support them (Bob 2005; see also Keck and Sikkink 1998). A common method to raise awareness about the group's cause is "dif-fuse consciousness-raising," consisting of speaking tours, interviews, media engagements, prizes, and so on (Bob 2005, 24). Social media strategies are also key to raising consciousness. The effectiveness of these efforts depends a great deal on the international standing of the group itself (Bob 2005, 43). Activists, opposition movements, and journalists challenging authoritarian governments from abroad therefore have strong incentives to limit "undesired news" about themselves and their associates so that funders and allies can support them without incurring backlash (Bob 2005, 52). If an authoritarian government can keep its critics out of the international spotlight and/ or undermine their credibility, they can keep potentially threatening causes off the international agenda, thus limiting the pressure that rebounds back on the government.

Often external critics of authoritarian regimes are (self-)exiles from that country. Oppositional exiles have long been a concern of authoritarian states, but today's exiles can take advantage of global communication tools to make links with domestic actors also interested in pressuring the government. Globalization means that "a national public sphere need not be co-terminus with territorial boundaries, and hence physical exit no longer necessarily implies exit from the national public sphere" (Glasius 2018, 81). However, the same technologies that give activists the opportunity to operate transnationally to pressure an autocracy afford authoritarian regimes "opportunities to monitor and respond to the activities of political exiles rapidly and on a large scale" (Michaelsen 2018, 249; see also Moss 2018).

Autocracies cannot perfectly reproduce the control they have domestically in foreign settings, but they target challengers abroad to enhance regime security. Doing so has both rhetorical and coercive dimensions (Glasius 2018). Rhetorically, authoritarian regimes can slander critics and attempt to undermine their reputation. They can also mobilize regime-supporting activists abroad to manufacture the image of critical exiles as malcontents or not representative of opinion within the state (Tsourapas 2020). They can use media campaigns overseas and at home to create a negative narrative about dissidents abroad, which helps justify repression against them and signals to the activists themselves that the state is keeping tabs on them (Lewis 2015, 146–147). For example, the government of Uzbekistan, in its efforts to target exiles from the 2005 massacre of protesters in its eastern city of Andijan, launched a media campaign against the movement leaders, including a documentary on Uzbek TV in 2010 that painted the activists as malign forces (Cooley and Heathershaw 2017, 201–209).

Coercively, autocracies can target political critics abroad so that politics "outside" the state do not infiltrate politics "inside" the state (Cooley and Heathershaw 2017, 191). The idea is to undermine the ability of external critics to influence domestic politics. The state can "extend its coercive power beyond borders" to target exiles by, for example, spying on activist groups, withdrawing their citizenship, detaining or harassing them, intimidating or arresting their families back home, or in extreme cases even beating or assassinating them (Cooley and Heathershaw 2017, 187–219; Lewis 2015; Glasius 2018). Silencing critics and activists abroad is part of a strategy to drive a wedge between external and internal activists so that they cannot effectively work together (Moss 2018). The motivation is to prevent anti-regime activities taking place abroad from mobilizing domestic challengers to weaken authoritarian rule at home.

The internationalization of authoritarian image management thus has a firm foundation in the quest for internal security. The logic of maintaining internal security demands that the frontiers of image management must be expanded transnationally. Doing so helps to bolster legitimation messages at home, to ensure that challenges to the regime's legitimacy emanating from abroad do not gain traction domestically, and to undermine the ability of critics abroad to gain support internationally.

External Security

Beyond directly preserving internal security, authoritarian states extend their image management abroad to help secure their external environment. They wish to render the regional and international context more conducive to their interests. While there is certainly overlap with the internal security logic, seeking external security through authoritarian image management also has distinct dimensions. Here we can conceive of an escalation of ambition and complexity ranging from (1) the minimalist goal of contributing to a regional political environment that does not become a domestic threat, to (2) the more ambitious goal of enhancing other foreign policy aims by improving the image of the authoritarian state abroad, to (3) the grand aspiration of forging an international normative environment conducive to the acceptance of authoritarian practices. Each level will be discussed in turn.

Governments care about the regime types and ideologies of other states (Owen 2010). Particularly in their immediate neighborhood, states prefer the familiarity that comes with similarly constituted neighbors. As Bader, Grävingholt, and Kästner (2010, 85) observe, "governments are not indifferent with respect to the political regime type of other states, but do develop a preference toward systems convergence, in particular in their regional environment." For this reason, authoritarian states, particularly global and regional powers, have incentives to promote the legitimacy of their own political system in their immediate neighborhood (Owen 2010; Kneuer and Demmelhuber 2016).

The most pressing external security motivation is to prevent the diffusion of democracy in the autocracy's immediate region. This sort of "democracy prevention" sees authoritarian regimes act to prevent spillovers of democracy from neighboring states (von Soest 2015). Given the tendency for democracy to diffuse geographically (e.g., Brinks and Coppedge 2006; Lankina, Libman, and Obydenkova 2016), authoritarian leaders are right to fear the advance of democratic norms on their borders. Despite globalization processes, the dynamics of authoritarian cooperation, diffusion, and promotion still tend to display geographical clustering that is at least partly due to shared language and/or cultural similarities (Jackson 2010, 109–110; Kneuer and Demmelhuber 2016; Bank 2017; Glasius, Schalk, and De Lange 2020).

While many scholars emphasize the forcible or manipulative dimensions of cooperation between regional autocratic regime elites, halting democratic advance can be ideational, for example, in "a less coercive, but nonetheless active, process through which an authoritarian regime presents itself and its policies as an autocratic role model for emulation by other states" (Hall and Ambrosio 2017, 152; see also Burnell and Schlumberger 2010, 10; Weyland 2017a, 1237). Autocratic powers can do this by, for example, "label[ing] their own regime as a 'new' or 'alternative' form of non-Western democracy and export[ing] the model to nations within their neighbourhood" (Kneuer and Demmelhuber 2016, 776; see also Ambrosio 2008). In addition to claiming such an alternative form of "democracy" as legitimate, democracy-resisters question the credentials and motives of democracy promoters to reduce the appeal of their messages (Whitehead 2014, 7). These rhetorical strategies aim to deflect pressure to change emanating from other states or international organizations.

This impulse for authoritarian regimes to promote their legitimating ideas in their immediate neighborhood for the minimalist goal of "diffusion proofing" their region resonates with studies of international aspects of autocracy that emphasize its defensive character (e.g., Ambrosio 2010; von Soest 2015; Bank 2017; Yakouchyk 2019). The aim is not necessarily to advance authoritarianism abroad, but rather to justify and stabilize authoritarianism by minimizing the appeal of democracy. From the perspective of authoritarian leaders, a reliably autocratic neighborhood is safer.

Beyond the minimalist goal of containing regional democratization processes, authoritarian states manage their image abroad to enhance other foreign policy objectives. We would expect the motivation to be different with
autocratic-autocratic dyads and autocratic-democratic dyads. For autocratic
states dealing with other autocracies, image management functions in a more
controlled information environment. The strategy is likely to be more elite-
focused rather than public-facing. Bader, Grävingholt, and Kästner (2010)
theorize that unless it comes at the expense of stability, autocracies prefer
to deal with other autocracies because in both cases the winning coalition
is smaller, and the outcome is therefore likely to result in private goods for
both sets of elites. Here the regional autocratic power uses "its external relations as one way to secure the resources necessary in order to strengthen its
domestic position" (Bader, Grävingholt, and Kästner 2010, 87). The lack of
accountability and oversight in autocratic systems mitigates the ability of the
public to learn about the details of foreign policy cooperation, but rumors
of exploitation or corruption are still likely to circulate, and outside powers
may criticize such cooperation. An autocratic state legitimating itself externally as a worthy partner or emphasizing shared values can help refute such
accusations. An ideologically permissive region can also help delegitimize
external criticism from "outsiders" and widen the scope of what is tolerated
domestically for autocracies to maintain power (Ambrosio 2008). This ultimately helps facilitate foreign policy goals for the state that successfully
manages its image abroad.

In relations with democracies, the motivation of authoritarian image
management is still to help achieve foreign policy aims, but the approach
is likely to differ. In a democratic partner state, the autocratic regime may
confront a skeptical public and feel compelled to present itself in attractive
and non-threatening terms in order to persuade public constituencies to not
frustrate its foreign relations with the host state. This is a form of what Adler-
Nissen (2014) calls "stigma management." States that deviate from accepted
norms, like democracy from the perspective of a democratic public, are frequently stigmatized and ultimately suffer from loss of status. This can frustrate their ability to achieve their objectives. However, stigmatized states do
not passively accept their lot. Instead, they actively cope with and manage
their stigma. An authoritarian state attempting to assuage stigma emanating
from democratic publics is likely to either reject the stigma ("we are not authoritarian") or counter-stigmatize ("we have problems, but you aren't perfect either"). This is a process in which the state will "selectively devalue the

performance dimensions that suggest that their group fares poorly and selectively value those dimensions on which their group excels" (Adler-Nissen
2014, 165).

Criticism of an authoritarian state's foreign policy goals or domestic system
is likely to be more visible in a democratic public sphere, but the protections
of that same public sphere mean that criticism can be responded to publicly.
The authoritarian state can take advantage of the free speech guarantees
afforded by democratic systems to present its case publicly. This is important because while foreign policy is often thought of as elite-driven, emerging
research suggests that public opinion is important to the formation of foreign policy, at least in democratic societies (Rothschild and Shafranek 2017).
People often take their cues about how their state should relate to other states
at least as much from their peers as they do from elites, which can ultimately
trickle up to change policy orientations (Kertzer and Zeitzoff 2017). An authoritarian state wishing to achieve foreign policy objectives with democratic partners therefore has strong incentives to legitimate its rule, or at least
respond to negative messages, directly to the publics of democracies.

Beyond the goal of achieving specific foreign policy outcomes lies the
grander ambition of promoting authoritarian norms globally. This entails
forging a friendlier international environment for authoritarian practices
and altering the standards upon which legitimate political authority is
judged. The international standards most likely to perturb authoritarian
powers are those that revolve around human rights and liberal democracy.
Authoritarian states would instead prefer norms associated with a strong
emphasis on security and a relativism tied to the prominence of "traditional
culture" (Cooley 2015). Norms about these concepts are malleable, though,
and are shaped in large measure by the political identities of major states in
the system (Gunitsky 2017). As Ambrosio (2010, 377) puts it, "as the legitimacy of authoritarianism increases, it is more likely that autocratic norms
and practices will spread throughout the international system."

Sometimes diffusion can happen without the specific intent of an authoritarian power. Elites in other states might find a rising authoritarian power appealing as a successful model and therefore adopt certain—or even many—of
its institutions domestically (Fordham and Asal 2007; Gunitsky 2017; Møller,
Skaaning, and Tolstrup 2017). This can reify the appropriateness of authoritarian norms so that authoritarian states can claim their systems rest on more
equal footing with the legitimacy of democratic states (Ambrosio 2010, 380–
381). In other words, "states with a high level of prestige can help to set the

tone about what is acceptable in the international system, a process which facilitates the diffusion of norms and values" (Ambrosio 2010, 386).

While this model of diffuse emulation does not result from the specific intent of an authoritarian state to coerce or induce other states to comply, it may stem in part from the state burnishing its image as a successful political model. Great powers actively shape their international image to help manufacture prestige (Fordham and Asal 2007, 33). States have incentives to influence global norms to their favor, and a more positive image helps them do that. Larson, Paul, and Wohlforth (2014, 19) note that states actively seek to get others to view them as high status, in part because esteem can bring material benefits: "High status . . . confers tangible benefits in the form of decision-making autonomy and deference on the part of others concerning issues of importance, including but not limited to security and prosperity." The prestige of a major authoritarian state can have impacts on the international system by altering the preferences and attitudes of other states (Ambrosio 2010, 386).

Studies on ideas and international norms in world politics often emphasize the importance of elite receptivity as the major driver of socialization processes (e.g., Ikenberry and Kupchan 1990; Owen 2010; Haas 2014). Elites have access to international currents of information and the power to shape institutions that entrench norms, even if the public is indifferent or unaware (e.g., Moravcsik 2000). Even norm change literature that focuses on grassroots activism stresses the need to change the decision-making calculus of elites (Keck and Sikkink 1998) and to rhetorically entrap elites in normative commitments (Risse, Ropp, and Sikkink 1999).

From this perspective, authoritarian states aiming to influence international norms are likely to focus on elite audiences because they have more influence than mass publics. The capabilities and beliefs of elites are important in determining whether authoritarian norms are promoted in or by a given state (Vanderhill 2013). Political elites are able to use international organizations, like the Shanghai Cooperation Organization (SCO), to diffuse and entrench norms friendly to the maintenance of authoritarian power, such as "no-questions-asked" extradition of political enemies, the stigmatizing of "extremist" political groups, and robust conceptions of state sovereignty (Ambrosio 2008; Melnykovska, Plamper, and Schweickert 2012; Lewis 2015; Cooley and Heathershaw 2017). Elites have agenda-setting capabilities and influence about which international norms their state should support, both at home and in international organizations. Writing about Central Asian autocracies, for example, Jackson (2010, 104) notes the importance of elite receptivity to norms:

> Wary of the West's promotion of democracy and human rights, many of Central Asia's political elite view the Russian government's ideas about legitimacy, authority, respect, order, and sovereignty as more similar to their own indigenous norms and practices, and a better fit with their desire to strengthen existing institutions and power structures, than Western ideas of liberal democracy and human rights.

The causal emphasis attributed to elites in shaping international norms is warranted, but incomplete. Ideas about international order are most influential when they have traction at both the elite and the mass level (Allan, Vucetic, and Hopf 2018). An authoritarian state wishing to see its preferred norms reflected in the international system therefore has incentives to not only gain support from political elites, but also to legitimize its image at the popular level among foreign audiences (Brazys and Dukalskis 2019). The aim is not necessarily to promote a change of regime type in the target state, but rather to generate mass attitudes receptive to the sending state's priorities in the international sphere. Norms associated with human rights, for example, benefit from awareness and acceptance at the popular level (e.g., Davis, Murdie, and Steinmetz 2012; Ron and Crow 2015;). If they are devalued or contested by other pro-authoritarian norms among foreign publics, then public demand that states prioritize them in international fora would decrease. Ultimately, the ability of norms to threaten authoritarian rule would be weakened. The international environment would therefore be safer for dictatorship.

Conclusion

While all states have incentives to manage their image abroad to some degree, authoritarian states have extra motivation to do so in the post–Cold War era. Democracy is rhetorically prized in international discourse, and even authoritarian leaders frequently articulate their right to rule in democratic terms (Maerz 2019). However, sometimes this claim strains credulity and at other times autocracies dispense with the pretense that they rule on procedural grounds. The rhetorical prominence of democratic values internationally means that authoritarian states have reasons to manage their image abroad in order to, at minimum, alleviate external pressure on their domestic political system, and more ambitiously to forge an international environment conducive to their interests and identities. Both aims entail authoritarian states promoting their claims abroad and potentially adding an extraterritorial dimension to their legitimation-protecting repression. This chapter has set a theoretical framework that can be used to explore why authoritarian states manage their image abroad and how they might go about the task. It has provided a theoretical foundation in the quest for internal and external security that motivates authoritarian image management.

Many questions remain unanswered. Most importantly, we want to know whether these theoretical considerations play out in the empirical world. Do authoritarian states behave in the ways that this chapter has posited? The next chapter will turn to this question by proposing a mechanistic approach to authoritarian image management. It will help us understand how these processes work and what to look for when we approach the empirical record.

3

Mechanisms of Authoritarian
Image Management

In January 2012, just one month after the death of its previous leader Kim Jong Il, North Korea allowed the Associated Press (AP) to open a bureau in the capital Pyongyang. The bureau was initially staffed by a North Korean reporter and photographer and was overseen by regular visits from an experienced foreign bureau chief and foreign photographer (Daniszewski 2012). The tension in this arrangement is obvious: North Korea is a highly authoritarian state with some of the world's most stringent systems of information control, while the AP is an international news agency that relies on the principle of the freedom of the press. Criticism followed the bureau's opening (Stone Fish 2014), but as of this writing it remains open.

During its short history, journalists involved with the project have been open about the limits the government puts on them. The original bureau chief, Jean Lee, remarked in an interview with the *Columbia Journalism Review* that there are strict rules on foreign journalists and that she "operate[s] under the assumption that everything I say, everything I write, everything I do is being recorded" (Sheffield 2012). The next bureau chief, Eric Talmadge, was also forthcoming about the restrictions on his reporting, which included limitations on where he could go and whom he could speak with (Farhi 2015). From the perspective of the AP, the aim of the arrangement is clear: even limited access to a state like North Korea is better than no access, and will hopefully result in better reporting from the country for its customers.

From the state's perspective, interesting trade-offs also arise. News by the AP from North Korea will have more credibility than Pyongyang's propagandistic state media, but the risk is that the AP may report negative stories that would have more credence because of the agency's increased access. It is an extreme case, but how do we make sense of why the DPRK would allow the AP to open a branch in Pyongyang? How are foreign journalists meant to function in this environment? What is limited foreign reporting

Making the World Safe for Dictatorship, Alexander Dukalskis, Oxford University Press (2021). © Oxford University Press.
DOI: 10.1093/oso/9780197520130.003.0003

meant to do for North Korea's image, and how is it meant to accomplish its aims? These types of questions have relevance not only for North Korea, but also for other authoritarian states attempting to influence how they are perceived abroad.

The previous chapter argued that authoritarian states have clear motivations to control their image abroad. In order to bolster their internal and external security, they are compelled to present a positive image of themselves to foreign publics and to protect that image from criticism by undermining unwanted messages and/or messengers. While the previous chapter answered "why" questions, this chapter turns to "how" questions.

How exactly do authoritarian states manage their image abroad, and what are the causal chains linking their activities to their desired outcomes of internal/external security? This chapter proposes four sets of mechanisms to explain how authoritarian image management is meant to have tangible effects for states. It specifies the causal chains through which authoritarian image management techniques benefit authoritarian states. The framework categorizes concrete actions (e.g., buying propaganda space in foreign newspapers, restricting the activity of foreign correspondents, or coercing exiles) into higher-order groupings of mechanisms. The idea is to create a framework that can facilitate case study and comparative causal analysis across a range of contexts.

The four mechanisms organize the multifarious tactics of international authoritarian image management into a coherent framework. The mechanisms vary along two dimensions: their form and their intended target. First, the chapter divides tactics into "promotional" and "obstructive" forms of image management. The former consist of disseminating content that is favorable to the government, while the latter aim to eradicate or undercut unfavorable ideas disseminated by other actors. Second, this distinction is layered onto the target audience for the tactic and divides potential audiences into "diffuse" and "specific" groups. The former consist of broad foreign publics, while the latter consist of particularly relevant or influential groups like journalists, activists, elites, or policymakers.

This exercise results in four mechanisms of international authoritarian image management. First, *promotional/diffuse* mechanisms are those that disseminate favorable messages or symbols about the state to foreign publics in the hopes that they are persuaded to see the state more positively and therefore act accordingly. Foreign propaganda inserts in foreign newspapers or externally facing TV outlets are examples of this form. Chapter 1 of this book described Kazakhstan's PR efforts as an example of promotional/diffuse authoritarian image management. Second, *obstructive/diffuse* mechanisms protect the state's narrative by censoring, obscuring, or refuting unfavorable information circulating in foreign public spheres in order to reduce criticism about the state and allow it to operate with less foreign pressure or opposition. Trying to block negative references to the country in foreign movies or flooding social media with distracting content to drown out a negative news story about the country operate on this logic. The RIRA "troll farm" example at the outset of this book exemplifies this mechanism.

Third, *promotional/specific* mechanisms attempt to persuade foreign elites or other relevant groups to view the state favorably so that they can in turn influence either foreign publics to view the state positively and/or policymakers to act in the state's interest. Offers of junket trips to journalists or policymakers are examples of this type of image management technique. My invitation to "learn" about China was promotional/specific authoritarian image management in action. Fourth, *obstructive/specific* mechanisms are the most coercive and see the state target individuals or groups beyond its borders (or foreigners within borders) that are critical of the state. The aim is to reduce their ability to critique the state, amplify critical messages, gain allies, mobilize resources, and build linkages with domestic dissidents, all of which might be used to exert pressure on the state. The apprehension of Saudi activist Loujain al-Hathloul in the UAE was an obstructive/specific action.

This chapter elaborates on these mechanisms and provides illustrative examples of each. The framework draws in particular on recent work that has attempted to theorize the extraterritorial dimensions of authoritarian state power (e.g., Lewis 2015; Dalmasso et al. 2018; Glasius 2018b; Tsourapas 2020), the sources of domestic authoritarian power (e.g., Gerschewski 2013), and literature on the role of ideas and narratives in international relations (e.g., Miskimmon, O'Loughlin, and Roselle 2013; Allan, Vucetic, and Hopf 2018). The result is a comprehensive framework that can be used to explain how authoritarian image management works.

Mechanism-based thinking emphasizes process, or the "how" question. By understanding the pathways through which one variable acts on another, researchers can better demonstrate causality (Hedstrom and Swedberg 1998). Instead of a correlational account, a mechanism-based approach to research attempts to explain the area between cause and effect by revealing and empirically evaluating causal chains (Hedstrom and Swedberg 1998).

Mechanisms can be thought of as "causal pathways" that explain a relationship (Gerring 2007; Brady and Collier 2005, 277). They are useful insofar as they aim to make the "black box" of a relationship more translucent in order to answer the question: "how does it work?" (Bunge 1997, 427–428).

To avoid being only descriptive, mechanisms must operate at some level of generality across contexts (Hedstrom and Swedberg 1998; Tilly 2001). Otherwise they can be accused of being retrofitted into an empirical account to claim "scientific" causal explanation (Norkus 2005). To be useful, mechanisms must be modular and able to shed light on seemingly disparate processes across a range of contexts.

A mechanism-based approach to the relationship between authoritarian image management and the internal/external security of autocracies emphasizes what dictatorships do to control their image, how they envision those tactics working, and whether they play out as imagined. In sum, rather than saying that "authoritarian image management can increase internal/external security x%," the idea is instead to say, "authoritarian image management operates across diverse contexts in the following frequently recurring ways." The remainder of this chapter lays the theoretical groundwork that will allow empirical analysis in the remainder of this book.

Mechanisms of Authoritarian Image Management

Authoritarian image management comprises efforts by the state and/or its proxies to protect and/or enhance the legitimacy of the state's political system outside its borders. Authoritarian states do so to enhance their internal and external security. By providing a mechanistic account, the focus is on the processes and sequences that operate between the cause (motivation for internal/external security) and the intended effect (enhancing internal/external security). To do so, it is useful to think about both the form of such tactics and the indented audience or target.

In terms of form, mirroring what authoritarian regimes do domestically, one can distinguish between "promotional" and "obstructive" forms of authoritarian image management. Promotional efforts include the dissemination of messages, symbols, arguments, stories, and so on. The general idea is to persuade listeners of the veracity or appeal of the message. Obstructive forms of authoritarian image management aim to eradicate or mitigate unfavorable ideas disseminated by other actors. This schematic recognizes that propaganda and censorship are related insofar as they sustain one another, and both aim to influence opinion (Taylor 2003, 10; Dukalskis 2017).

"Promotional" forms of authoritarian image management encompass publicity efforts to present a favorable image of the state and/or its political system abroad. The domestic analogue is publicity or propaganda aiming to foster positive affinity for the government among citizens. The idea is to bolster the attractiveness, appeal, and legitimacy of the autocracy so that it is highly regarded. Extending the concept extraterritorially, promotional authoritarian image management practices can include investments in international media to influence international perception of the state, large showpiece events like hosting the World Expo, educational diplomacy like Confucius Institutes, the use of symbols like animals or historical figures, the elevation of particular celebrities, and so on. These are the tools of state-driven soft power: they are methods of attraction. They are sometimes part of a broad "branding" strategy and are sometimes disseminated through public diplomacy initiatives in which the state "targets the general public in foreign societies and more specific non-official groups, organizations and individuals" to advance its interests and values (Melissen 2005, 5). Promotional authoritarian image management tactics include the broad array of efforts the state undertakes to make itself and its sociopolitical system look good abroad.

"Obstructive" forms of authoritarian image management encompass acts of extraterritorial censorship, distraction, or even repression if aimed at silencing critical voices. These resonate with what Glasius (2018a) calls "authoritarian practices," which she defines as "patterns of actions" that sabotage accountability "by disabling access to information and/or disabling voice" (Glasius 2018a, 527). Relatedly, illiberal practices infringe "on the autonomy and dignity of the person" (Glasius 2018a, 530). The extraterritorial extension of such practices is of interest when it comes to authoritarian image management (Glasius 2018b). Here the state attempts to silence critics or censor information beyond its borders through authoritarian and illiberal practices.

Obstructive forms of authoritarian image management have their domestic analogue in the restriction of "coordination goods" such as freedom of speech (Bueno de Mesquita and Smith 2010), the censorship of news media (Stier 2015) and the internet (King, Pan, and Roberts 2013), and the repression of groups or individuals who might challenge the state's legitimating narrative (Ghodes and Carey 2017). Beyond the state's borders, this may include pressuring international companies to censor undesirable content, attempting to manipulate scholars or journalists, directly targeting exiled dissidents, and so on (Glasius 2018b; see also Lewis 2015). Authoritarian states cannot always replicate their authoritarian and illiberal practices abroad directly, but they adapt and adjust them for external deployment (Dalmasso et al. 2018).

In sum, authoritarian image management as an overarching concept manifests itself in "promotional" (i.e., soft power initiatives, public diplomacy, nation branding, framing) and "obstructive" (i.e., extraterritorial authoritarian and illiberal practices) forms. Promotional and obstructive forms of authoritarian image management are meant to work together insofar as the latter shield the former from criticism. When critical ideas are sheltered or the material upon which to build critical arguments is harder to find, marshalling a critique of an autocracy is rendered more difficult (Kuran 1995). However, it can also be the case that if obstructive tactics like repression are exposed, they can become a liability for the image of the source state. In this case, promotional tactics are required to repair the damage and bolster the image of the state by justifying the obstructive practice and/or distracting from it. The following section will unpack these basic distinctions further and present the theoretical work that underpins them.

Along with disaggregating the form of authoritarian image management, one can also distinguish between two ideal types of audiences: diffuse and specific. "Diffuse" audiences consist of the general public, while "specific" audiences concern an influential category of people, such as journalists or decision-makers. As discussed in the previous chapter, analyses of ideational change in world politics, especially early studies, often emphasized the role of elites. For example, Ikenberry and Kupchan (1990, 293) argue that public opinion can influence elite decisions but that elites must ultimately take on board ideas for deeper socialization to occur; in other words, "socialization is principally an elite and not a mass phenomenon" (Ikenberry and Kupchan 1990, 314).

Elites are self-evidently important for shaping public discourse and beliefs, but this only tells part of the story insofar as "the more deeply an elite ideology connects with mass common sense, the stronger and more robust it will be" (Allan, Vucetic and Hopf 2018, 847; see also Pu 2012, 352–353). In most contexts, even authoritarian ones, decision-makers cannot too frequently and too obviously make decisions that radically deviate from mass beliefs or else they will lose support (Allan, Vucetic, and Hopf 2018, 851). Should this happen, they would have to resort to coercion, which carries risks of backfire. This helps explain why even highly authoritarian states attempt to legitimate their rule domestically to a broad audience (Dukalskis and Gerscehwski 2017; Gerschewski 2018).

Therefore, including both elite and mass audiences in the framework provides a fuller picture of authoritarian image management. States aiming to persuade audiences of their messages must adjust the content and form to suit the beliefs and interests of the audiences (Miskimmon, O' Loughlin, and Roselle 2013, 12; Brazys and Dukalskis 2020). One would expect methods to differ when an autocracy is projecting its message to the public and when it is trying to convince influential elites. Likewise, one can posit that obstructive tactics of censorship and repression will be adjusted for different targets.

Putting these two dimensions together yields Figure 3.1, which shows the causal logic of how different mechanisms of authoritarian image management are meant to work. Virtually any tactic of authoritarian image management can be placed in one of these more general cells. The advantage of this approach to explanation is that it provides expectations about causal processes and sequences that can be used to evaluate the empirical record.

The authoritarian image management approach is beneficial in part because it avoids some of the pitfalls of existing frameworks and related concepts. For example, by incorporating obstructive tactics, it avoids criticisms of soft power and public diplomacy which posit that the concepts downplay their relationship with repression or censorship (for a critique of soft power, see Bially Mattern 2005). By disaggregating targets, it addresses criticisms that studies of ideational change in world politics are too elite-focused. It is a comprehensive analytical framework that folds several tactics and patterns into one account and specifies relations between them. It captures the multidimensional reality of what authoritarian states do to try to make their worlds safe for dictatorship.

Each of these cells deserves more explanation. The following four subsections take each of these categories in turn, explaining what effect they are meant to have on the internal and/or external security of the autocratic state that deploys them. Each will explain the general logic and provide some examples to help clarify. In subsequent chapters, a range of empirical material will be systematically evaluated using this framework, but some general examples will be included in this chapter to illuminate the mechanisms.

	Diffuse Audience	Specific Audience
Promotional Form (e.g., external propaganda, nation branding, soft power initiatives)	Disseminate positive messages/symbols ↓ Improve how the state is perceived abroad ↓ (1) Reduce pressure for domestic change emanating from abroad, and/or (2) reduce opposition to foreign policy objectives	Show positive image of state to elites ↓ Elites more favorable to state as they pursue their work ↓ Opinion-shapers reproduce positive images and/or political elites favorably influence policy ↓ (1) Public opposition or pressure on state reduced, and/or (2) policies friendlier to state's interest
Obstructive Form (e.g., extraterritorial repression, censorship, authoritarian practices)	Remove/obscure/distract from negative information about the state ↓ Reduce resonance of criticism about the state ↓ (1) Foreign publics not inclined to pressure state, and/or (2) do not voice opposition to state's foreign policy goals	Silence, verbally or with coercion, messengers of criticism ↓ Frustrate their ability to credibly criticize state ↓ Messages do not reach intended domestic or foreign audiences ↓ (1) Reduce pressure from foreign publics to change, and/or (2) reduce opposition to foreign policy goals, and/or (3) sever linkages between external critics and internal dissidents/activists

Figure 3.1. Mechanisms of authoritarian image management.

Promotional/Diffuse: Improving Public Opinion

The promotional and diffuse category of authoritarian image management is perhaps the most familiar type. Indeed, in many cases this category appears as not so different from what democratic states do to improve their image abroad. It contains messages or symbols meant to improve the image of the state sending them, but they are not necessarily directed at any specific group beyond broad publics. Rather, they are designed to have more general appeal. The causal logic underpinning promotional/diffuse image management is that the state disseminates positive messages or symbols about itself to improve how it is perceived among the populations of other states. The idea is that those populations are then not inclined to pressure that state to change domestically and/or do not frustrate the state's foreign policy goals by voicing opposition.

In his work on state-led public relations, Kunczik (1997, 12) documents hundreds of examples in which states engaged in the "planned and continuous distribution of interest-bound information . . . aimed (mostly) at improving the country's image abroad." They "brand" and market their distinctive positive attributes to improve their reputations (van Ham 2001). In a general sense, virtually all states make some effort to be seen positively abroad. Authoritarian states are no different, and thus the first link in the causal pathway described earlier, namely disseminating positive messages or symbols, is relatively straightforward. For example, nondemocratic states create foreign media outlets that report positively on their government (Kunczik 1997, 252–256), maintain government websites that signal the state's modernity and legitimacy (Maerz 2016), host international sporting events to showcase their preferred image (Cha 2009), and highlight their economic achievements (Zakaria 1994). For example, Saudi Arabia has recently invested in a multifaceted public relations campaign that includes publishing positive content on social media, press releases, and public events "to promote the changing face of KSA [Kingdom of Saudi Arabia] to the rest of the world and to improve international perception of the kingdom" (Kerr 2017, n.p.).

It is an open question how these efforts influence the public opinion of foreign countries about the disseminating state. Given the diffuse nature of this mechanism, it is difficult to link empirically these general efforts and support among foreign publics (exceptions include Schatz and Levine 2010; Bailard 2016; Custer et al. 2018; Brazys and Dukalskis 2019). Public images of a state may be influenced by any number of factors, including that state's political and economic record (Gunitsky 2017) or even idiosyncratic factors like the perceived quality of its products or the style of play of its international athletes (Kunczik 1997, 2). The general empirical effect of tactics like foreign-facing propaganda or hosting showcase international events is likely to vary by state and across time. However, it is likely to work at least some of the time, and on the scale of state budgets it is relatively cheap (Sharp 2005, 107). States frequently behave *as if* promotional/diffuse image management techniques work to shape foreign public opinion.

There are at least three ways in which promotional/diffuse image management techniques can benefit the state. First, the idea of soft power suggests that the ability of states to get foreign actors to want the same thing as them is powerful if it can be achieved (Nye 1990, 2008). Promotional authoritarian image management can help a state set its preferred agenda internationally by reducing skepticism about its intentions and by gaining acceptance for its preferred concepts and goals. Doing so may come in the form of a "strategic narrative" in which the state "describe[s] how the world is structured, who the players are, and how it works . . . [and] set[s] out what the story of the state or nation is, what values and goals it has" (Roselle, Miskimmon, and O'Loughlin 2014, 76). Spinning the strategic narrative so that it reflects positively on the state helps to frame the state's goals, capabilities, and intentions to minimize pressure for domestic change and maximize latitude to pursue foreign policy aims.

Second, scholarship on status in international relations emphasizes that since status is subjective, states attempt to influence how others perceive them, in part to secure more power (Larson, Paul, and Wohlforth 2014, 11; Larson and Shevchenko 2010; Pu and Schweller 2014; Pu 2019). At minimum, they attempt to mitigate the effects of having negative images to avoid being marginalized in the international community (Adler-Nissen 2014). But more ambitiously, they strive for higher status by making claims in their rhetoric, diplomacy, and symbolism (Larson, Paul, and Wohlforth 2014, 22). Acquiring high status can be materially beneficial for a state insofar as other states may defer to a high-status state in some areas (Larson, Paul, and Wohlforth 2014, 19). At a deeper level, states care about status in part because it helps determine "who gets to constitute and participate in making international order" (Clunan 2014, 296), the very same order in which the domestic political structure is embedded.

The desired result of promotional/diffuse methods is that foreign populations are convinced to not pressure the state to change domestically and to not oppose the state's foreign policy goals. The links can operate either directly, by a foreign public not objecting to a particular policy, or indirectly, by a foreign public becoming used to the changed international order such that the policies of an authoritarian state do not seem out of place. This is a distinction that Miskimmon, O'Loughlin, and Roselle (2013, 152) draw between "conversational power" and "environmental power." The former is about actors getting others to do what they would not otherwise do in a specific interaction. The latter is about shaping the context in which the interactions take place, which helps determine the standards on which the interaction is judged, how the interaction is communicated, and what actors are deemed relevant to speak.

Third, promotional/diffuse authoritarian image management provides images and information that can rebound back to the domestic sphere to help solidify authoritarian resilience. As discussed in the previous chapter, information and images about how a political system is respected by foreign publics can be reproduced domestically to help generate political legitimacy (Hoffmann 2015). If a political regime is able to demonstrate positive responses abroad to its political ideas, this can help justify its domestic rule insofar as it validates the acceptability and prestige of the ideas on which the political system is based (Holbig 2011, 170). This can help generate cohesion domestically and marginalize criticisms of the government's political rule (Edney 2014). Del Sordi and Dalmasso (2018, 101) describe this process well:

> on the one hand, authoritarian elites observe the international context and produce discourses and policies that aim to create a positive country image, or brand. On the other hand, authoritarian leaders use the international recognition they consequently obtain as a means to legitimize their rule at home, by presenting themselves as internationally praised role models and, therefore deserving of support by the local population.

In sum, the first mechanism of authoritarian image management sees states disseminate desired messages or symbols with the aim of shaping international public opinion to relieve domestic pressure and/or minimize resistance to foreign policies. When it is successful, the state secures increased status, and thus deference, and can frame international processes in ways that are helpful to its goals. It may also solidify its standing among the domestic audience and thus improve its internal security.

Obstructive/Diffuse: Protecting the Narrative

Obstructive/diffuse image management techniques are meant to shield the sending state from criticism and/or undermine alternatives. Rather than disseminating positive messages about the state, they are designed to eliminate negative information about it, undermine opponents, respond to criticisms, impugn accusers, or muddy the waters of public discourse. They appear not only as observable communications, but also as efforts to censor or remove undesirable information from public circulation. The causal chain is to respond to, remove, obscure, or distract from negative information about the state, in order to reduce the resonance of criticism about the state among the general public. The desired results are the same as promotional/diffuse techniques insofar as foreign publics are not inclined to pressure that state to change domestically and/or do not frustrate the state's foreign policy goals by voicing opposition.

The obstructive/diffuse mechanism immediately complicates any simple model of external authoritarian propaganda or authoritarian soft power. States disseminate positive messages and images of themselves abroad, true, but they also attempt to expunge or obscure negative images of themselves in the public discourse through authoritarian practices. Despite the attempts by many autocratic states to construct an authoritarian public sphere domestically, the speed and intensity of global information flows means that the barrier between internal and external public spheres is not entirely impenetrable (Glasius 2018b, 181). Being located outside of the state does not completely impede meaningful participation in discussion about a state's politics. But conversely, extraterritoriality also does not completely protect discussion from techniques of censorship or manipulation deployed by the state. Authoritarian states attempt to influence transnational communication flows to censor information, but there are limits, insofar as "they are unable to censor as effectively as they might do within the borders" (Glasius 2018b, 190–191). A modified approach, facilitated by digital communication technologies, is to "censor" potentially damaging narratives by "flooding" the public sphere with information to obscure the threatening message or narrative (Roberts 2018, 87). For example, the RIRA troll farm techniques that obscure or distract about bad news from Russia or its invasion of parts of Ukraine take this approach. They confuse public discourse about these topics, attack the credibility of Russia's accusers, and so on. The result is to deflect from negative criticism about Russian policies.

If the authoritarian state cannot censor or drown out undesirable messages abroad, it may be compelled to respond to them in some way. Here it can draw on some of the legitimating elements that authoritarian states frequently deploy in the domestic sphere (Dukalskis 2017). It can frame events or processes so that they are consistent with its legitimating messages, blame other actors for negative events attributed to it, or use rhetorical devices to conceal its own harmful or dubious actions. For example, it may deploy moral equivalence arguments along the lines of "yes, we have problems, but look at all the bad things that democracies do—who are they to judge us?" Or it may present itself as a passive bystander or even a victim of some harmful process, rather than a contributor to its cause.

Either by censoring, obscuring, or rhetorically responding to negative images of it abroad, the authoritarian state hopes to inhibit the resonance of criticism about its practices among the public. Perhaps the censorship or flooding buries a negative story so that it never comes to public light, or perhaps the rhetorical tactics it uses work to assuage concerns that members of foreign publics have about its actions. The logic is to protect the image of the state abroad by erasing damaging information or mitigating its impact.

The last step in this causal chain sees the reduced effectiveness of criticism contribute to frustrating wider efforts at putting pressure on the authoritarian state. Awareness-raising by activists about issues like human rights abuses in the target state, for example, will be less likely to be effective if they face a public that is either not primed to be sympathetic and/or is armed with rhetorical justification for ignoring those abuses. The latter is powerful insofar as people can easily fail to do anything about injustices if they have cognitive tools to help justify their lack of agency or the inevitability of atrocities (Cohen 2000). Relatedly, inhibiting or mitigating negative stories or criticisms of the state allows it to pursue its foreign policy agenda with less popular resistance.

Promotional/Specific: Cultivating Opinion-Shapers and Influencers

Authoritarian image management involves more than just disseminating messages to broad audiences and shielding those efforts from criticism. Promotional authoritarian image management, or what Cooley and Heathershaw (2017, 77–78) call "image crafting", can also be targeted at particular groups or persons. The idea is to present an image of the state to specific influential groups so that they act on and/or reproduce that image to the benefit of the state. The logic is that the autocratic state shows a positive image of the state to opinion-shapers and/or policymakers so that they pursue their work with that positive image in mind. With opinion-shapers, the second half of the chain is that they will reproduce that image to the wider public in order to reduce pressure among the general public on the state to change domestically and/or to gain support for foreign policy object-ives. Alternatively, the end of the causal chain may be more direct insofar as targeted political elites may influence policy so that it is in the state's interest, so that ultimately direct political pressure on the state to change domestically is alleviated and/or the foreign policy goals of the state are achieved.

In other words, promotional/specific mechanisms target individ-uals or groups who have some capacity to shape a wider discourse and/or policy environment. The logic resembles that of authoritarian co-optation at the domestic level insofar as it ties strategically relevant actors to the re-gime (Gerschewski 2013). Co-optation, however, usually relies on material payoffs, which may happen in the case of promotional/diffuse image man-agement, but could also include methods that do not rely on payments or institutional power, such as flattery or access.

The first link in the causal logic of this mechanism is to convince specific actors or groups to ratify the state's image. In practical terms, this may in-volve influencing the work of foreign journalists in the country so that they present a more positive image of the state to international readers (Edney 2014, 81–83), stage-managed tourist visits (David-Fox 2012), junkets for for-eign politicians or journalists (Young 2015, 114), cultivating international opinion-shapers who can tell the country's story (Brady 2015, 53–54), and/or funding academic research that shapes the scholarly view of a state (Cumings 1996). As mentioned in the opening chapter, South Africa's Apartheid gov-ernment did all of these things to try to convince American and European opinion-shapers that its system of racial segregation was legitimate and that sanctions would disproportionately hurt black South Africans (Nixon 2016).

The second link in the causal mechanism then sees the positive image of the state reflected in the influential person's work. Politicians after a junket may keep that sense of indebted hospitality in mind when discussing foreign policy toward that state or defending its human rights abuses, academics may choose research topics or deliver lectures that reify positive images, and so on. The implication of junket trips for journalists is that they will report more positively about the host country when they return to their work at home. The hospitality extended is implicitly expected to be returned.

Here the process can follow two causal branches. The first branch pertains to opinion-shapers such as journalists and academics who lack direct policy-making influence. Their role in this chain is to reproduce the positive image, or at least downplay negative images, of the state within their discourse communities and/or to the wider public. In an admittedly extreme case,

US journalist John Barron reflected on how some opinion-shapers told the story of Stalin's Soviet Union abroad after they had visited on stage-managed tourist programs:

> Viewed in retrospect, the results . . . achieved surely must be classified as brilliant. At a time when the secret political police were murdering hundreds of thousands of Soviet citizens, and when countless others were being herded into concentration camps where ghastly conditions ensured the deaths of most, famous Western authors, scholars, journalists and lawyers acclaimed Soviet feats of "human regeneration" and "social correction." (quoted in Kunczik 1997, 252)

While the example is extreme and not representative of all Western thought leaders at the time, it lucidly describes a link in this causal process, insofar as some opinion-shapers presented a favorable image of the Soviet Union after they had been the willing targets of promotional/specific efforts (David-Fox 2012; McNair 2015; White 2019). They were flattered with hospitality and were shown a manicured image of the Soviet Union such that they could report positively back home. Their opinions would furthermore carry the credibility that comes with being a firsthand witness. The next link in the chain is for the effects of that wider public image to reduce pressure among foreign publics for the authoritarian regime to change its policies and to gain support, or at least to reduce opposition to the state's foreign policy goals. In the Soviet case, the aim was to reduce opposition to communism in the West so that at maximum it could spread there, but at minimum Moscow would face less pressure against its foreign policy.

The second branch of the promotional/specific causal pathway is more direct. If policymakers or politicians are compelled to view the state in question positively, then they can influence policy directly in their domain. The direct mechanism helps the autocratic state reduce pressure on itself, and thereby enhance its security, by ensuring that sympathetic voices circulate in influential policymaking circles. It also means that its foreign policy priorities can get a better hearing. The link to these effects may be subtle insofar as a positive image of the state may lead some policymakers to emphasize or de-emphasize some issues related to the state. Or the positive image held by the policymaker may lay dormant in normal times but become salient and useful in times of heightened pressure for the state, such as after a crackdown or amid bargaining over a bilateral foreign policy issue.

Obstructive/Specific: Targeting Critics

Authoritarian states frequently have critics abroad who may irritate their official narrative and tarnish the government's image. Sometimes this can come in the form of (self-)exiled citizens who choose to criticize their home state government from abroad. But critics abroad need not be exiled citizens. Foreign activist groups, intellectuals, or journalists sometimes critique the politics of autocratic states or present information seen as threatening to the state's image. The obstructive/specific mechanism of authoritarian image management aims to silence critics either by attacking their reputation or by intimidating them or even violently repressing them. The causal story is to silence or influence, either verbally, with cumbersome administrative procedures, or with coercion and/or threats, the voices of critics or purveyors of negative information. This will damage their ability to credibly criticize the state or present damaging information. The messages they communicate become less likely to reach or resonate with foreign or domestic publics. This can have numerous effects, such as reducing pressure from foreign publics on the regime to change domestic policies, reducing opposition to foreign policy goals, and/or severing linkages between external critics and internal dissidents.

The ability of critics abroad to articulate and disseminate their messages, gain support, and mobilize resources presents a challenge to the authoritarian state (Lewis 2015, 144). The logic of the obstructive/specific mechanism of authoritarian image management is a silencing one. While the obstructive/diffuse mechanism protects the state's narrative in general terms, the obstructive/specific mechanism targets the carriers of critical messages. This form of image management is designed to protect the state's legitimation efforts through targeted silencing, discrediting, and/or repression.

The first step is to silence the sources of negative information about the state outside the state's borders. This can entail "extending the scale of domestic political controls across borders" (Lewis 2015, 141). In practical terms, this can take many forms, including monitoring and harassing critics, attacking their reputations, hacking activist websites, threatening families of exiles if the former remain in the home country, and possibly even physically harming or assassinating the sources of criticism (see Collyer and King 2015; Lewis 2015; Cooley and Heathershaw 2017, 195–201; Moss 2018; Michaelsen 2018; Glasius 2018b). These sorts of measures, as with traditional conceptions of territorially bound state repression, are meant to work by "imposing a cost on the target as well as deterring specific activities and/

or beliefs perceived to be challenging to government personnel, practices or institutions" (Davenport 2007, 2).

The threatening beliefs and/or activities may be taking place outside of the state's borders, so the state's ability to repress them is constrained both by its own resource limitations and by the sovereignty of other states. While "the authoritarian state has ample opportunities to extend its coercive power beyond borders," it cannot repress the ability of people in foreign locales to communicate with the same efficiency that it can domestically (Glasius 2018b, 186, 190–191). Extraterritorial repression aimed at critics of the state is likely to be more targeted and less effective than its territorial equivalent, although the very fact that the criticism emanates from abroad limits its resonance domestically. Moreover, a determined state can still exert enormous power. As mentioned in the previous chapter, the digital infrastructure that has shrunk the world for activists and challengers has also given authoritarian regimes new tools for obstructive/specific targeting. Moss (2018, 276) illustrates this point well regarding the Syrian diaspora challenging the government of Bashar al-Assad:

> the very mechanisms that link members of the diaspora to their home countries and make them vital members of transnational advocacy networks also expose diasporas to authoritarian systems of surveillance, repression, and social control that operate through [internet communication technologies] and are pervasive across social media.

If the sources of critical messages can be repressed, then this can enhance the state's ability to control its narrative beyond its borders. Silencing critics abroad makes it more difficult for them to oppose the state's policies and/or present negative information about it, or to share critical information with domestic actors. If the message is not able to be produced, then it cannot reach the audiences necessary to have the desired effect of putting pressure on the state's political system or frustrating its foreign policy goals. The state's preferred image of itself is therefore shielded from direct criticism and can circulate with less resistance, thus boosting the regime's security.

However, exiled activists are not the only target for obstructive/specific authoritarian image management. In theory, it could apply to anyone critical of the authoritarian state. A special category of people, alluded to in the introduction of this chapter about North Korea, are foreign journalists reporting from the state in question. Instead of preventing messages from entering the state, like in the case of exiled activists, the objective with regard to foreign journalists located in the state is to prevent negative messages from emanating outward. Foreign media thus present a unique and salient category for the state's obstructive image management.

Most violent coercion against journalists around the world is targeted at domestic journalists, not foreign correspondents (Ghodes and Carey 2017, 163). Authoritarian states appear less willing to violently repress foreign journalists given the possibility for international backlash. Their obstructive/specific image management techniques when foreign journalists are the target usually rely on subtler forms of information denial. They may include restrictions on access to sites, information, and people.

The final links in this causal mechanism result from the message being silenced. If the repression is indeed effective in silencing the messenger and preventing the message from reaching its intended audiences, then this ultimately has three effects. The first two are similar to the final outcome of the other causal chains outlined thus far. First, it reduces pressure from foreign publics for the government to change since the former is now deprived of potentially resonant arguments and/or stories that can be used in their work. As mentioned in the previous chapter, in the "market" of transnational activism, participants must craft compelling stories and travel to spread their message to earn support (Bob 2005). If they are repressed or harassed by the governments they are targeting, then these activities are more difficult to undertake. Funders select issues to support partly based on how salient they are among public audiences (Bob 2005, 29), so if an authoritarian government can keep its challengers off the international stage, then they can keep their causes off the agenda and ultimately shield the state from activists' foreign pressure. International media coverage amplifies human rights activism on salient and visible issues (Ron, Ramos, and Rodgers 2005), so inhibiting critical activists abroad from communicating their message is a powerful tool for authoritarian states.

Second, it reduces the resonance of criticisms about the state's foreign policy. For example, activists often use state visits or summits to highlight their criticisms of the visiting figure's home state and relations between the two states. Frustrating critics' ability to use high-profile events as a platform for criticism means that the state's foreign relations can proceed with fewer impediments.

Third, and particularly germane to the obstructive/specific mechanism of targeting activists, silencing critical voices abroad erodes or even severs their links with domestic dissidents so that their messages cannot penetrate domestic society (Michaelson 2018; Moss 2018). Linkages to international networks are key to the ability of domestic activists to influence authoritarian governments (Keck and Sikkink 1998). Access to international networks provides information, points of leverage, financial resources, tactical or strategic support, and so on. Domestic activists are much better placed than international activists to use these resources to change the state's policies because they are located in the context, immersed in domestic networks, have access to local media platforms and physical spaces, and may be able to cultivate sympathizers within the government. If the state can sever links between international and domestic critics, then the messages of the former will be much more difficult or even impossible to communicate to the latter and vice versa. If domestic activists are disconnected from those contacts, then their ability to effectively criticize or pressure the state from a domestic standpoint is reduced.

For instance, Cooley and Heathershaw (2017) detail how Central Asian autocracies look abroad to target former regime insiders-turned-critics, opposition leaders, alleged religious extremists or banned clerics, and human rights activists (Cooley and Heathershaw 2017, 190). This helps prevent political opponents based abroad from gaining traction domestically. The governments use threats and warnings, arrests and detentions facilitated by like-minded autocracies, and finally, rendition, disappearance, attack, and/or assassination (Cooley and Heathershaw 2017, 195–201). For example, Uzbekistan looked abroad to target exiles wishing to mobilize and seek accountability for the country's 2005 massacre of protesters in the city of Andijan (Cooley and Heathershaw 2017, 201–209). Tajikistan's authorities targeted a nascent opposition movement led by a former regime insider Umarali Kuvvatov; he was ultimately assassinated in Istanbul in 2015 (Cooley and Heathershaw 2017, 209–217). The aim of all these activities is to eliminate the threat posed by external critics to the image and the internal security of the regime.

Combining Mechanisms and Contexts

In practice, authoritarian states use combinations of these mechanisms to manage their image abroad. The most attentive deploy a comprehensive strategy of authoritarian image management. Saudi Arabian efforts, for example, range from putting on art or cultural exhibitions (promotional/ diffuse) to manipulating online conversation (obstructive/diffuse) to staged meetings with key opinion leaders (promotional/specific) to murdering critical dissidents abroad (obstructive/specific) and everything in between. How might different target contexts influence the strategies of authoritarian states?

Recognizing that there is a sizable gray area on this spectrum, the targeted contexts can be distinguished as more democratic or more authoritarian. Given that democratic societies have larger winning coalitions and more liberal public spheres, one would expect the more diffuse mechanisms to be more commonly deployed in democracies, while the specific mechanisms are likely to be more common in autocratic states where the winning coalition is smaller, and impact can be attained by influencing a smaller circle (e.g., Bueno de Mesquita et al. 2005; Bader, Grävingholt, and Kästner 2010). Furthermore, the obstructive mechanisms in theory are more likely to backfire in more democratic contexts because they can be more easily exposed. Censorship or repression by an authoritarian state in a democratic one may thus ultimately damage the former's image, which would recommend a more promotional strategy. The Khashoggi murder by Saudi agents, for example, eliminated a critic, but especially in the democratic West it drew attention to Saudi Arabia's human rights abuses and "derailed the crown prince's carefully crafted rebrand" (Hall 2019, n.p.), at least for a short period of time. Russian government-linked assassinations of exiles on UK territory seriously damaged British-Russian relations (Blake 2019).

There are therefore good reasons to expect the promotional/diffuse mechanism to be prominent in democratic targets. Authoritarian states can take advantage of the liberal public sphere afforded by democratic societies to disseminate their messages and viewpoints. Furthermore, democratic publics are likely to be the most active in criticizing authoritarianism abroad because it clashes with their own political norms and because citizens of other authoritarian states are likely to target their activism domestically. The example of Russia's television networks in the United States and Europe, for example, aptly illustrate this configuration. The host societies are committed to freedom of speech and so restricting those networks is difficult for them to manage, thus allowing official Russian perspectives to circulate.

The obstructive/diffuse mechanism is likely to manifest itself in different ways in democratic and autocratic contexts. In democratic contexts it may be more necessary to base this mechanism on rhetoric, refutation, and distraction, rather than outright censorship. Democratic states generally censor the media less than autocracies (Stier 2015), so it is more difficult to rely on a tactic of outright censorship in democratic contexts. An authoritarian state asking a counterpart government to censor or restrict information is likely to have a more difficult time convincing a democratic leader to comply, but an authoritarian leader may do so. For example, in 2017, Turkish authorities apparently agreed to censor "anti-China" material at the behest of the Chinese government (Reuters 2017). A similar bilateral censorship tactic with a more democratic regime, committed to freedom of expression, would be more difficult and so the authoritarian state might employ different tactics to influence foreign public discourse. It is also the case that obstructive tactics like censorship are more likely to backfire in democratic contexts because they can be more easily exposed.

The promotional/specific mechanism will be actively deployed in both contexts, but it may garner greater returns on investment in an autocratic context. In democratic public spheres, friendly opinion-shapers are likely to have a more difficult time breaking through the "noise" to communicate the state's image effectively, although they may sometimes succeed or may simply lobby other elites privately. Perhaps more importantly, the more transparent context of a democracy means that the connections between the speaker and the authoritarian state itself can be revealed more easily. Ongoing debates about the Chinese Communist Party influencing elites in Australia and New Zealand, for example, would be much more difficult to base on solid information if the latter two states were not democratic, with avenues like freedom of information requests or protections for investigative journalists. Furthermore, in terms of policymakers, given the smaller circle of influential elites and the reduced transparency in authoritarian regimes, it is likely that a promotional/specific strategy akin to co-optation can yield quicker results.

Finally, the obstructive/specific mechanism is likely to be more common when the target state is autocratic. This mechanism relies on repression and silencing activities that are easier to carry out with the protection that can be offered by an authoritarian host. However, when extraterritorial repression does take place in a democratic state, it is more likely to be discovered and publicly exposed than if it took place in an authoritarian state. This means that publicly available data about authoritarian extraterritorial repression will likely give the impression that it is less common in dictatorships than it actually is because information about actions in autocracies is more difficult to obtain.

Conclusion

Returning to the example described at the outset of this chapter, we can use the vocabulary established so far to better understand North Korea's partnership with the AP. Clearly, it has a promotional/diffuse aspiration from Pyongyang's standpoint. The idea is to present North Korea positively and credibly to international audiences. However, to achieve success, the government perceives that it needs to control the AP bureau itself with obstructive/specific tactics. It uses obstructive/specific methods by inhibiting the work of the foreign correspondent, including restricting where s/he can go, limiting available information and access to sources, and so on. In this way, the government hopes that fewer negative stories about North Korea will reach foreign readers and undermine the regime's security. The mechanisms proposed in this chapter help us describe and understand the techniques of authoritarian states in new ways that go beyond existing widely used concepts.

The next step is to evaluate the proposed causal pathways to see if they indeed do have the desired effects. In other words, we want to move from "how do they work?" to "*do* they actually work?" Of course, the mechanisms are more likely to work when they are resourced appropriately. More resources and professionalism can help reduce the likelihood that authoritarian image management efforts are seen as mere propaganda. This may involve "media specialists and perhaps propaganda departments" (Whitehead 2014, 22) and/or foreign public relations firms or fixers (Cooley and Heathershaw 2017; Cooley, Heathershaw, and Sharman 2018). Regimes with higher capacity to adapt to varied information environments and to change with the times are likely to be better at authoritarian image management (see Morgenbesser 2020b).

Beyond these basic points, there is much to investigate. Authoritarian states of all stripes use a range of tactics to influence how they are perceived abroad. The following chapters turn to empirical examination of these mechanisms in concrete cases. They aim to assess whether the motivations and pathways discussed in this and the previous chapter occur empirically and to understand how they unfold.

4

Selling Dictatorship and Silencing Dissent

A Global Snapshot

Authoritarian states can never quite control things as efficiently abroad as they can at home. It is more difficult for them to censor information abroad or to compel foreign audiences to consume state media. Foreign audiences have not been socialized in the state's school system to identify with national images or heroes. Indeed, foreign audiences may be downright skeptical of any given state's political system or policies. This means that authoritarian image management will always be a pale imitation of the domestic authoritarian public sphere. And yet, authoritarian states try to portray their political systems positively in search of enhanced internal and external security.

The previous chapters have outlined the theoretical and conceptual underpinnings of authoritarian image management. Subsequent chapters will present detailed case studies focusing on China, North Korea, and Rwanda, each chosen because they illustrate different aspects of authoritarian image management. The purpose of this chapter is to provide a global, cross-national snapshot of two dimensions of authoritarian image management efforts, one promotional and one obstructive.

First, to capture primarily the "promotional" mechanisms of authoritarian image management, the chapter presents data on public relations (PR) and lobbying of authoritarian states in the United States. The United States requires that agents engaging in political activities on behalf of foreign principals register with the Department of Justice (DoJ), which means that the public has access to documents with details about how authoritarian states try to burnish their image among the public at large (promotional/ diffuse image management) as well as among elites and policymakers (promotional/specific image management). Analysis of 113 filings from 33 countries active in 2018 and 2019 reveal a glimpse of what authoritarian states do with the tens of millions of dollars they invest in trying to cultivate a positive image of themselves in the United States in order to bolster their internal and/or external security.

Making the World Safe for Dictatorship, Alexander Dukalskis, Oxford University Press (2021). © Oxford University Press.
DOI: 10.1093/oso/9780197520130.003.0004

Second, to illustrate the "obstructive" side of authoritarian image management, this chapter presents the Authoritarian Actions Abroad Database (AAAD). The AAAD reveals nearly 1,200 individual cases in which an authoritarian state attempted to threaten, attack, abduct, arrest, detain, or assassinate one or more of its citizens abroad who were perceived to be politically threatening. The aim of these actions is to silence the messages that critical exiles share with the wider world and to prevent their activities from influencing domestic politics and undermining regime security.

The purpose of this broad, cross-national data is to emphasize two main points. First, the data reveal the dual nature of authoritarian image management. Authoritarian states do not just engage in insipid marketing campaigns to make themselves look good abroad. As the AAAD reveals, authoritarian states take concerted and coercive actions outside their borders to silence critics. Even the lobbying and PR activities contain some deception and obfuscation that is not quite captured by concepts of soft power, public diplomacy, or branding. Second, the data are meant to underscore how many different types of authoritarian states engage in these activities. While subsequent chapters focus on China, North Korea, and Rwanda, and journalistic attention often covers Russia's usage of these activities (e.g., Blake 2019; Pomerantsev 2019), analyzing PR documents and the AAAD reveals that a variety of dictatorships engage in authoritarian image management techniques of both the promotional and obstructive varieties. Indeed, the two data sets, both reported in more detail in the appendices to this volume, reveal the activities of 48 states, and this is only using publicly available information (self-reported in the case of the PR data). Given that some aspects of authoritarian image management are designed to be hidden or obscured, the true scope of these activities is likely to be wider and the intensity deeper than publicly available data suggest.

Selling Dictatorship: Public Relations and Image Management

Authoritarian states regularly engage in public relations and lobbying abroad to try to advance their goals. The opening sections of this book's first two chapters featured the example of Kazakhstan (Schatz 2008; Cooley and Heathershaw 2017, 77–78) and the previous chapter briefly discussed Saudi Arabia's recent PR blitz (Kerr 2017). A report by the advocacy group

Corporate Europe Observatory (2015) details in 18 case studies the ways in which repressive states use PR firms in Europe to improve their image and discredit their opponents. The global consulting firm McKinsey has worked in a variety of capacities with authoritarian regimes around the world (Bogdanich and Forsythe 2018). The examples are numerous, but there are few systematic studies of the topic in academic literature (Cooley, Heathershaw, and Sharman 2018).

The use of PR firms to burnish the image of dictatorships is not new. Philippine dictator Ferdinand Marcos was an early adopter of this technique, spending $500,000 in 1977 to enhance his image in the United States (Morgenbesser 2020a, 10). What seems to have changed over the years is that now dictatorships keep PR firms on retainers to work for them on a continuous basis. While early adopters like Marcos may have contracted with a PR firm for a distinct campaign or to influence a specific piece of legislation, something which still occurs today, many of today's dictatorships also keep PR firms working for them year-round to improve in more routine ways how they are perceived abroad (Morgenbesser 2020a, 11). This is part of a broader shift after the Cold War that saw dictators and their elite allies using "the West's institutions and brokers" to launder both their ill-gotten gains and their reputations (Cooley, Heathershaw, and Sharman 2018, 42).

In the theoretical language of this book, the companies that take on dictatorships as clients most commonly engage in promotional/diffuse methods (e.g., public relations, "media outreach," advertising) and promotional/specific image management (e.g., lobbying, "government relations," "reaching out to key opinion leaders"). Sometimes they may also engage in obstructive/diffuse image management (e.g., public relations "crisis management") or even in obstructive/specific methods (e.g., discrediting critical NGOs or exiles), as in the case of "black PR" that targets political opponents of wealthy clients (Cooley, Heathershaw, and Sharman 2018, 45). In general, the aim of using a foreign PR firm is to portray the dictatorship positively in the firm's host country so that decision-makers there facilitate the client's foreign policy and the general public does not frustrate its aims.[1]

The use of PR firms is a global phenomenon about which it is often cumbersome and sometimes impossible to gather data. Some jurisdictions,

---

[1] Others focus on the reputation management and laundering of specific elites (Cooley and Heathershaw 2017; Cooley, Heathershaw, and Sharman 2018). This book is more concerned with how the authoritarian state and its representatives, rather than specific individuals, are portrayed.

however, have transparency laws that allow a glimpse into the world of marketing dictatorship. In the United States, entities working to advance the political goals of foreign actors must register with the DoJ. The Foreign Agents Registration Act, known as FARA,

> requires certain agents of foreign principals who are engaged in political activities or other activities specified under the statute to make periodic public disclosure of their relationship with the foreign principal, as well as activities, receipts and disbursements in support of those activities. Disclosure of the required information facilitates evaluation by the government and the American people of the activities of such persons in light of their function as foreign agents. (Department of Justice 2020a)

The DoJ maintains a public FARA database of all registrants and foreign principals and reports to Congress periodically. Registrants are generally US-based firms that provide lobbying, legal, public relations, consulting, and strategic planning services. Foreign principals are companies, individuals, state bodies, or other entities based outside the United States that contract with registrants for their services. The database can be searched by agent or foreign principal within date ranges or for the entire period. In most cases, copies of Exhibit A and/or Exhibit B are available. Exhibit A is a form that registrants must complete when they contract with a new foreign principal. Exhibit B stipulates that copies of written agreements or summaries of oral agreements with the foreign principal must be provided (Department of Justice 2020b).

This chapter reports on data from active foreign principals in 2018 and 2019.[2] As of December 31, 2019, the database listed 701 active foreign principals in the United States with links to Exhibit A/B or amendments that may contain more information. To get a snapshot view, all registrations on behalf of foreign authoritarian entities that stipulated that activity was undertaken in 2018 and/or 2019 were included. Using the same list as the AAAD (see the following and Appendix 2 for more details), cases were included if they were defined by major comparative politics data sets as non-democratic. Where necessary, extra searches were conducted by registrant to get up-to-date materials as filings are sometimes amended with more information. This

---

[2] The FARA database stretches back to the 1940s. Systematic analysis over time is not done here, but those wishing to get a briefer comparison of 2018 and 2019 with previous years can see semi-annual reports to Congress here: https://www.justice.gov/nsd-fara/fara-reports-congress.

does not include most independent companies from authoritarian states, individuals from authoritarian states that are in opposition to the relevant regime, or strictly tourism-related work. This procedure yielded 113 filings from 33 states that were active between January 1, 2018, and December 31, 2019. The complete list, including links to copies of the registrations, can be found in Appendix 1. The total annual value of the contracts using this method is between about $153 million and $172 million spent on PR and lobbying fees by authoritarian states in the United States.

Several clarifications are in order. First, these data provide an extremely conservative picture of authoritarian image management activities in the United States. These are only overt self-reported efforts registered with the US government. They do not include foreign government funding to think tanks or research institutes, which is generally not required to be reported under FARA but which a *New York Times* investigation found to be in the tens of millions annually (Lipton, Williams, and Confessore 2014). In general, the filings do not include corporate intelligence groups that approach or even cross legal boundaries as they gather information on their clients' political opponents (Burgis 2017). They do not capture many religious activities that facilitate the foreign policies of the sending state (Öztürk and Sözeri 2018). They do not capture covert efforts, social media strategies managed by entities outside the United States, informal networks and relationships, events organized by embassies themselves, cultural outreach institutions like Confucius Institutes, and so on. While foreign agents and principals have a duty to self-report their activities, this is not always well policed, and there are certainly gaps. This information is just the tip of what is obviously a much larger iceberg.

Indeed, as a testament to the difficulty and ambiguity of gathering PR and lobbying information even with strong transparency laws, the data for this section were compared to the "Foreign Lobby Watch" tool provided by the Center for Responsive Politics.[3] The tool lists governmental and nongovernmental spending for all countries, but for this exercise only the 33 countries for which data were obtained from FARA are used. For those same 33 countries, the Center for Responsive Politics lists zero spending for nine of them. However, for others, such as China when *China Daily* is included, or Russia when its media arms are included as government spending despite layers of intermediaries (see later discussion), the totals are much closer to those

---

[3] Available at: https://www.opensecrets.org/fara/countries (data analyzed May 2020).

found using the search methods of the FARA website described earlier. For still others, such as Saudi Arabia and the United Arab Emirates, the Center for Responsive Politics totals are much higher. However, if we aggregate all the outlays for 2018 and 2019 as reported by the organization, we get an annual total of just over $112 million for the countries on the list. Adding the missing data from the other nine countries would bring the total closer to the numbers reported earlier. The discrepancies are likely due to gray areas as to what counts as "government" spending, as well as missing data.

Second, in terms of financing, the data should be viewed as a conservative estimate. With some notable exceptions, fees for most reported filings here do not include expenses, but only consulting or retainer payments. This means that the actual money spent under most listed contracts is much higher than the number listed here. For example, if a country is paying a firm a $120,000 fee to organize a conference, this sum usually does not include expenses like renting the venue, paying for travel, speaker fees, purchasing advertising space to publicize the conference, and so on. The Center for Responsive Politics attempts to track receipts for expense outlays, but as of this writing the coverage is incomplete, especially for 2019.

Third, the registrations vary considerably in terms of their specificity. Some contain just a few sentences with general terms like "government relations" or "public relations." A few are quite granular and list specific activities, dates of conferences or meetings, number of articles to be placed in media outlets, and so on. Most registrations are somewhere in between these poles.

Fourth, authoritarian states are by no means the only entities that register their PR and lobbying efforts with the DoJ. Indeed, they may not even be the most active. Entities from democratic states—and sometimes the states themselves—like South Korea, India, Japan, Canada, Taiwan, and Australia all have active contracts. Furthermore, sometimes anti-authoritarian individuals or entities, such as opposition parties or governments-in-exile, register their efforts.

Fifth and finally, these documents generally only bear on activities in the United States. Excluded are PR contracts with firms based outside the United States. Most importantly, this excludes the cluster of London-based firms that are well-known for laundering the reputations of autocratic leaders (Corporate Europe Observatory 2015; Segal 2018). This underscores the point made earlier that the activities and funding reported in the FARA database provide only a small glimpse of the efforts of authoritarian states to press their case to publics and elites abroad.

These considerations aside, what do the registrations tell us? Most obviously, they confirm that authoritarian states regularly spend money in the United States to bolster their image among policymakers and the public. The registrations have a minimum total annual value of over $153 million. This figure excludes 12 of the 113 agreements which have either unspecified values or hourly fee structures. Two contracts are also explicitly pro bono. If we assume the 12 unspecified or hourly contracts are similar to the average annual value of the 101 contracts for which sums are listed, then the total annual value is about $172 million. Again, for the reasons discussed previously, this should be viewed as a very conservative estimate.

There are a few notable states that spend exceptionally large amounts. Saudi Arabia's registrations for this period total over $21.5 million in fees. These included a $1.5 million annual value contract with LS2group for government relations and for the company to "inform the public, government officials and the media about the importance of fostering and promoting strong relations between the United States and the Kingdom of Saudi Arabia" including "media outreach and engagement efforts across select media markets throughout the U.S."[4] A $1.4 million contract between Saudi Arabia's sovereign wealth fund and KARV Communications promises to conduct "outreach and relationship-building to various stakeholders in business and the media."[5] A nearly $6 million contract between the embassy and Qorvis Communications describes the latter's services as "media monitoring, outreach activities, content development, research and analysis, and event planning and support."[6] These outlays coincided with Saudi Arabia's global PR push under Crown Prince Mohammed bin Salman. Journalist Richard Hall gives an example of what a PR investment of this sort provided:

In early 2018, the royal embarked on a high-profile media tour of the US— billed as a coming out party after assuming de-facto leadership of Saudi Arabia from his father. He held meetings with President Donald Trump, Jeff Bezos and Bill Gates, Hollywood stars, Wall Street financiers and Oprah Winfrey, to name a few. He appeared on the flagship news programme *60 Minutes* for a sit-down interview, and attracted faint praise from columnists in *The New York Times*. (Hall 2019)

[4] https://efile.fara.gov/docs/6749-Exhibit-AB-20191112-1.pdf (all FARA links in remainder of chapter last accessed September 1, 2020).
[5] https://efile.fara.gov/docs/6162-Exhibit-AB-20190225-3.pdf.
[6] https://efile.fara.gov/docs/5483-Exhibit-AB-20191030-69.pdf.

Saudi Arabia's neighbor, Qatar, spent at least $6.9 million during this period, despite its small population of under 3 million people. This included contracts for promotional/specific image management. A $480,000 contract with Third Circle, Inc., focused on fostering exchanges between Qatar and US states and cities, as well as "developing bilateral exchange programs for young leaders."[7] A related agreement with the same company stipulated that it would assist in "arranging for state and local elected officials to participate in delegations traveling to Qatar for meetings with government officials, business and trade representatives, and representatives of other organizations and institutions."[8] A $360,000 contract with Mercury Public Affairs agreed to provide "research, advice and assistance to [the] Embassy regarding the work of nongovernmental policy institutions and academic institutions active in studying Middle East issues." This contract included an optional clause that the embassy could exercise for "planning, organizing, staffing and attending two separate 'thought leader' events in Qatar."[9] These specific targeted agreements involving Qatar were in addition to millions spent in general lobbying and public relations agreements.

The Russian and Chinese cases deserve special attention. The US DoJ in recent years has made the external propaganda arms of each state register as foreign agents. This includes the externally facing television stations of each state, namely Russia Today (RT) and China Global Television Network (CGTN). Both television stations present themselves as ordinary news outlets, but given the relationship between each station and its respective host state, as well as the content of their broadcasting, they can both be considered external propaganda. Yet they have somewhat different approaches (Rawnsley 2015). RT generally does not extoll Russia's virtues directly and instead focuses on presenting a negative picture of the United States and "the West." It presents Russia as a "global underdog" to the United States and fosters conspiracy theories about the latter and criticizes US influence abroad (Yablokov 2015). CGTN often portrays the United States negatively as well, but it focuses more on showing positive aspects of Chinese society and politics (Rawnsley 2015). Both CGTN and RT maintain active YouTube channels and social media accounts in multiple

---

[7] https://efile.fara.gov/docs/6540-Exhibit-AB-20190326-3.pdf.
[8] https://efile.fara.gov/docs/6540-Exhibit-AB-20190122-2.pdf.
[9] https://efile.fara.gov/docs/6170-Exhibit-AB-20191210-72.pdf.

languages to disseminate their messages globally. Both stations also have free live streaming services on their websites. Externally facing authoritarian TV and radio stations are a hallmark of "sophisticated authoritarianism" insofar as they advance the messages of authoritarian states without having to rely on censorship or repression (Morgenbesser 2020b, 46). They seize on protections afforded by the liberal public sphere in democracies to advance their messages.

In the United States, the FARA filings reveal substantial investments by each state in reaching American audiences.[10] The Russian documents for 2019 include a $9.4 million registration for Radio Moscow, the wire service and website Sputnik, and other assorted activities. The contract is highly detailed and runs to nearly 60 pages, with an itemized budget.[11] Russia runs RT in the United States through a company called T&R Productions LLC. Its 2019 filing shows that during the three-year window from 2014 to 2017, RT's parent entity contributed just over $70 million, or about $23.4 million annually.[12] This went to pay for RT's salaries, office space, wardrobes, production, and so on. Of course, the United States is just one audience for RT, which also has Arabic, Spanish, and French content (Orttung and Nelson 2019). RT's global budget in 2017, according to a spokesperson, was $323 million (Erlanger 2017). Perhaps more importantly for Moscow, Russian-language TV in neighboring states can influence political views there to be friendlier to Russian policy objectives (see Peisakhin and Rozenas 2018; Chapman and Gerber 2019). The US operation of RT, while highly publicized, is a small part of Russia's attempt to shape its image abroad—or perhaps more accurately, to delegitimize "the West"—around the world.

CGTN, which is overseen by China Central Television (CCTV), runs its organization in the United States through CGTN America and an organization called MediaLinks TV, LLC. The documentation seems to suggest that CGTN resented having to register with FARA as its application contains careful language noting that according to FARA's interpretation CGTN America is a foreign agent: "the FARA Unit has concluded that CGTN America engages in 'political activities' as defined by FARA, requiring it to register." It further argues that "CGTN America performs news gathering

---

[10] Unlike most other registrations, the financial figures for RT, CGTN, Sputnik, Radio Moscow, and *China Daily* do include expenses.

[11] https://efile.fara.gov/docs/6524-Exhibit-AB-20190314-3.pdf.

[12] https://efile.fara.gov/docs/6485-Amendment-20190211-2.pdf.

and reporting activities like those performed by other Washington news bureaus, including those of other foreign news organizations that broadcast or publish in the U.S."[13] This line is consistently used across CGTN's various filings. Its most recent financial statement as of this writing shows that in 2018 CCTV transferred a total of $19.5 million to "defray CGTN America operating costs." This was made in six separate transfers. The first transfer of 2019 is also listed and is for the same amount as the first transfer of 2018, suggesting that CCTV's investment will continue on a similar scale. A subset of CGTN's content, namely how it frames politics in Xinjiang, will be analyzed in Chapter 6.

Beijing also invests heavily in print media to convey its viewpoint, often purchasing "advertorial" inserts in major international publications and making copies of its own papers freely and widely available. Advertorials are advertising inserts made to look like ordinary journalism. The Chinese government has purchased advertorials in publications like *The Economist*, the *Washington Post*, the *New York Times* International Edition, the *Wall Street Journal*, the *Los Angeles Times*, and many others (Lim and Bergin 2018). In its most recent FARA filing as of this writing, the China Daily Distribution Corporation reported an outlay of just over $5 million for the previous six-month period for the "distribution of 'China Daily' pursuant to an exclusive distribution rights contract" as well as "advertising campaigns in Wall Street Journal, Washington Post."[14] The idea behind advertorial inserts in newspapers read by opinion shapers is to get China's viewpoint into the mainstream of elite discourse. It surely also reaches the eyes of a few readers who may not know that the *China Daily* or its associated brands are pushing official Chinese propaganda.

The documents show that the Chinese government also engages in more targeted efforts to portray China positively in the United States. Bearing in mind that these are only the self-reported documents, which do not include most of the off-the-books aspects of the "political influence" operations in which the Chinese Communist Party and its United Front Work Department engage (on these themes, see Brady 2018; Hamilton and Ohlberg 2020), they reveal targeted efforts at promotional/specific image management. For example, in a $120,000 contract with Capitol Counsel LLC, the "US-China Transpacific Foundation" agreed to arrange travel for members of the US

Congress and/or their staff to China. The aim was to give those on the trips the "opportunity to enhance their understanding on the cultural, economic, political and social developments of the People's Republic of China."[15] An agreement between BLJ Worldwide and the China-United States Exchange Foundation (CUSEF) showed that $356,400 was for maintaining the ChinaUSFocus.com website, which has pro-Beijing content, but also for facilitating delegations to China.[16]

A $168,000 filing between CUSEF and Wilson Global Communications LLC focused specifically on the African American community. This included arranging student visits and leadership delegations from historically black colleges and universities. The activities were meant to facilitate "building, enhancing, and retaining positive relationships with key opinion leaders in African American communities, students from underserved communities, and African American media outlets." The ultimate goal, according to the agreement, "is to enable these audiences to better understand China, preferably first-hand, in an effort to inform them and provide background knowledge to formulate personalized perspectives that can be articulated as balanced opinions when presented with Sino-US relationship issues."[17] This is precisely the logic of promotional/specific authoritarian image management: cultivating individuals to be advocates for the government's preferred positions and images. This strategy has the advantage of the messenger not being directly tied to the relevant state, which makes it more difficult to dismiss the message as propaganda.

Staying with promotional/specific image management, but moving on from China, a contract between the Agency for Information and Mass Communication in Uzbekistan's president's office and Frontier Consulting LLC described its promotional/specific image management project in an almost refreshingly direct way. The plan was to "invite western journalists to Tashkent for a 3-day tourism press tour in November 2019" and to "handle all communications with the media representatives, including ensuring that the journalists publish supportive and on-message articles following the trip."[18] The trip was organized around an investment conference held in Tashkent on November 15, 2019. A search of Google News and Lexis Advance UK for relevant terms from the days surrounding this period reveal a few articles that report on the conference, although it is rarely clear if

[15] https://efile.fara.gov/docs/6328-Exhibit-AB-20190320-10.pdf.
[16] https://efile.fara.gov/docs/5875-Exhibit-AB-20170921-53.pdf.
[17] https://efile.fara.gov/docs/6584-Exhibit-AB-20190201-9.pdf.
[18] https://efile.fara.gov/docs/6753-Exhibit-AB-20191120-1.pdf.

the articles were linked to this PR effort. One possible exception is an article in EmergingMarkets.me written by the partner of Frontier Consulting himself, which reports that "Uzbekistan is on a roll with its economic reforms" and that "the momentum of positive change is strong" (Martin 2019). It is unclear how effective articles like this are, given that they are in relatively obscure—although targeted—publications, but the method of generating positive news coverage is clear.[19]

Regardless, many authoritarian regimes clearly believe that public relations and lobbying projects work to secure their goals. If they did not, it would be unlikely that they would give tens of millions of dollars to foreign firms to that end. Generating positive messages for diffuse audiences and cultivating friendly opinion shapers able to communicate the state's viewpoint are common methods of authoritarian image management. The states that put major money behind these efforts and think through their targeting in a sophisticated fashion undoubtedly reap benefits for their image management and thus for their foreign and domestic policy goals, and ultimately their internal and external regime security.

Contracting PR and lobbying firms reflects a strategy of adapting authoritarian image management to the open public sphere and liberal economic markets of most of today's democracies. As noted in previous chapters, when an authoritarian state wishes to bolster its image in a democratic state, it must appeal to a broader audience relative to an authoritarian state. In the latter it can deal almost exclusively with its counterpart government and needs to worry less about its image in the broader public because the public and independent pressure groups have less input in policymaking. While it is a challenge for an authoritarian state to improve its image in a foreign democracy, it can use the institutions and protections of liberal democracy, as well as the relatively unregulated nature of PR and consulting industries, to its advantage. Some firms in the United States and Europe are only too happy to accept money from authoritarian regimes to help them do that. Thus, even with transparency mechanisms like FARA, which allow for scrutiny and investigation by journalists and researchers, many authoritarian states calculate that it is money well spent to propagate positive images of themselves in democratic public spheres.

---

[19] The contract was also cheap by the standards of the other filings, totaling only $10,000 plus expenses. This would be a relatively small investment if the right person were to see one of those articles.

Silencing Dissent Abroad

As discussed in previous chapters, authoritarian states have an interest in trying to silence their exiled critics. This is not new (Adamson 2019, 4–8). The famous 1940 assassination of Leon Trotsky in Mexico City by a Soviet-backed secret police agent using an ice pick is among the most remarkable historical examples. The murder of Saudi journalist Jamal Khashoggi in the Saudi Arabian embassy in Istanbul in 2018 is a particularly gruesome and dramatic recent instance of an authoritarian state targeting its (self-)exiled enemies abroad.

More recently, scholars have tried to come to terms with understanding what is variously termed extraterritorial repression, extraterritorial authoritarian practices, extraterritorial security practices, long-distance authoritarianism, or transnational authoritarianism (see, among others, Collyer and King 2015; Lewis 2015; Moss 2016; Cooley and Heathershaw 2017, 195–201; Moss 2018; Michaelsen 2018; Glasius 2018; Adamson 2019; Adamson 2020; Tsourapas 2020). The basic idea is that the state tries to extend its coercive reach beyond its borders to control dissidents abroad. Or, as Cooley and Heathershaw (2017, 190) put it: "as politics moves beyond borders, so too does repression." As discussed in the previous chapter, the aim of obstructive/specific authoritarian image management tactics like this is to silence the messenger so that her/his messages critical of the dictatorship do not reach their intended audiences and do not damage the regime's internal or external security. It also helps sever informational and organizational ties between exiled journalists or activists and their domestic counterparts, thus directly improving the regime's internal security.

Sovereignty makes extraterritorial repression more difficult than domestic repression. It is more challenging for states to intimidate political actors in other countries than doing so at home, given that the apparatus of the state is controlled by a third party. The threatening state must rely on networks of informers, surveillance organized at embassies, and/or online monitoring to keep an eye on political threats in other countries (Adamson 2019). Its actions abroad are not as shielded from international accountability as are its actions domestically. However, if local authorities in the "host" country cooperate in arresting or extraditing dissidents, then the state's job is made easier (Tsourapas 2020). One way that states try to do this is through Interpol Red Notices. Red Notices are essentially blanket requests by states to extradite the named person. They are meant for international fugitives, but authoritarian states increasingly use them to target and to limit the movements of exiled political opponents (Lemon 2019).

Despite challenges that come with sovereignty, authoritarian states nonetheless try to intimidate, silence, or even assassinate their exiled critics. Data on this underworld is scare because of its secretive nature, but the Central Asian Political Exiles (CAPE) database has pioneered an effort to systematically collect information of this sort. It captures the ways in which five states—Tajikistan, Uzbekistan, Kazakhstan, Turkmenistan, and Kyrgyzstan—attempt to "track and ultimately detain, capture or assassinate an *exile* who is deemed a threat to the regime in power" (Heathershaw and Furstenberg 2020, emphasis in original). The typology defines an "exile" as "an emigrant who has settled or spent a prolonged period overseas for reasons which are wholly or partly of a political character" (Heathershaw and Furstenberg 2020).

The Authoritarian Actions Abroad Database (AAAD) builds on the logic, methods, and research of the CAPE database, but modifies its approach in some important ways (for the full AAAD codebook, data-gathering procedures, and instructions to access to the data, which are freely available, see Appendix 2). First, the universe of states is all authoritarian states between 1991 and 2019. To define authoritarian states, the data set draws on typologies of authoritarian spells by Geddes, Wright, and Frantz (2014) and Wahman, Teorell, and Hadenius (2014). This approach sacrifices some of the depth that the CAPE database provides for a broader scope. Second, the AAAD uses some different definitions from CAPE, eliminating for example the "banned cleric" category, separating journalist and activist categories from one another, and adopting a more relaxed approach to what kinds of exiles are politically salient. Specifically, on the latter point, the AAAD incorporates people who left their country for non-political reasons such as work or study, but whom their home state regards as threatening to the state's political image abroad. The most common types of people that fit this description in the AAAD are North Koreans, who usually defect for economic reasons, and Uighurs, many of whom found themselves abroad for business or educational reasons but became political targets of the Chinese state, particularly amid a post-2014 crackdown. Third, the AAAD is event-based rather than case-based, which means that instances are organized based on delimited actions rather than by individual histories of the exiles themselves. Two different attempted assassinations of the same person at different times, for example, are recorded as two separate events in the

AAAD, whereas in CAPE they would both be rolled into the case history of the individual.

The AAAD contains publicly available information regarding authoritarian states' attempts to silence critics abroad from 1991 through the end of 2019. It contains information about cases in which authoritarian leaders try to suppress their critics abroad through threatening the dissident's family back home, threatening the dissident directly, arresting/detaining, attacking, abducting, extraditing, and/or assassinating the target. For the latter three actions, attempts are recorded as well, such as an attempted but ultimately unsuccessful assassination. The target categories are journalists, activists, opposition members, former government officials, and, as discussed earlier, a residual category of citizens.

Searching for information was done using a four-stage process. First, where similar databases existed, their content was incorporated. Most prominently, the CAPE database was drawn upon to categorize most cases from the five relevant Central Asian states, but other databases, such as the Front Line Defenders (2019) database of human rights defenders and the Xinjiang Victims Database (2019), were also used, given that researchers had already gathered the information and made it public. Second, Google news and Google search terms were utilized to identify a population of texts that contain information about the actions of authoritarian states against exiles abroad. A complete list of search terms can be found in in the "search procedure" section of the codebook in Appendix 2, but term combinations like COUNTRY THREATENED EXILES were queried. The search terms were designed to cast a wide net and therefore required readers to determine the relevance of each article. Third, given the possibility of recency bias in Google search terms, Lexis Advance UK was mined with a focus on earlier years in the data set, using similar search terms as those from the Google news and Google search procedures. Fourth, this was all done in English initially, but follow-up searches were completed in Arabic, Chinese, French, Korean, Turkish, and Russian to capture new cases and to illuminate more details on existing cases for verification purposes.

Information from credible NGOs, international watchdog groups, and credible journalistic sources were sought. Where news articles were found, attempts to corroborate each incident were made, given that multiple news sources report on the same event. Usually it was not difficult to find multiple credible sources reporting on the same incident. If the report was uncorroborated but the source is a credible organization and the claims resonate with broader patterns, then the source was included in the database. Authoritarian actions abroad are often inherently secretive—indeed, they are usually designed as such—and so in cases where responsibility was not always clear, the coding team discussed the case and used its best judgment to determine whether the case should be included or excluded. The database was cross-checked and validated by the coding team and the author to ensure reliability.

These procedures yielded 1,177 cases in which 35 authoritarian states took direct actions abroad to silence their (self-)exiled critics, including 52 assassinations and 30 attempted assassinations between 1991 and the end of 2019. The earliest case recorded in the AAAD is the assassination in April 1991 of Abdel Rahman Boroumand, an associate of the former Iranian prime minister Shahpur Bakhtiar, who himself was killed in Paris four months later (Riding 1991). The most recent case recorded comes from the final days of December 2019, when two school employees associated with the opposi- tional Turkish Gulenist movement were detained in Kyrgyzstan, with Turkey seeking their extradition (Putz 2019).

As with all data-gathering efforts, clarifications, caveats, and limitations need to be made explicit. First, and most importantly, the database relies only on publicly available digital information. Given the secretive nature of authoritarian actions abroad, as well as the fact that some dissidents may not want to publicize threats or attacks against them for safety reasons, the AAAD is radically incomplete. This is inevitable due to the nature of the sub- ject matter. The issue is compounded by the fact that there is a politics to the ways in which human rights NGOs and journalists gather information on human rights abuses, with some states gaining more attention than others (Ron, Ramos, and Rodgers 2005). Large states with ties to Europe and the United States are likely to be over-represented if previous research on NGO information politics is accurate. The data should therefore be viewed as a glimpse of a much larger universe of events that may never be recorded in a wholly representative way, and certainly not ever recorded in their entirety. Nevertheless, it is a useful glimpse because it shows how active authoritarian states are when it comes to targeting critical citizens abroad.

Second, some events involve multiple targets. Where possible, the effort was made to disaggregate events into their most specific possible version: one event happening to one person. Sometimes, however, this was not possible due to information limitations. For example, a Human Rights Watch report detailing how the UAE intimidates the families of dissidents described how the families of four exiled critics were threatened in the UAE, but no separate names or details were provided (Human Rights Watch 2019a). This was recorded as one event affecting four exiles. Sometimes it is not possible to disaggregate information because the action itself is targeted at an entire group. For example, in July 2015 Thai authorities sent more than 100 Uighurs, who had apparently fled repression, back to China (Holmes 2015). No individual details are readily available, and the action was taken at one time, so this is recorded as one event involving 109 persons. Most of the events in the AAAD are recorded at the individual level, but these group cases are included because they fit the relevant definitions. The alternative is to record each of the 109 cases in the Thailand/China example as 109 rows in the AAAD, but this option was generally not chosen unless names were available in order to keep the focus on the event as the unit of analysis. However, if all events in the AAAD were re-coded so that events involving multiple people were disaggregated, then the number of recorded events would increase from the current 1,177 to approximately 2,585.

Third, often the perpetrators of authoritarian actions abroad are not easy to identify. This is by design. Authoritarian governments often use "thugs for hire" to intimidate or attack dissidents domestically. Ong (2018) specifies three conditions in which the use of thugs is particularly likely: when the actions are illegal or unpopular, when the state wants to evade responsibility, and when states have weak capacity where they are operating. Taking action against critics abroad satisfies all three of these conditions: in most cases, states do not want to be seen to violate the sovereignty of other states; they do not want to be linked back to their repressive actions abroad; and they have far weaker capacity abroad than they do domestically. This means that the attribution of responsibility for authoritarian actions abroad is made intentionally difficult. Sometimes details about cases only come to light or are confirmed years later. There are undoubtedly cases in the AAAD where responsibility is misattributed, but for each case the preponderance of evidence was considered, and a judgment was made.

Fourth, sometimes authoritarian states accuse exiles of non-political crimes to tarnish their reputations and/or to justify their extradition or arrest. However, sometimes the relevant target really has committed non-political crimes for which their home state wants to pursue justice. This makes it difficult to determine when a terrorism charge, for example, is a politically motivated smear on a nonviolent political opponent or is a genuine and plausible accusation. Muddying the waters in this way is a tactic of authoritarian states to discredit their detractors. But even when the waters are clear, distinguishing between types of anti-government activists is sometimes difficult (Young and Shellman 2019). For the purposes of the AAAD, when there is evidence that an exiled dissident really has committed violent actions, or that corruption allegations are legitimate and the primary reason for being targeted, then those cases are not included. For example, the state abducting a militia commander in a neighboring state would not be included, but if the same state were to abduct a nonviolent opponent, then this would be included. The global dimensions of China's massive anti-corruption campaign present a difficult case. It is likely true that most of the targets are indeed guilty of corruption; however, it is also true that Chinese elites with personal ties to Xi Jinping are more likely to be shielded from the consequences of the anti-corruption drive (Lorentzen and Lu 2018). While recognizing that there is abundant gray area in many cases, anti-corruption extraditions and related actions are generally not included unless corruption accusations are a readily identifiable mask for other political motivations. This helps provide a more conservative estimate of authoritarian actions abroad than if all anti-corruption cases were deemed politically motivated.

With these clarifications in mind, the data are revealing of the scope of authoritarian actions abroad. Table 4.1 shows the top 10 cases, broken down by the offending country. These top 10 comprise about 80% of all the cases in the AAAD, while the top five alone comprise nearly 60%. The phenomenon of extraterritorial repression appears to be disproportionately driven

Table 4.1 Ten Most Frequent Source Countries in AAAD

Country	Total	Percentage of All Cases
Uzbekistan	195	16.6%
China	167	14.2%
North Korea	156	13.3%
Turkey	111	9.4%
Russia	74	6.3%
Tajikistan	72	6.1%
Iran	55	4.7%
Syria	43	3.7%
Thailand	37	3.1%
Egypt	37	3.1%

by a small number of states. The five most frequent offenders are Uzbekistan, China, North Korea, Turkey, and Russia. Uzbekistan (first), China (second), and Turkey (fourth) together illustrate the impact of repressive campaigns extending beyond borders, with many cases in these three countries coming in the aftermath of the Andijan massacre of 2005, repression of Uighurs after 2014, and after a 2016 coup attempt, respectively. Together, the Central Asian states of Uzbekistan (first) and Tajikistan (sixth) account for nearly 23% of the cases in the database. This may be partly a product of the detailed data gathering by the CAPE research team, but it also has to do with the fact that Russia and Central Asian states cooperate with one another to control one another's dissidents. All states in the region share an interest in squelching anti-authoritarian critics, which fosters collaboration between them (Cooley and Heathershaw 2017).

China is second, accounting for over 14% of the cases, which is perhaps not surprising given that it is by far the world's most populous authoritarian state. As noted earlier, these cases generally exclude Xi Jinping's anti-corruption drive. More details about China's obstructive/specific tactics will be discussed in Chapter 6, so here it will suffice to say that the post-2014 security crackdown in Xinjiang has a wide-reaching transnational dimension that is reflected in these data. The government looks upon Uighurs with international connections as suspicious and broadened its repressive net internationally during the crackdown, targeting ordinary students and workers abroad in addition to suspected violent actors (Allen-Ebrahimian 2019; Greitens, Lee, and Yazici 2020, 19–20). The aims are "to persuade citizens to return to China for re-education; to create mistrust among diaspora members and thereby limit collective mobilization; and to discourage Uyghurs from making appeals for host-country support or engaging in public advocacy" (Greitens, Lee, and Yazici 2020, 20).

North Korea is third in terms of verifiable actions. It regularly seeks the return of people who defect across the Chinese border (and beyond) and threatens the families of those who defect. North Korean defectors constitute an inherent threat to the governance system there because it is so tightly controlled and there is a de facto prohibition on leaving the state. There is no civil society to speak of domestically, so human rights and oppositional activism about North Korea necessarily takes place outside the state (Yeo and Chubb 2018). The North Korean state knows this, and so takes measures to deter defection and to mitigate its impacts once it has already occurred. It particularly targets vocal or high-level defectors, but throughout its history it has attempted to silence or intimidate virtually all defectors. Defectors are treated as an inherent threat to regime security in the North Korean case because "the very act of defection or border crossing announces the limitations and failure of the state. Without saying a word, border crossers articulate the varied failures of North Korea" (Fahy 2019, 131).

Turkey appears as the fourth most active state, which is remarkable given that in these data it is only coded as "authoritarian" after 2014, whereas the other four states in the "top five" were all authoritarian for the entire 30-year period under analysis (on post-2013 Turkey, see Bayulgen, Arbatli, and Canbolat 2018). Turkey's domestic crackdown after a failed 2016 coup attempt was breathtaking in scope, with nearly 100,000 people detained, almost 50,000 formally arrested on terrorism charges, almost 150 media outlets closed, and roughly 1,700 civil society organizations shuttered (Bayulgen, Arbatli, and Canbolat 2018, 357). The response had a global dimension (Schenkkan 2018). Turkish authorities unsuccessfully attempted to upload 60,000 names to Interpol's Red Notice System (Lemon 2019). Turkey also unsuccessfully pressured the United States to extradite Fethullah Gulen, the alleged mastermind of the coup, and the leader of a spiritual civil society movement (Gall 2018). Beyond extradition, it took other measures, such as branding exiles as terrorists and forcing the closure of critical newspapers abroad (Russell 2018; DW 2016). In one case, it appears that groups with ties to the Turkish state were preparing to assassinate a critical journalist in Denmark only to have their plans thwarted by Danish intelligence services (Bozkurt 2019; Öhman and Kavak 2018). The aim of this extraterritorial campaign, as summarized by Russell (2018, n.p.), is to "sow discord among diaspora communities, to create an atmosphere of fear and mistrust, and to prevent individuals from criticizing the government."

Russia is the fifth most frequently appearing case, with 74 instances, representing over 6% of the total cases in the AAAD. Vladimir Putin's Russia has become adept and brazen at targeting enemies abroad, particularly in Europe, but also with the cooperation of Central Asian states (e.g., Blake 2019). As mentioned in the following, this includes at least 21 assassinations or assassination attempts. Russian authorities appear disproportionately concerned with former regime insiders abroad relative to most other states. About 28% of its targets are former government officials, whereas in the entire AAAD only about 9.5% are. Former insiders may have secrets and the connections necessary to spread their messages that the authorities wish to keep hidden away.

Table 4.2 AAAD by Target

Target	Total	Percentage
Citizen	439	37.30%
Activist	390	33.14%
Journalist	163	13.85%
Former government official	112	9.52%
Opposition	73	6.20%
Total	1,177	100.00%

Table 4.2 breaks down the data by target. Just over 37% of those targeted are citizens. Many of these are from North Korea where, as explained earlier, the very fact of defection is viewed as politically threatening by the government even if the persons leaving are doing so for economic reasons, as most North Korean defectors do. China has also harassed citizens from Xinjiang abroad who left for non-political reasons, and Uzbekistan has done the same to some of those who fled the Andijan massacre. The second most prominent category are activists of various stripes, who constitute over 33% of the cases. The vignette at the outset of this book about the experiences of Saudi women's rights activist Loujain al-Hathloul details a prominent case in this category. Journalists who have fled constitute about 14% of the cases. Journalists have the skills and knowledge to publicize regime abuses to wide audiences and so are suspect for authoritarian regimes. We know that autocracies threaten and kill journalists domestically (Ghodes and Carey 2017), but these data show that they regularly target their exiled journalists as well. Former government officials and members of the formal opposition together account for nearly 16% of the targets in the AAAD. Despite their relatively small numbers, these two categories are important because in any direct confrontations about authoritarian rule at elite levels they are likely to have a high degree of influence.

Table 4.3 lists the actions that authoritarian states take to silence their exiled critics. For each category, an illustrative example will help explain the logic and consequences of the action. Examples from China, North Korea, and Rwanda will be set aside for now, as those three cases are discussed in more detail in subsequent chapters.

There is a high degree of parity in terms of the actions recorded, but the most common type of action is threats against exiled critics. This count probably vastly underestimates the amount of threats that are made because they

Table 4.3 AAAD by Action

Action	Total	Percentage
Threatened	222	18.86%
Arrested/detained	215	18.27%
Extradition attempt	203	17.25%
Extradited	174	14.78%
Family threatened	173	14.70%
Abducted	70	5.95%
Assassinated	52	4.42%
Assassination attempt	30	2.55%
Attacked	27	2.29%
Abduction attempt	11	0.93%
Total	1,177	100.00%

are rarely reported and because anonymous online "trolling" is not included. Threats are common for critics of authoritarian rule. As anti-government protests in Syria grew in 2011, for example, the Syrian authorities intensified their harassment and threats against activists and critics living abroad. In its report on the subject, Amnesty International (2011, 17) details the threat against a vocal exile in Sweden:

Iman al-Baghdady, who moved from Syria to Sweden one year ago and has previously been in contact with Amnesty International, was interviewed by the Swedish newspaper *Dagens Nyheter*. In its edition of 30 July 2011, Iman al-Baghdady said that when the mass pro-reform protests began in Syria, she began video-blogging and spreading information through social media from her apartment in Stockholm and that she and her husband participated in several pro-reform demonstrations in the city. On 27 May a letter arrived on her door mat. It was written in Arabic and the message was clear: 'Keep quiet or neither you, nor your family in Syria is safe'. The sender used Iman's maiden name, which the couple say only the embassy would have known.

The second most common action is arrest or detention in a foreign state. Sometimes the arrest leads to an extradition, while at other times the subject is released. The action is usually not carried out by the home state itself, but rather by the host state at the request of the home state. A recent example happened in November 2019 in Southeast Asia. That month, Cambodian opposition leader Sam Rainsy, living in exile in France, announced that he would return to Cambodia to contest the 34-year-long dictatorship of Hun Sen (on the Cambodian regime, see Morgenbesser 2019). Rainsy was ultimately prevented from boarding his flight from Paris to Bangkok because the Thai government announced that it would not allow him to transfer in Thailand. The Cambodian government pressured its neighbors to arrest fellow members of Rainsy's banned Cambodia National Rescue Party (CNRP). Malaysian authorities detained CNRP's deputy leader Mu Sochua in Kuala Lumpur as she was ostensibly attempting to travel from the United States to Cambodia. Two others, Ngoeum Keatha and Heng Seang Leang, were also detained (Amnesty International 2019a). All three were eventually released, but still Hun Sen was successful in hindering their goals and preventing their messages and organizational networks from being spread further in Cambodia.

Threats against the exiled critic's family account for nearly 15% of cases. Again, it is highly likely that the instances recorded here are immeasurably undercounted. Authoritarian regimes often tightly control information such that threats of this nature do not become public. Exiles themselves also may not wish to publicize such instances because they may judge that it would put their families at more risk. The category "family threatened" in the AAAD is really a catch-all for a variety of types of threats and coercion that the families of exiled critics face, ranging from administrative hassles to being imprisoned.

Egyptian authorities under Abdel Fattah el-Sisi, for example, routinely harass family members of exiled critics. A Human Rights Watch (2019b, n.p.) report on the subject concludes that "authorities have carried out arrests, house raids, interrogations, and travel bans against dozens of relatives of dissidents who live abroad, apparently in reprisal for their activism." The brother of high-profile activist Wael Ghonim, for example, was arrested in Egypt apparently after Ghonim refused to be silent after a threat from the Egyptian embassy in Washington, D.C. Ghada Naguib, a political activist based in Turkey, reported that her brothers and brother-in-law were arrested in Egypt in 2018 and held incommunicado for several days. The aim of this tactic is to impose costs on the exile and to get members of the exile's family to pressure him/her to silence their criticism in exchange for the family's safety. It is a clear way in which authoritarian states can use sovereignty to their advantage when attempting to silence exiled critics because the state retains control over the exile's relatives who remain in the country.

Extradition and attempted extraditions together account for just over 32% of the cases recorded. Sometimes attempted extraditions are requests by the home government that are rebuffed before anything happens, but at other times they are resolved only after an arrest/detention. The case of Hussein Osman Said, an Eritrean and cofounder of the group Eritrean Diaspora for East Africa (EDEA) in Kenya, illustrates how even an attempted extradition can be a major impediment not only for activism but also to ordinary life. On a business trip to South Sudan in 2013 he was arrested and told by the police that they had orders to extradite him to Eritrea. He was eventually released, but his passport had been invalidated by the Eritrean embassy in Kenya, so he was stranded in a foreign country with no valid documents. While he was eventually able to make it back to Kenya, it took three weeks to do so (Amnesty International 2019b, 9).

Abductions and attempted abductions together account for only about 7% of the reported cases. This relatively low number is likely because it is meant to capture "informal" kidnappings or extraordinary renditions. To capture an exiled critic, authoritarian states will first try to get the host state to do their work for them by arresting/detaining the person, hopefully (from the state's perspective) to extradite them. Abductions are also difficult to verify because they are meant to leave behind no evidence and, if successful, the victim cannot alert anyone about it. Nevertheless, evidence about some abductions and abduction attempts is available. For example, in December 2012 two men tried to force a Sudanese activist into their car in Cairo, Egypt (Amnesty International 2013). Laotian political activist Od Sayavong was apparently abducted in September 2019 in Thailand and has not been heard from as of this writing, a year later (Lamb 2019). In May 2015 Tajik political activist Ehson Odinaev was apparently taken off the street in St. Petersburg, Russia, while he was on the way to the pharmacy (CAPE 2020).

The AAAD records 27 instances of physical attacks that were not apparent assassination attempts or abductions, just over 2% of all cases. For example, an Amnesty International (2013) report provides details on attacks of several Sudanese activists in Egypt. An unnamed activist was beaten twice—once in 2005 and once in 2011—by people he believed to be working with the Sudanese government. In another instance from the same report:

A female activist, who had been working on Darfur human rights issues, described to Amnesty International how she was kidnapped on a Cairo street by three men dressed in plain clothes. After forcing her into a car, the men—who she believes were Egyptian—took her to a remote location and raped her repeatedly before leaving her on a Cairo road. The woman told Amnesty International that a few days after her rape she received a menacing phone call from a Sudanese security agent who had previously arrested her in Sudan.

Finally, assassination of critics abroad is the most decisive silencing action available to authoritarian governments. The AAAD records 52 assassinations and 30 attempts, together totaling almost 7% of all cases. Russia is responsible for 15 of the 52 assassinations and 6 of the 30 attempts, many of which happened in the United Kingdom (Blake 2019). The targets were often former government insiders-turned-critics who had damaging information about Vladimir Putin's rise to power and/or government abuses. A close second, Iran is responsible for 14 of the 52 assassinations and 5 of the 30 attempts. During the late 1980s and 1990s, the Iranian government undertook a concerted effort to eliminate many of its critics abroad, including the murder of former Iranian prime minister Shahpur Bakhtiar and his associate Abdel Rahman Boroumand. Four Kurdish opposition figures were killed in September 1992 in Berlin. They were meeting at a Greek restaurant and so the case came to be known as the "Mykonos Murders." In 1997, German courts concluded that Iranian intelligence was responsible for the assassinations (DW 2004). A more recent assassination involving Iran saw activist Massoud Molavi shot dead while walking in Istanbul (Reuters 2020). Molavi had publicized allegations of corruption against Iran's Islamic Revolutionary Guard Corps. Iran is known to have extensive intelligence operations in Turkey, and some sources have confirmed that Iranian intelligence was behind the murder; however, reflecting the shadowy nature of authoritarian actions abroad, Iran's culpability for the assassination cannot be confirmed with absolute certainty.

Clearly authoritarian states engage in a variety of tactics to silence their critics abroad (Tsourapas 2020). The AAAD reveals that these actions can escalate from threats all the way up to assassinations and everything in between. Exiled critics often know that these risks accompany their activities and so one wonders how many would-be critics abroad are deterred by the prospect of violence. Even if some courageous activists or journalists continue their work after having been threatened, many more people likely conclude that a life of intimidation, threat, and the prospect of extradition is not worth criticism that only stands an uncertain chance of being effective.

Conclusion: Multidimensional Authoritarian Image Management

This chapter has provided a global snapshot of two sides of authoritarian image management: "promotional" PR and "obstructive" repression. It described data on the public relations and lobbying efforts of authoritarian states in the United States. These activities are important for shaping the image of authoritarian politics, cultivating elite opinion leaders to think positively about the state in question, and facilitating the foreign policy goals of the foreign principal. The goal is for authoritarian leaders to enhance their internal and external regime security. It is hard to know how effective these efforts are in aggregate, but clearly many authoritarian states themselves think they are effective given that they hand over tens of millions of dollars annually to American companies to engage in these activities. Special attention was given to RT and CGTN as foreign television arms of large, powerful authoritarian states seeking to influence how authoritarian politics is talked about and how democracy is viewed globally. In sum, the liberal public sphere of the United States is awash with information that authoritarian states pay to put there. As the Corporate Europe Observatory (2015) details, similar processes are at play in Europe.

Far from only disseminating promotional messages, authoritarian states regularly try to silence their exiled critics. The data in the AAAD reveal how analytically unsatisfactory notions like "authoritarian soft power" really are. Authoritarian states protect their narratives by repressing messengers who might challenge those narratives from the outside. This mirrors what they do domestically to control information insofar as they supplement propaganda with legitimacy-protecting repression such as censorship (Dukalskis 2017). Critical journalists, activists, former government officials, opposition members, and even ordinary citizens can become targets of authoritarian states even when abroad if they threaten the image of the state. Authoritarian states cannot repress as effectively abroad as they do at home, but they adapt tactics that allow them to try to silence criticism abroad. The result is not only that the messages are often silenced, but also that many exiles and their families live in the shadow of intimidation and threat.

In some cases, such repression may backfire. The state attempts to prevent this from happening by obscuring responsibility and discrediting the exile. The scope of actions and the range of states reported in the AAAD, however, indicates that states mostly do not pay high prices for their authoritarian actions abroad. The governments in the AAAD mostly escape serious consequences for intimidating or attacking their critics abroad. China's international campaign against the Uighurs has not led to serious consequences for Beijing, although the domestic repression in Xinjiang has certainly reinforced its image as human rights–abusing state. The case of Rwanda detailed in Chapter 7 will show that even a small resource-poor state can assassinate critics abroad and evade severe consequences if the rest of its authoritarian image management strategy is effective. After widespread condemnation for the killing of Jamal Khashoggi, the Saudi government was heavily criticized initially, but eventually business returned for the most part to normal (Jaafari 2019).

This chapter has provided a wide empirical overview and several illustrative examples, showing the breadth of authoritarian image management efforts. The following chapters, drawing on some of the data presented here, turn to more detailed case studies to illustrate the depth and outcomes of authoritarian image management.

5

Controlling Critical Messengers

Foreign Correspondents in China

A 2013 museum exhibit in Shanghai titled "Red Star Over China: Chinese Communists in the Eyes of Foreign Journalists" extolled the reporters who wrote about the Chinese Communist Party's (CCP) revolution in the 1930s (Green 2013). The exhibit celebrated a handful of sympathetic foreign journalists from that period, opening with stirring praise for their virtues: "With their pens and their cameras, [they] presented to the world a fair and true image of the Chinese Communists and the People's Army, who, though equipped with inferior arms, were fighting heroically at the forefront in the struggle for national liberation" (Green 2013, n.p.).

The exhibit is a small example of a much larger reality: the Chinese government cares a lot about what foreign journalists say about it. For the CCP, influencing the work of foreign journalists, in particular those who work for outlets in the West, has long been part of a "deliberate strategy to manage, and where possible, control foreigners' presence and activities both in China and beyond" (Brady 2003, 1). Chapter 6 will detail the motivations and scale of China's external propaganda efforts and the practices designed to protect those messages from criticism. But first, this chapter focuses on a much more specific aspect of the Chinese government's image management: its efforts to influence the reporting of foreign correspondents for Western news outlets operating in China.

Foreign correspondents are people "who are stationed in other countries than that of their origin for the purposes of reporting on events and characteristics in the area of their stationing, through news media based elsewhere" (Hannerz 2004, 5). The boundaries of this definition can become blurred, but the core of the category can be thought of as journalists from elsewhere who are reporting from a country in an outlet managed externally of the host state. The audience comprises largely foreign readers, listeners, and/ or viewers. The journalists memorialized in the 2013 Shanghai exhibit were mostly correspondents for British and American newspapers, for example.

Making the World Safe for Dictatorship, Alexander Dukalskis, Oxford University Press (2021). © Oxford University Press.
DOI: 10.1093/oso/9780197520130.003.0005

While it is obvious that not everybody consumes the work of foreign correspondents, they are nonetheless important actors in the global media ecosystem. Major news outlets in general have long been theorized to have an agenda-setting function (McCombs 2005). Foreign coverage can help shape how a country or episode is understood by international audiences (Wanta and Hu 1993). While the number of foreign bureaus with bases in European and North American states has declined precipitously and has changed the nature of foreign reporting (Hamilton and Jenner 2004; Kaphle 2015), foreign correspondents have a new role in the age of social media and superficial stories, namely to deliver in-depth coverage and unique stories (Archetti 2013). Indeed, in some ways, social media have amplified the visibility of correspondents as they use Twitter to engage with their audiences and provide unique content or perspectives alongside their institutional coverage (Cozma and Chen 2013).

Foreign correspondents are therefore of special interest to authoritarian states, and they face challenges in doing their work in such contexts (Kester 2010). Chinese authorities have a keen interest in influencing how the country is presented in virtually all areas of the world. To influence the environment in which its external propaganda messages are received, the party-state aims to shape the independent messages that emanate from China. Controlling the independent information that leaves China provides a foundation on which its other authoritarian image management methods can be built. In terms of the mechanisms of authoritarian image management elaborated in Chapter 3, foreign correspondents are specific targets. Controlling them can come in both promotional and obstructive forms. Promotional forms may entail, for example, flattery, special access, or junket trips. Obstructive forms of influence may range from restricting access to information up to threats of, or even actual, violence and everything in between.

The chapter finds that for journalists working for European and North American outlets in China, the Chinese government is far more reliant on obstructive forms of image management to shape how China is presented by agenda-setting foreign correspondents. It attempts to use some promotional tactics, such as publicity tours, but since contemporary journalistic ethics prevent many reporters from engaging in this way, in general it relies on more restrictive and censorious practices to influence what reporters cover and how they do so. Its aim, at minimum, is to reduce the number of stories critical of the Chinese political system from reaching international audiences and thereby tarnishing the state's image. The ambition is to either keep certain issues off the agenda, or failing that, for Chinese state-produced or influenced content to fill the information void left by the reduction of stories on "sensitive" topics in the international sphere. Doing so is meant to enhance Beijing's internal and external security.

Historical Context and Legal Framework

Although the most immediately relevant group of journalists for the CCP to control are those who write for a domestic audience (see Repnikova 2017), the CCP has a long history of managing its relations with foreign journalists. Perhaps the most famous foreign journalist to ever report on the party remains the American Edgar Snow. His book *Red Star Over China*, the namesake of the 2013 Shanghai exhibition described earlier, is based on his time spent with the communist rebels in 1936, including extensive interviews with Mao Zedong himself (Lovell 2019, 60–87). Snow was treated to extraordinary hospitality when he arrived at the communist base area, which his diaries reveal left a highly emotional impression on him (Brady 2003, 44–45; Lovell 2019, 78). The book's content was shaped by Mao and other CCP elites (Lovell 2019, 76–77). Interview transcripts with Mao were scrutinized, and Snow consented to requests by Mao and Zhou Enlai to change some of the book's content to reflect the changing party line (Brady 2003, 47).

The book was a major success for the CCP "because it established Mao as both a national and an international figure and promoted the Chinese revolutionary cause" (Brady 2003, 46). The book portrayed "Mao and his comrades as idealistic patriots and egalitarian democrats with a sense of humour" (Lovell 2019, 61). It was translated into Chinese and was influential both at home and abroad (Lovell 2019, 82–87). Indeed, in 2016, the book was made into a 30-part television series screened in China (China Daily 2016). The combination of Snow's initial sympathy to the cause (although he was not a party member), hospitality designed to flatter him, and textual scrutiny and revision by the party proved to be an effective formula. In another book about his 1960 visit to China, Snow again aided the CCP by denying that mass starvation had occurred in China during the Great Leap Forward, a claim that is demonstrably false (Brady 2003, 122; on the Great Leap Forward, see Yang 2013). This strategy of using foreign journalists and writers to amplify CCP messages is framed as "using foreign strength to do propaganda work for China" (Brady 2003, 19). During the Mao period there were few writers from democratic states in China, and those who were allowed to stay were often sympathetic to the CCP, usually lived a privileged lifestyle, and were frequently financially and politically dependent on the party.

As China opened up in the post-Mao period, the problem facing the party became less about cultivating a small number of sympathetic journalists, as in the 1930s, but rather about managing the larger number of foreign journalists reporting in the country (see Brady 2008, 160–163). The perks available to "friendly" journalists were substantially less impressive than the lavish welcome and extensive access to top leaders that Snow enjoyed (Brady 2003, 233). Rather, the focus became on how to guide or control journalists who would report critically about China. In patterns that would continue to the present, foreign journalists were detained, expelled, scolded in the party press, and faced interviewees who had been primed by the party to be cautious or unresponsive to foreign journalists about certain issues (Brady 2003, 232–233). Indeed, as of this writing, journalists from major American and Australian media outlets are being expelled from China en masse (e.g. Tracy, Wong, and Jakes 2020). Bound up with the US-China rivalry and tense Australia-China relations, the expulsions are a significant escalation of Beijing's effort to control foreign journalists, but there is a deeper history.

Legally, the system governing foreign correspondents in China liberalized in 2008. Prior to that time, foreign journalists were governed by rules promulgated in 1990. Decree 47 of the State Council, titled "Regulations Concerning Foreign Journalists and Permanent Offices of Foreign News Agencies," contained provisions designed to control the work of foreign journalists. Many of these were carried over in the 2008 revision of the law, but some were scrapped. For example, the 1990 version of the law contained broad language such as that found in Article 14:

> Foreign journalists and permanent offices of foreign news agencies must observe journalistic ethics and may not distort facts, fabricate rumours or carry out news coverage by foul means. Foreign journalists and permanent offices of foreign news agencies may not engage in any activities incompatible with their status or the nature of their profession, or detrimental to China's national security, unity or social and public interests. (State Council 1990)

Furthermore, according to the pre-2008 regulations, journalists wishing to cover stories outside of the city where they were based had to apply for advanced permission (State Council 1990, Article 15). These regulations erected additional barriers to the work of foreign correspondents. They gave cautious local officials grounds to reject foreign investigations in their jurisdiction. Short of rejecting a request, the regulation gave security officials advance notice of a foreign journalist's presence and gave the former time to prepare a plan to monitor the correspondent if necessary. In practice, many journalists ignored this regulation at various times; however, this made them and their employers vulnerable to punishment. Article 19 gave the state the ability to decide "on the merits of each case, [whether to] give them a warning, suspend or stop their journalistic activities in China, or revoke their Foreign Journalist Identity Cards or Certificates for Permanent Office of Foreign News Agency" (State Council 1990, Article 19).

In October 2008, the Chinese government promulgated a revision to these laws in the form of Decree 537 of the State Council. Requirements to give advanced notice for coverage of most areas of China were eliminated. The language about "rumours" and "foul means" was eliminated, although the regulations still stipulate possible penalties for the violation of "other laws, regulations or rules of China," many of which themselves contain vague language that can be flexibly deployed (State Council 2008, Article 19). The new language on the parameters of journalists' reporting is more toned down:

Permanent offices of foreign media organizations and foreign journalists shall abide by the laws, regulations and rules of China, observe the professional ethics of journalism, conduct news coverage and reporting activities on an objective and impartial basis, and shall not engage in activities which are incompatible with the nature of the organizations or the capacity as journalists. (State Council 2008, Article 4)

The rules are less restrictive than the 1990 version. Despite this liberalization, several provisions are still relevant to China's efforts to limit or influence the work of foreign journalists. More will be said later about how things unfold in practice, but two elements of the regulations deserve brief mention because they are both specifically mentioned in the law and are important in practice. First, the visa regime requires that journalists reapply for visas and press cards every year, which entails applying to both the Foreign Ministry and the security services. This gives the authorities an annual opportunity to review the work of the journalist and/or the media organization, which contains an implied right to reject the application if the coverage has run afoul of explicit or implicit limits. The government has refused to renew visas with increased frequency in recent years.

Second, the regulations stipulate that if foreign news organizations wish to hire Chinese citizens, the latter must come from an organization approved by the Foreign Ministry (State Council 2008, Article 18). This means that news assistants and researchers working with foreign outlets must be registered with the government. In practice, this means that foreign media outlets either hire from a pool of pre-approved applicants or hire on their own and then seek approval from the authorities. This regulation gives a unique mechanism of control to the state because Chinese citizens are more vulnerable to repression than their foreign colleagues. The law means that the state can pressure Chinese employees of foreign news agencies, or even their families, if the coverage in which they participate is deemed off limits by the party.

As the interview data in the following will make clear, correspondents manage these restrictions in different ways. They look for ways to uphold their journalistic standards while operating in a political environment that has a different understanding of what journalism should be. The Chinese government's vision is one in which journalists work within the party-state system to not only guide public opinion in support of the party, but also provide internal criticisms and investigations designed to improve party performance (Repnikova 2017). They are not meant to question the CCP's rule or to report on issues the government deems out of bounds. This understanding, and the controls that come with it, sits at odds with journalism premised on the idea of being a critical check on powerholders.

Interview Sample and Data Sources

To gain a better understanding of how these regulations as well as the less formalized practices of the party-state in this area operate, this chapter presents data on semi-structured interviews with foreign correspondents based in China. Interviewees were contacted directly by the author via email or social media channels. Sampling aimed to ensure a broad diversity of outlets in terms of medium (e.g., newspaper, broadcast, radio), size of bureau, and time period spent in China. The aim was to ascertain a broad range of experiences.

One sampling frame in which the group is not representative is country of origin. For theoretical reasons, the interviews were all with foreign

correspondents from European and North American news outlets. This pur-
posive sampling strategy, with a snowball/chain-referral element (Tansey
2007), was chosen for two reasons. First, I was interested in how the CCP
aims to control messages that significantly influence international discourse.
The CCP has long complained that "Western" media is biased against China
(d'Hooge 2005, 91; Wang 2008, 265; Hartig 2016). It understands Western
news organizations to have disproportionate influence in driving the international news agenda (Wang 2008, 265; Liu 2020, 280–283), and so these
interviews focused on how the state attempted to influence their reporters as
important transmitters of China's image. However, there is variation within
the sample of journalists as to the size of the country of origin, the nature of
the bureau, and the topics the reporter gravitated toward.

There is a practical element limiting the sampling as well. European and
North American correspondents are often public facing on Twitter, and their
email addresses are easy to obtain from institutional websites. Contrast this
with news agencies from non-democratic states which may have more positive relations with Beijing. The Fars News Agency of Iran, for example, does
not typically use bylines in its English language stories, and no bureau information is available on its English-language website as of this writing. This
renders it difficult to obtain access for interviews, even if those journalists
would speak to a researcher. These realities influenced the representativeness
of the sample, but this limitation is palatable given the theoretical aims of the
interviews.

Details of the interview sample are reported in Table 5.1. Names and
other identifying information are withheld to protect the privacy of the
respondents. Some interviews were conducted in China while others were
conducted via Skype, and the time frame was from November 2018 to
January 2019. Exact dates and locations of interviews are not provided here
in case the journalist her/himself was under surveillance that day. Some
respondents were still correspondents while being interviewed and so their
time span is open-ended as of the interview. Other respondents were former
correspondents and were reflecting on their time in China. When discussing
events that occurred, general language such as "bureau chief for European
newspaper" or "correspondent for North American news outlet" will be
used, along with gender-neutral pronouns, such as s/he or him/her or they,
to further mask the respondents' identity. This sometimes results in awkward
syntax, but it is worthwhile to protect the sources trusting the researcher
with their experiences.

Table 5.1 Details of Interview Sample

Code	Media Outlet Location	Media Type	Time in China
Respondent 1	North America	Newspaper	2–5 years
Respondent 2	Europe and North America	Newspaper	10 years+
Respondent 3	North America	Newspaper	Less than 1 year
Respondent 4	North America	Newspaper	5–10 years
Respondent 5	North America	Newspaper	10 years+
Respondent 6	Europe	Multimedia	5–10 years
Respondent 7	Europe	Multimedia	Less than 1 year
Respondent 8	Europe	Newspaper	1–2 years
Respondent 9	Europe	Newspaper	5–10 years
Respondent 10	Europe and North America	Multimedia	10 years+

In some cases, current or former correspondents have written publicly about their experiences dealing with the Chinese state, and the chapter draws on that information. When these sources are used, it does not imply that the author has interviewed or met that person, rather only that the information was found through monitoring the news for these topics. Finally, to supplement the interview data, some reports from the Foreign Correspondents Club of China (FCCC) are used.

Controlling Key Messengers

Foreign journalists work within a legal regime that gives significant control to the Chinese authorities. However, even beyond the letter of the law, journalists must navigate a set of shadow strictures designed to limit their access to information and steer the content of their reporting. During interviews, at least eight themes arose that illuminated the ways in which various authorities within the Chinese party-state attempt to manage the image of China via Western foreign correspondents.

These will be presented roughly in the temporal order in which the journalist encounters Chinese attempts to exert authority or influence over her/his reporting. When reporting from China, a journalist must (1) obtain and renew his/her visa, (2) usually hire news assistants or researchers who are Chinese nationals and manage the sensitivities of that arrangement,

(3) come to terms with geographical areas of the country that are "off limits," and (4) consider requests by Chinese officials at various levels to attend publicity tours. When the correspondent begins researching and producing his/her stories or analysis, s/he will find (5) that it is difficult, if not impossible, to contact elite-level sources. If s/he or one of his/her colleagues writes a story or produces content that runs afoul of someone within the Chinese state, s/he might (6) receive complaints from the foreign ministry. In some cases, the foreign ministry might meet to cultivate more positive relations with a journalist or outlet as well. If a correspondent produces a story that catches the attention of the Chinese embassy in his/her employer's home country, (7) the embassy might complain to the outlet, try to influence its coverage, or even publicly insult the reporter. Finally, in the most extreme cases, the foreign correspondent (8) may find that s/he is detained, harassed, surveilled, and/or intimidated.

Recalling the theoretical mechanisms discussed in Chapter 3, this is a case of a state using authoritarian image management tactics on a specific group. Of course, not all journalists have been subject to all these methods, but these represent the toolbox of attempted control measures that Chinese authorities appear to use to influence the coverage of foreign correspondents for Western outlets.

Visa Process

The most regularized aspect of state power over foreign correspondents can be found in the visa application and renewal process. The application for a visa renewal gives the state an opportunity to communicate to reporters directly about what kind of coverage it would like them to pursue or avoid. In the most extreme cases, the renewal application allows the government to effectively remove journalists from China without having to pro-actively deport them. Simply denying a visa without comment prevents journalists from continuing their reporting from within the country.

Visas are generally granted on a one-year renewable basis. The first application is made from the reporter's home or residence country. Renewals can be made in China. For the renewal process, the journalist must get his/her press card reapproved by the Ministry of Foreign Affairs. This entails submitting paperwork at the ministry and sometimes being interviewed.

Once the press card is renewed, the applicant must then obtain a visa, which requires approval by the Public Security Bureau. The process used to occur in December for every foreign journalist, but now applications are processed on a rolling basis.

The experiences of journalists with the visa process vary. Some have had virtually no difficulties and have not been asked any substantive questions at the interviews (Respondent 8). One correspondent was asked what kind of stories s/he planned to write in the coming year and was able to answer truthfully that "slice of life" stories and stories about relations between China and his/her home country were of special interest (Respondent 6). Others report that the Ministry of Foreign Affairs has directly told them during the visa renewal process which stories the journalist had written that upset the government (Respondent 10). In this latter case, a journalist spent months trying to obtain visa renewal and ultimately received it after significant effort to gain diplomatic support from the journalist's home government.

In some cases, the government has elected to not renew the visas of journalists it viewed as troublesome. The FCCC attempts to keep track of expulsions and visa issues, noting an uptick in difficulties in 2019 and 2020 especially, although there were issues prior to that (see FCCC 2018, 2020). In 2012 American journalist Melissa Chan was denied a visa for her work with *Al Jazeera*, while in 2015 French journalist Ursula Gauthier was denied a visa for her work with the magazine *L'Obs*. In both cases, the refusal to renew visas followed critical stories, in Chan's case about forced labor in Chinese prisons and in Gauthier's case after reporting about Xinjiang (Rauhala 2015). In Gauthier's case, the officially backed Chinese tabloid *The Global Times* ran an article accusing her of being unprofessional, unethical, and showing "support to terrorism in Xinjiang" (Global Times 2015). In August 2018, *BuzzFeed* reporter Megha Rajagopalan had her visa renewal application denied after her reporting on Xinjiang (Graham-Harrison 2018a). Again, *The Global Times* wrote that Rajagopalan "has written distorted reports about a variety of things that have happened in [Xinjiang], feeding the Western media narrative that favors stories critical of how China governs the autonomous region" (Global Times 2018). It continued to opine that Western journalists generally are obsessed with presenting China in a negative light. In March 2020, the government expelled American journalists working for the *New York Times*, *Wall Street Journal*, *Washington Post*, and *Time*, as well as the US government–funded *Voice of America* (Tracy, Wong, and Jakes 2020). The measure and its aftermath affected at least 17 journalists, bringing the total of expelled journalists between 2013 and 2020 to around 30 as of this writing. This number does not include those who were denied a visa in the first instance.

It is possible that denying journalists visas can serve as a signal to other reporters to stay in line. Self-censorship is hard to measure, so there is no direct evidence that this tactic is effective, but one can imagine that some journalists think carefully about risking their visa given that they often have their families in China with them. Annoyance with the visa process from journalists usually revolves around lengthy delays or holding of passports, rather than the threat of non-renewal, although the latter is becoming rapidly more common.

Chinese National Colleagues

Virtually all Western news agencies in China rely on professional input from Chinese citizens in their news-gathering operations. Chinese nationals can be producers, contributors, fixers, researchers, news assistants, camera operators, and so on. Chinese nationals legally cannot be correspondents for foreign outlets, and those working in roles directly contributing to producing the news must be cleared and approved by the Chinese government. Sometimes in the visa-renewal process the authorities would confirm with the foreign correspondent the identities of the Chinese nationals working with them. These procedures mean that when a Western journalist works with a researcher or producer, s/he must either select applicants from a pre-approved list of journalistic professionals or hire somebody and then seek government approval.

This arrangement requires the foreign correspondent to consider carefully in what kind of projects the news assistant or producer should be involved. The prevailing sense among respondents is that Chinese nationals are much more vulnerable to intimidation by the Chinese government. They have families in China who can be pressured, and they do not have the diplomatic backing of a foreign state. They are in a difficult position, torn between compulsion from the Chinese state and society to present China well and from their international colleagues to adhere to journalistic standards that may reveal information critical of China. These cross pressures are most acute on stories that the Chinese government is most eager to censor. Journalists working on stories about Xinjiang or dissidents, for example, sometimes do not involve their Chinese colleagues so as to insulate them from any insistence or intimidation from the state (Respondent 3; Respondent 5; Respondent 9). The theory is that if they do not know any details about the reporting, then they cannot be pressured.

Yet, some news professionals are intimidated by the Chinese state. In one case, a Chinese news researcher for a North American outlet went to Xinjiang on an assignment that was not about the repression of Uighurs, but when s/he returned s/he was still detained (Respondent 1). S/he was detained while in Xinjiang but released and apparently followed by state security or recognized by surveillance cameras because s/he was apprehended upon her/his return after leaving a subway station. Local police detained her/him, beat her/him up, and left her/him in a cold dark room for a period before releasing her/him. It is unclear what permission the local police had from higher authorities to take these measures. Regardless, this targeted repression had its intended effect. The bureau cancelled his/her upcoming trips and the journalist remained in the profession but no longer wished to work on stories that might draw negative attention from the state.

In another instance, a Chinese researcher for a different outlet received a call one night from the security services requesting that s/he come meet them (Respondent 3). S/he was preparing to go out of town for holiday the next day, so s/he suggested meeting upon return. However, the security authorities demanded that s/he come to the meeting immediately or else they would be waiting at the train station the next day. The correspondent managing this researcher advises Chinese colleagues to be vague about reporting when talking to the authorities but to tell the truth when pressed. In general, though, foreign correspondents who were interviewed did not talk in much detail with Chinese colleagues about the latter's interactions with the state.

These strictures on Chinese nationals working for foreign media impact on the ability of correspondents to report on China. They help to narrow the field of qualified people willing to work for foreign media outlets. It is a difficult job in which the employee faces significant cross-pressures not only from their employers and the state, but also from society. Nationalistic voices sometimes accuse them of being traitors and blame them for letting down their country by working for the "enemy" (Respondent 9). By stifling the domestic expertise available to foreign journalists, the state can deprive foreign news media of information and insights that might help them craft their stories about China. Particularly with stories about repression or dissidents, the regime governing Chinese news professionals provides another point of pressure that the state can use to clamp down on reporting. The overall aspiration is to keep foreign reporting about China within acceptable bounds so that the state's official messages have fewer critical voices to compete with.

Off-Limits Areas

Some areas of China are off limits to foreign journalists unless they are on a specially arranged tour (see next section). Tibet is the most well-known such area. Xinjiang is not officially off limits as of this writing, but journalists face onerous obstacles in reporting from there. Some areas of the North Korean border are restricted, and other areas might sometimes be difficult for foreign journalists to access. These restrictions evolve over time as political sensitivities shift.

Prior to 2008, foreign journalists were required to obtain permits for reporting trips to any areas outside their home city. This meant that local and/or provincial security services were alerted to the presence of a foreign journalist in advance and were able to arrange an escort from the Foreign Affairs Bureau to accompany the journalist. This put serious limitations on the work of foreign reporters wishing to cover stories of which the government would not approve. In this instance, reporters would sometimes go without requesting permission, although this then put them in a vulnerable position because they had violated official rules. A meeting with a dissident or the source for a story critical of the government could then be broken up on the grounds that the journalist had violated administrative protocol. This meant that reporters had a calculation to make: "every time we did a story outside Beijing, we would have to decide whether it was a big enough story to warrant breaking the rules of the road. And sometimes we would. Sometimes we wouldn't" (Respondent 10). Even so, there appeared to be considerable sub-national variation, as some provincial offices were known to be liberal in granting permission to cover topics like protests or dissent, while others were less forthcoming.

In the post-2008 environment, the geographical scope for reporting is much more open. Only a few areas remain firmly off limits, although many topics remain functionally off limits. Yet, much like Respondent 10's observation about the costs and benefits of pursuing stories in such areas, some take the risk anyway.

The repression of ethnic Uighurs has become a topic that many journalists feel is worth the risk of perturbing the Chinese authorities. When they decide to report from Xinjiang, reporters take measures to reduce their own exposure and that of their sources (Respondent 2, Respondent 4, Respondent 5). For example, they take temporary mobile phones and laptops, rent cars so that they can drive themselves, avoid making hotel reservations in advance so as not to alert the authorities, and, as mentioned earlier, in most cases they do not ask Chinese nationals from their bureau to attend due to the repression they may face.

Reporting from places like Xinjiang involves considerable hassle and risk to personal safety. This is part of the Chinese state's attempt to control the messages and information emanating from these places to international audiences. Since domestically there is little space for independent reporting on these sorts of issues, foreign correspondents are among the few individuals able to shed light on Chinese policy in these areas. The Chinese state therefore takes an interest in controlling their messages by restricting access to the location and its sources. Even this method has its limitations, however, and information about state repression inevitably escapes. Restricted access is therefore just one of the message-controlling tactics the government uses. The next chapter details the Chinese government's effort to fill the resulting void in Xinjiang information by disseminating positive stories and responses to criticisms through its own propaganda streams.

Official Publicity Tours

In addition to dissuading journalists from going to certain areas or reporting about them, the government wishes to highlight what it sees as favorable news stories. This is the "promotional" side of the Chinese government's efforts to influence its image via Western reporters. It is generally not as prevalent as the more obstructive tactics discussed throughout this chapter, but nonetheless various arms of the party-state attempt to show themselves positively to foreign journalists. As the next chapter will make clear, positive tactics are used much more systematically with journalists from the Global South on Chinese government programs.

Every correspondent interviewed recalled being invited on official tours on at least one occasion, and usually on a regular basis. Often these invitations were sent to many journalists, or even the entire foreign correspondent community, and sometimes they are even posted publicly on a central website. Two examples shared by interviewees illustrate the tenor of these invitations:

Dear journalists,

To better understand the revolutionary base areas in Jiangxi province, the social and economic development, poverty alleviation policy in Jiangxi, the International Press Center (IPC) of the Ministry of Foreign Affairs, together with the Office of Foreign and Overseas Chinese Affairs of the Jiangxi provincial Government, has the pleasure to invite resident foreign correspondents to visit Jiangxi from August 21 to 25. Please refer to the draft itinerary (Appendix I, pending for changes) for your information.

...

Dear journalists,

To better understand the protection and utilization of old factories for expanding cultural space and upgrading the industrial structure in Beijing, the International Press Center (IPC) of the Ministry of Foreign Affairs has the pleasure to invite resident foreign correspondents to a half day group reporting trip with the theme of "New story of old factory buildings in Beijing" starting from 13:30, October 10th. The field trip will feature Langyuan Vintage cultural and creative industries, Laijin cultural and creative industries and Chaoyang Museum of urban planning.

Usually the invitations would stipulate that the inviting agency would cover the expenses for the attendees. As the sample messages reveal, these trips generally attempt to show positive attributes of China from the government's point of view. They may be organized at the central level, or sometimes in conjunction with different ministries or provincial authorities wishing to highlight their work.

Journalists in the interview sample did not regularly attend these sorts of events. They were usually perceived as being of little value, highly scripted, and boring. On occasion, however, these trips could offer access to public officials or to a site that could only be obtained via the trip. Some journalists therefore reported going on trips to see an emerging industry or new government program as part of their research. For example, some went to see preparations for the summer Olympics in 2008 or for the 2022 winter Olympics. However, all the correspondents interviewed reported that their organizations paid their own way on these occasions and that an ethical red line would be to accept expenses from the Chinese government.

Some promotional trips take place in areas that may bear on the issue of government repression. The following invitation involves a trip about ethnic Tibetan culture and economic development, a connection the Chinese government is eager to enforce its narrative about:

> The first Silk Road (Dunhuang) International Cultural Expo will be held in Dunhuang on September 19–21, which aims to promote cultural exchanges for all-round cooperation and development in multichannel and high level, and carry forward the Silk Road Spirit—"peace and cooperation, openness and inclusiveness, mutual learning and mutual benefit." It is co-sponsored by Ministry of Culture, the State Administration of Press, Publication, Radio, Film and Television, National Tourism Administration, China Council for the Promotion of International Trade and Gansu Provincial People's Government. The Expo will be attended by government delegations from countries along the Belt and Road, foreign diplomats in China, media, heads of international organizations, representatives of sister cities of Gansu Province, dignitaries of international cultural communities and business leaders.
>
> . . .
>
> The International Press Center (IPC) of the Ministry of Foreign Affairs, together with Foreign Affairs Office of Gansu Provincial People's Government, has the pleasure to invite resident foreign correspondents to a group reporting trip visiting Dunhang city and Gannan Tibetan Autonomous Prefecture, Gansu Province, from September 19 to 23. The Itinerary (Appendix I) is only for your information, pending for final version. The correspondents group will first go to Dunhuang to report on the Cultural Expo and then visit Gannan Tibetan Autonomous Prefecture to gain knowledge about the economic and social development and ethnic culture there.

Some journalists attended trips organized to Tibet itself because there is no other way to report from the region. However, once there, they often attempt to evade their minders to get information for stories (Respondent 10). The state attempts to restrict journalists from conducting independent reporting on Tibetan trips by having security agents stand guard in the hotel where journalists are staying and follow them if they leave the premises. Even so, occasionally correspondents can evade these strictures. One reporter, for example, was able to leave the hotel and interview two sources, one of whom was a shopkeeper, and the other was someone with foreign connections whom the government would likely view as suspicious (Respondent 4). They were willing to speak, and after checking back with them in the future, they were still willing to speak and were unafraid, which indicated to the journalist that they did not face harassment and that s/he therefore had not been followed on those occasions.

Although these publicity tours were generally offered on a first-come, first-served basis, access was sometimes more restricted. For example, one respondent applied for a trip in the west of China, not to report on repression or contentious ethnic issues, but rather to report on how a particular factory complex was coping with changing economic trends in the context of China's larger economic plans (Respondent 9). S/he was not invited to join the trip and became curious as to why. After informally asking a contact in the Chinese state media, s/he learned that the trip included only journalists from outlets of states friendly to the Chinese government, such as Central Asian states, Iran, and Pakistan. It is difficult to verify, but this kind of tour may have been the foundation to produce a genre of content that is often seen in China's external propaganda streams, and which will be briefly highlighted in the next chapter, namely stories about foreigners uncritically impressed with some aspect of China's development or policy.

Publicity tours provide a way for the Chinese government to reveal what it wants to reveal to selected audiences. It gives the state an opportunity to control the message about restricted areas like Tibet or to promote initiatives that it thinks will be of benefit. Reporters from Western news agencies generally ignore invitations to these sorts of trips unless they are of specific interest or if they think they can still report with a critical eye from restricted areas. In all cases in which this occurred, the media outlet did not allow the Chinese government to pay for expenses, as this would be seen to compromise journalistic independence.

Cultivating Sources

Perhaps the most consistent pattern in reporting from China is the difficulty foreign journalists have in gaining information from high-level sources. All the reporters interviewed described facing severe difficulties in cultivating professional relationships with political actors that would result in the latter commenting to the former, even off the record. While getting high-level sources in any country is difficult, the CCP's discipline is formidable, and most journalists face a veritable brick wall in gaining insider insights from party sources.

For example, a reporter from a European paper who had been in China a bit less than two years observed, "my colleagues who have been in this business longer than me say they've never come across a place that's as tight-lipped as this. People with experience in other communist states they come here and they say 'nobody is talking politics'" (Respondent 8).

One journalist from Europe reflected in detail on his/her several years of experience reporting from China:

> Yeah I've only ever really had one [case] where I think we were getting something close to an inside view from somebody who is, you know, not relatively senior in terms of rank or position but in terms of connections. For example we got a steer from him long before the whole "extension of term" limits thing—maybe even 18 months before that happened.[1] I mean of course those rumors were there but the sort of insight he had and the detail he was able to give us now with hindsight makes me realize that he really did know something. But it is rare and our ability to find people like that, it was kind of chance. It came as a result of a particularly skilled and connected local producer. You know one of my Chinese colleagues culti-vated that relationship through a story we were doing and then we built and built this sort of rapport and it kind of worked but other than that in all of the years I've been here I'd say that's an exception that proves the rule. It's sort of none. (Respondent 6)

One way to mitigate this lack of access is for reporters to seek com-ment from academics at respected Chinese universities (Respondent 3, Respondent 4). For example, scholars who advise the government on policy sometimes have insights on internal politics or the thinking of policymakers. However, interviewees reported that since Xi Jinping has taken power, even this has become more difficult. According to these journalists, academics are increasingly reticent to talk, and even more hesitant to go on the record about Chinese political developments. One way around this is to contact academics who appear on Chinese state media such as CGTN because presumably they

---

[1] This refers to the government removing term limits in 2018 for China's head of state, which was widely taken as an indicator that Xi Jinping will rule indefinitely. On the causes and consequences of this development, see Shirk (2018).

have been authorized to speak on these issues to international audiences (Respondent 3). But even this method only really reproduces the party line and gives little insight into what is happening behind closed doors. One group that is sometimes able to give insight is foreign diplomatic staff, but they of course have limited access themselves.

According to a survey by the FCCC about working conditions for foreign journalists in the year 2017, 40% of respondents reported that conditions for information-gathering in China had deteriorated relative to 2016 (FCCC 2018). This included perceived increasing unwillingness of sources to speak with journalists. As one correspondent who had been in China more than 10 years noted, "getting *anybody* to talk to you now is really hard" (Respondent 2). In practice, this means that foreign journalists often get their information from local media, from China's international-facing prop-aganda outlets, or from highly scripted press conferences. The result is that the official Chinese perspective is communicated in a disciplined fashion, with few domestic voices willing to publicly dissent in international media. The appearance of such unity benefits the Chinese state because it enables it to exert more control over its self-presentation, even in foreign news stories.

Complaints to Bureau and/or Reporter

Because Chinese authorities generally do not give comment to journalists except in press conferences, correspondents often look to Chinese party-state media for the official perspective if they wish to include it in their story. In some circumstances, however, Chinese authorities complain to the bureau or to the reporter him/herself about certain stories after they are published or broadcast. Several respondents had experiences of this kind.

Bureau chiefs are generally targeted for this tactic more than correspondents themselves. Reporters often noted that while they had not been called into the Ministry of Foreign Affairs or the State Council Information Office for their reporting to be scrutinized, their bureau chiefs had (e.g., Respondent 5, Respondent 7, Respondent 8, Respondent 10). The bureau chiefs generally attempt to insulate the individual reporters from such pressure, but in cases of small outlets sometimes the bureau is only one or two people so functionally there is little difference.

Two bureau chiefs for North American outlets had similar experiences pertaining to coverage in their publications (Respondent 1, Respondent

3). In both cases, they were summoned to the Ministry of Foreign Affairs. Incidentally, it is common knowledge that when officials from the ministry want to talk to reporters and float more constructive ideas like asking a question at a press conference or covering a story, the meeting takes place at a coffee shop near the ministry (Respondent 3, Respondent 4). However, when officials wish to put pressure on journalists or scold them, then the meeting takes place in the ministry itself.

In these two episodes, each bureau chief was queried about an opinion piece that had been printed in their newspaper that was deemed to be offensive to Chinese authorities. In both cases, the bureau chiefs had to explain that they had no control over what happens in the opinion pages of their newspapers and that there was commonly editorial independence between the op-ed pages and the news pages of Western outlets. Nonetheless, on both occasions, the officials had read the story closely and/or had it translated for them so that they could confront the bureau chief with their complaints. On both occasions, the issue was left there and so far as the journalist could tell there was no further action. Indeed, in one of the cases, the official admitted that he really had to do this to satisfy his boss so everyone could move on (Respondent 1).

In a more direct approach, the authorities called a reporter from a North American outlet to the ministry to complain about their coverage (Respondent 4). The official had printouts of their recent articles with an analytical cover sheet containing the translated headlines of all the reporter's stories, as well as a pie chart dividing up the articles s/he had written by theme. The complaint was that the journalist was spending too much time writing negative stories about China and should instead vary his/her coverage and present positive stories. The tone of the meeting itself was contentious.

These ad hoc meetings appear relatively rare for correspondents, and most complaints seem to be filtered through bureau chiefs, central headquarters, embassies (see later discussion), or occur at the annual press card renewal meeting. Yet, they do happen occasionally, and they are another way in which Chinese authorities attempt to influence what stories reporters tell. The meetings are sometimes about specific stories and are sometimes more general conversations about how to cover China positively or select stories that will highlight China's positive aspects. Regardless, the Chinese government is active in complaining about coverage directly to foreign news outlets.

Complaints via the Chinese Embassy in the Home Country

There have been several instances in which the Chinese embassy in the journalist's home country has complained or otherwise exerted pressure regarding the correspondent's reporting. Some of these instances are well publicized (see Reporters Without Borders 2019). For example, in March 2018, the Chinese embassy in Sweden verbally attacked Swedish journalist Jojje Olsson in a public statement (Embassy of PRC in Sweden 2018, n.p.). It claimed that he had entered China on the wrong visa for journalistic activity, which was "deceptive and shameful behavior [that] fully indicates that he is not an honest or credible person." The statement continued to say that "people with even just a little common sense and independent judgment have no difficulty in seeing that the articles he wrote about China are filled with false and exaggerated content intended to maliciously smear China. He does not understand the situation in China but poses as a 'China expert.' Where is the credibility of those fabricated articles?" Letters to the editor by Chinese diplomats to newspapers that run critical stories appear, and sometimes they do single out the reporting of the correspondent to try to pressure him/her to present a more favorable image of China.

Several respondents indicated that the Chinese embassy in their home countries had contacted their employers. One respondent for a European outlet indicated that it was indeed so ordinary that s/he did not hear about every instance when it happened, but rather heard about them while visiting the central offices (Respondent 9). Another recalls that officials from the Chinese embassy set up a meeting with their bosses in the home country to complain about their reporting (Respondent 6). Others had been singled out in public speeches, statements, and/or letters to the editor by Chinese embassies in their home states.

Yet, sometimes embassies impugn the reporter in more private ways. In an effort to overcome the difficulty of cultivating sources in China, correspondents try to build contacts with the Chinese embassy in their home states because often a major focus of their reporting is on the relations between that state and China. It is therefore useful to have contacts in the Chinese embassy for comment or for information. Communication of this sort is facilitated by WeChat. In private communications like this, embassy officials sometimes indicate their displeasure at the correspondent's reporting or questions. For example, one respondent was accused of bias and of "hurting the feelings" of Chinese officials and of her/his questions being designed to "deliberately provoke China, which is extremely disgusting and unacceptable" (Respondent 4).

The experience of one correspondent writing about ties between the home country and China reveals how this can work and is worth reporting at length in the correspondent's own words. S/he recounts how the people profiled in the article, who were Chinese nationals living in the correspondent's country, seemed to be persuaded by the embassy to condemn the story:

> What happened there was when that piece went out which contained [critical] quotes and I think the headline was also quite strong. And I'd had really good exchanges with those [sources] up until then. They were really friendly and I spoke and chatted to them on WeChat and over email and everything. I knew that they had very strong nationalistic feelings, which is very typical of Chinese people. And then I spoke to them when I saw the piece because I hadn't written the headline. When I saw the piece, I thought, "I wonder if they're going to be concerned about that." I spoke to them and they said, "Oh yes. Thanks. Thanks very much. I really like it. Really nice to know you." All positive. And I also spoke to another [source] as well to say, "I hope you like the piece there's obviously you know some controversial points in it but you know this is kind of what we do. It's just a standard report here." And then literally 24 hours later I got an email . . . and one of them said I spoke to my good friend XXXX at the Chinese embassy here who found it full of untruths. . . . Full of untruths and prejudice. And then he went on for another couple of paragraphs basically supporting how they also found it prejudiced and full of untruths and said that they had not said it originally when they spoke to me because in China they have this feeling that you shouldn't directly criticize somebody after they've done some work. Go figure. So, you know I said "for this this and this reason it's not prejudice and it's not full of untruths" and I stood by it and my editor also stood by it and we exchanged emails a few times and then eventually it just stopped. And the guy from the embassy XXXX had actually friended me on WeChat before the article went out and then when I tried to send him a message once I got the complaint I found that he had de-friended me [laughs]. (Respondent 7)

As this is a relatively specific story about Chinese nationals in another country, this was the only instance in the interview sample of sources outside of China being pressured by the government. However, respondents unanimously reported that interviewing sources within China is becoming increasingly difficult, so it may be the case that this chill has extended extraterritorially (see Reporters Without Borders 2019).

Sometimes, Chinese embassies hold preemptive meetings at the headquarters of foreign media outlets. The goal is not to complain about a report or story, but rather to nurture a positive image more generally for China so that it is reflected in that outlet's coverage. As noted earlier, this has a domestic analogue in that bureau chiefs are sometimes invited to the Ministry of Foreign Affairs or the State Council Information Office to discuss achieving what they perceive as fair reporting about China.

Surveillance, Detention, and Intimidation

At the most extreme end of the spectrum constraining journalist's work in China lie surveillance, police detention, and threats or intimidation. While surveillance is sometimes difficult to detect, at other times it seems intentionally visible to signal to the targets that they are being watched. It is also possible that authorities engage in digital or electronic surveillance, but if this is successful then the target would usually not be aware of it.

However, sometimes the correspondent knows for sure that s/he is being monitored. For example, surveillance is virtually guaranteed on trips to especially repressive areas like Xinjiang. The surveillance is often accompanied by detention in a police facility and/or intimidation by security forces, often in plain clothes. Indeed, several of the interviewees in this sample had been detained by police during their reporting (e.g., Respondent 2, Respondent 4, Respondent 10). Even short of detention, however, intimidation can occur. One correspondent recounts a story from his/her trip to Xinjiang in which a plainclothes police officer visited his/her hotel:

> I went back to the hotel and . . . I couldn't get Wi-Fi of course I couldn't get internet at all, but I went down to the lobby to see if I could get something. And then I ordered a beer and two beers came. This guy came out and sat down opposite me. He said, "do you feel safe here?" That's a thing you hear a lot from police, particularly in Xinjiang, "do you feel safe here?" It's very unsettling. Then he said, "you speak English, right?" And I said, "yep." And he said, "I speak English, too listen: One. Two. Three. Four. . . ." And he proceeded to count to five hundred and something, five or six

hundred. Staring at me. I thought, "what's going on here?" And every time I'd go, "very good very good," he'd go [puts finger up] and would keep going. And then he produced this child's book. And he started to read this story . . . kind of along the lines of the "the quick brown fox jumps over the lazy dog" or whatever it is. One of these sort of verbal tricks. And he started reading these things out to me and I thought, "what's going on?" They must be searching my room, but normally they'll just do that when you're out. Also, I had my computer with me. Then he went off and kind of left me there feeling very uneasy. And he says, "I come to Beijing every so often, maybe I'll look you up." (Respondent 2)

Indeed, journalists have written publicly about surveillance and detention when reporting from Xinjiang (e.g., Zand 2018; Vanderklippe 2018; Mozur 2019). Foreign journalists are watched closely in their hotels, on the road, and walking in public places. This has a chilling effect on residents being willing to speak with them, in addition to blocking off areas where journalists can visit. Police frequently make journalists delete photos from their cameras or phones, although there are ways to mitigate this obstacle.

Another sometimes "sensitive" place is the border area with North Korea. One reporter from a North American outlet recalls that it became obvious s/he was being surveilled because the police would visit sources after the journalists met with them:

But the most obvious thing . . . I remember one guy in particular who was very friendly to us who we'd seen several times during the course of a week and he said that the police have been asking about us and what we were doing. To see him in his office. And then there was a local guy, a Korean Chinese guy, who had been our fixer in XXXXX and had been arranging for us to speak to businesspeople and things like that. And over the course of like three or four trips he became more and more . . . like it became clear . . . it must have been after a third trip, when we called him about going again, he was just like "no," you know it became clear that they'd gone to him. They knew he was helping us. (Respondent 3)

Sometimes, though, surveillance is not determined by geographical factors, but rather by the type of story the journalist is working on or the contact s/he is meeting. For example, one journalist recalls that s/he had arranged to meet with a former political prisoner for a story. In her/his own words:

I arranged to speak with him, and I met his wife in a mall. We went out and suddenly her phone rings and she just like leaps into action. We run outside and he had arrived. I think in a taxi. And immediately unknown people, presumably security agents, take him out. They drag him into a car, the car goes peeling away as I show up. His wife was quite brilliant. Because these security guys don't look like anybody except for criminals. They really resemble criminals in their tactics and in their appearance and all the rest. And so, she started freaking out and started getting the local cops involved, "he's been kidnapped, he's been kidnapped," and made a big stink of it. So at that point, I couldn't interview the guy. I ended up interviewing him online. OK so I did get through, but not in person. Yeah, then we went back to a coffee shop and chatted for a while again. And that was fine. But then we, as I was going to leave, I had driven a rental car and the rental car was in the basement of this shopping mall. And I got a bit lost. And I started to realize people were following me. . . . Anyway, I got to the car and then they would not let me go in the car. And they took me off [to] the police station and that was the first time I've really been detained in China. It was a few years ago and I was, that was quite nerve racking. And basically, they wanted to make sure I didn't have pictures of this guy which, I hadn't gotten. That's the thing about some of these tactics: they often succeed. (Respondent 4).

Similarly, a correspondent on a trip involving reporting on human rights activists recalls catching authorities in the act of bugging his/her hotel room. The story is darkly humorous:

And we got to the hotel and then I left to go get a taxi and it was raining so I couldn't, and I had to come back up to the room. And the staff says "you can't go in." So I sort of said "yes I can . . . watch me." I went in the room and there they were, bugging the room. They had the chair in the corner of the room turned over, with kind of like wires sticking out of it. So, I was thinking, "why are there wires in these chairs?" I asked the guy and he just said "it's broken." (Respondent 2)

This type of topic-based surveillance is not always centered on the journalist but rather on the subject. As Respondent 4's story about the shopping mall illustrates, it was not s/he who was under surveillance initially, but rather the person and family s/he was attempting to interview. In cases like this, the journalist encounters state surveillance as a third party. Respondent

10 captured this point: "I think often the surveillance was more surveilling the dissidents and people we were interviewing than us although, you know I think we did also at some points have surveillance on us."

In general, most respondents report that surveillance is assumed, although they are usually not able to identify it so readily as in these instances. Yet, small signs sometimes emerge that surveillance is more common. For example, one respondent reports that in the annual visa interview the authorities would sometimes reveal personal details, such as romantic relationships, to signal that s/he is being watched (Respondent 5). Others report instances in which their offices were bugged, or colleagues found listening devices in their apartments (Respondent 10). Some have written publicly about how surveillance has increased recently, even on reporting trips to unremarkable areas about non-"sensitive" topics (Mozur 2020).

Conclusion: An Obstructive Foundation for Promotional Methods

This chapter has analyzed the Chinese government's efforts to influence the global ideational context in which China's rise is viewed by focusing on how it controls Western correspondents reporting from the country. Foreign correspondents are a key group for any authoritarian state because they disproportionately shape the international image of that state in the minds of foreign audiences. It is therefore not surprising that Chinese authorities pay close attention to influencing the coverage of this group in their efforts to craft China's image abroad. The chapter discussed eight ways in which the Chinese party-state attempts to influence the work of foreign journalists, ranging from inducements like junket tours to repressive measures like detention or intimidation.

In general, for major Western outlets, the government relies on obstructive tactics such as making information unavailable or detaining journalists, rather than promotional tactics such as privileged access. The strategy in dealing with Western journalists from credible independent outlets seems to be to attempt to limit their ability to write negative stories about China so that the information void can be filled by Chinese state outlets. However, as discussed at more length in the next chapter, the Ministry of Foreign Affairs also attempts to cultivate friendly journalists from Africa, Asia, and Latin America with lengthy fellowship programs in China (Krishnan 2018;

Reporters Without Borders 2019). The implication is that these journalists will then say positive things about China, which will in turn be reproduced in China's foreign-facing party-state media. Combined, the strategy appears to be to inhibit critical journalists, particularly from "the West," and promote friendly ones, particularly from the Global South.

To discourage critical reporting about the Chinese political system, the CCP will also take on entire news organizations over their coverage, as when it suspended new visas for *New York Times* journalists after its reporting about the personal and familial wealth of Chinese premier Wen Jiabao (Wemple 2014), or when the state blocked *Bloomberg News* after a report on the wealth of Chinese political elites and seemingly succeeded in inducing self-censorship among its editors (Wong 2013). Most recently, the Chinese government expelled journalists from several major American outlets (Tracy, Wong, and Jakes 2020). The obstructive strategy helps create a void about certain issues that can either be left empty or filled by China's external propaganda outlets like CGTN or friendlier foreign journalists. Filling the void is a topic to which the next chapter turns.

The question remains about whether China's efforts to control foreign correspondents are effective. Do we see the obstructive/specific causal mechanism playing out in this case to improve China's internal or external security? On one level, the answer is clearly yes. China's restrictive measures effectively deprive journalists of facts and sources that they need to investigate stories in the country. Dissidents are hard to access, political elites will not talk to foreign correspondents, and mechanisms like freedom of information requests for some issues do not exist in any meaningful way. Journalists need access to information to write stories, and the Chinese government is committed to restricting information. Putting areas like Tibet "off limits" means that journalists cannot regularly visit there and write stories that might keep Chinese government policies in Tibet in the headlines. Surveillance and repression may not deter some intrepid foreign journalists from covering stories, but it might deter some and it likely deters many potential sources from cooperating with them. Clearly, the Chinese state prevents many stories from reaching international audiences by restricting the work of foreign media outlets, even if it is difficult to measure the absence of content. This reality improves the CCP's internal and external security at first glance.

However, on a deeper level, it is unlikely that these tactics ultimately achieve a more ambitious objective: generating more positive coverage of China in Western outlets. Journalists do not appreciate being harassed or intimidated, and the lack of information (including censored internet) is a persistent complaint of foreign correspondents. They do not wish to be pressured or scolded, and in general would prefer to do their work without these inconveniences. Indeed, the FCCC annually publishes its grievances with government policies and practices that inhibit their work and sometimes endanger themselves or their colleagues (FCCC 2018, 2020). It is worth considering that China's interference with foreign correspondents therefore may backfire by alienating them. In other words, surveillance, repression, harassment, strident complaints, and so on, may have the effect of making foreign correspondents less likely to report favorably about China.

The Chinese party-state, however, does not rely only on obstructing foreign journalists to cultivate its image. This is only the preparatory work for its broader ambitions. It also generates a tremendous amount of foreign-facing propaganda to disseminate its messages to foreign audiences. Controlling foreign correspondents is an effort to shape the information environment so that China's preferred messages face fewer counter-narratives and so China's critics are looked upon with more skepticism. The next chapter turns to the proactive efforts that the CCP takes to ensure that its messages are heard in international discourse.

6

Promoting and Controlling
the China Dream

China's External Propaganda and Repression

It is easy to forget that Mao Zedong's cult of personality, which so saturated Chinese politics up to the 1970s, also found adherents scattered around the globe. In some sense, the international dimension is harder to explain than its domestic analogue. Domestically, many Chinese citizens acted as if they worshiped Mao in public, even if they had private complaints or doubts about his rule. Internationally, however, Mao and his brand of politics appealed to an assortment of far left-wing groups around the world, ranging from European and American cities to rural areas of Latin America and South Asia. This appeal was in no small part due to the Chinese government's efforts to promote Maoism as the ideology that would lead the world revolution.

Part of the reason it is easy to forget Maoism's one-time appeal outside of China, as Julia Lovell so astutely points out, is because today's CCP is eager to downplay Beijing's bid for global leadership (Lovell 2019, 11–12). The official line is that China will "never seek hegemony" and that it does not interfere in the politics of other sovereign states. China's aspiration for global leadership under Mao sits at odds with this argument, rendering it important for the contemporary party to downplay legacies of interference and ambition (Lovell 2019, 13).

Lovell details how the CCP under Mao spent a good deal of time, effort, and resources to make itself, and Mao himself, look good to foreign audiences. It operated "a lavish and exhaustively orchestrated hospitality machine" designed to flatter key foreign guests in the expectation that they would support the CCP's aims (Lovell 2019, 78). From the 1960s, the CCP attempted a charm offensive in the Third World (Lovell 2019, 147). In several African states, for example, this manifested itself in inviting select leaders to meet Mao himself, broadcasting radio propaganda, providing aid, and

Making the World Safe for Dictatorship, Alexander Dukalskis, Oxford University Press (2021). © Oxford University Press.
DOI: 10.1093/oso/9780197520130.003.0006

disseminating millions of copies of the "Little Red Book" of Mao quotations (Lovell 2019, 187–193). These authoritarian image management efforts were fed back into domestic propaganda to motivate people to work for the revolution. Again, Lovell (2019, 142) writes: "The idea of an approving foreign gaze—that events in China were inspiring revolutionaries all over the world—was intensely important to those propelling the revolution." Despite today's party partially distancing itself from Maoism and the CCP's previous global revolutionary ambitions, those efforts were real, and they influenced the way millions of people around the world perceived Maoist authoritarianism.

The authoritarian image management techniques of the Mao era provide some key building blocks for contemporary China's efforts. The importance of hospitality, for example, has remained a key feature of Beijing's strategy, even if the guests are now far more numerous and therefore generally do not receive attention from the pinnacle of leadership. The main difference from the Mao era, of course, is the material context of China. While during the Maoist era China was poor and its population was subject to grand schemes aiming to achieve great leaps or permanent revolutions, the China of today is powerful and successful in ways that would have seemed unimaginable during Mao's life.

This chapter focuses on contemporary China's effort to shape its image abroad through both promotional messaging and obstructive control techniques. The previous chapter focused specifically on how the CCP tries to control the narrative emanating from within China's borders by influencing correspondents from European and North American news outlets. This chapter widens its focus to capture the myriad ways in which the Chinese government is packaging its image for international audiences (promotional/diffuse), cultivating messengers capable of conveying that image (promotional/specific), trying to respond to or downplay criticisms about its policies in international discourse (obstructive/diffuse), and intimidating and threatening activists outside its own borders (obstructive/specific). To do so, it will draw on a variety of data, including speeches and documents from the leadership, close attention to China Global Television Network (CGTN) content, interviews conducted by the author with targets of China's promotional/specific efforts, and China-relevant data captured in the AAAD presented in Chapter 4. First, however, background about Beijing's attempts to shape its image in recent years will help situate the data in a broader conversation.

Soft Power, External Propaganda, and "Telling China's Story Well"

It is not an exaggeration to say that the Chinese government is preoccupied with how China is perceived abroad (Pu 2019, 34). The CCP attempts to put a positive gloss on China's achievements and to counter negative images (Hartig 2016, 661; Brazys and Dukalskis 2020). It attempts to police the boundaries of discourse about its policies with a vigilance matched by few contemporary states. The Chinese government has backed its image management efforts with considerable sums of money. As Lim and Bergin (2018, n.p.) put it in their long-form journalistic piece on the topic: "China is trying to reshape the global information environment with massive infusions of money—funding paid-for advertorials, sponsored journalistic coverage and heavily massaged positive messages from boosters."

The underlying cause of these efforts stems from the realization that if China was going to rise and be respected as a great power, it needed to improve its image (Brady 2015, 51). China's communist authoritarian political system means that its political values deviate from the purported values of most of the international community (Zhao 2015, 195). Some argue that this limits its political appeal internationally (Economy 2018, 221). Perhaps more importantly, citizens of many states are wary of what a powerful China will mean for them and, from the Chinese government's perspective, need to be convinced to see Beijing positively, or at least to not think about China in political terms.

The CCP's domestic political power is bound up with its global status and the ease of enacting its foreign policy priorities. However, the Chinese leadership understands that if China is seen as too powerful and threatening abroad, then other states may take corresponding actions to counter it. As Brady (2008, 151) put it, "the more China opened up to the outside world, the more important foreign propaganda work became." There are exceptions (Pu 2019, 44), but in general Beijing has strong incentives to present itself in a benign manner abroad. To do so, it sometimes intentionally downplays its material power, arguing instead that China is a poor developing country focused on domestic development, not regional or global dominance (Pu 2019). Regardless, the leadership wants China's political system to have a positive image, or at least to be grudgingly accepted abroad as powerful and inevitable. Rolland (2020, 5) summarizes the CCP's efforts to counter what it calls the "so-called China threat theory" externally: "this is done mainly by helping provide a soft pulp of peacefulness and benign intentions relentlessly applied on top of—though barely concealing—a hard core that is mostly about the party's unhampered power and aura."

The party's legitimating narratives to the domestic audience feature heavy doses of nationalism and a discourse highlighting the government's performance (Dukalskis and Gerschewski 2020). Delivering national glory and material development are both eased if China's external environment is friendlier to its interests. As such, the core priorities of Chinese foreign policy are to ensure continuity of the CCP's power through creating external conditions conducive to economic development and security (Heilmann and Schmidt 2014; Buzan 2014). Part of this effort entails "defend[ing] the domestic political project from internal and external ideological threats" (Edney 2014, 102). Indeed, China's success and prestige abroad are fed back into domestic propaganda streams to enhance the CCP's legitimacy at home (Holbig 2011; Pu 2019, 40; Rolland 2020, 46).

In some ways, these fundamental concerns have been with the CCP since its seizure of power, and particularly since reform and opening began. Between Mao's death and the more assertive foreign policies of the Xi Jinping era, the CCP used techniques of authoritarian image management to dampen criticisms of some of its internationally unpopular policies (Zhao 2015). For example, it retained a public relations firm after the 1989 Tiananmen Square crackdown to try to soften its image abroad (d'Hooge 2005, 92), and highlighted "foreign friends" who defended China (Brady 2008, 159-160).

A leaked 1993 document titled "China's Public Relations Strategy on Tibet" details the discussions of a meeting of external propaganda officials in Beijing and gives a glimpse into how the CCP deals with criticism of its repression. The document stresses the importance of securing the loyalty of Tibetans living abroad, and where this is impossible, to isolate and discredit critics. It recommends aggressively reporting on Buddhist religious ceremonies in Tibet to foreign audiences, but not within Tibet itself. In a foreshadowing of what was to come during a repressive campaign in Xinjiang from 2014 onward, the documents recommended that cultural outreach, such as dancing and art exhibitions, should be used for political purposes to show the CCP as an enlightened ruler of Tibet. Foreign reporters should be welcomed on a discerning basis: "select some relatively objective and fair-minded persons and journalists to visit Tibet and only request them to report objective facts. Being truthful to facts is very convincing. The number of people doesn't have to be large, but the selection must be well made" (quoted in d'Hooge 2005,

101). This strategy ultimately did not prevent pro-Tibet protesters around the world from using the 2008 Olympic torch journey for the Beijing games from becoming a site of mobilization and embarrassment for the CCP; this despite the party's retention of public relations firms to help with its external propaganda efforts (Clifford 2008). It did, however, along with China's growing power, help take support for Tibetan independence or even genuine autonomy off the mainstream international agenda.

Since the early 1990s, "promoting a positive image on the world stage has been a top priority of the Chinese government" (Pu 2019, 35; see also Brady 2008, 151–174). In the 1990s and early 2000s, influential Chinese intellectuals and eventually the Chinese government itself began to discover the conceptual device of "soft power" (Edney et al., 2020). At the 17th CCP Congress in 2007, General Secretary Hu Jintao's report mentioned soft power in the context of enhancing culture (China Daily 2007). Hu's understanding of soft power from the report is bound up with promoting and strengthening culture domestically in order to strengthen unity as the foundation from which to project an image of a strong and cohesive China (Edney 2012, 908). As Wang (2008, 258) put it, "few Western international relations phrases have penetrated as deeply or broadly into the Chinese vocabulary in recent years." The concept provided the language and formulations to underpin the strong desire of the Chinese government to "shape a favorable external environment" by presenting China as a non-threatening rising power (Wang 2008, 258; Ding 2010).

The prevailing understanding of soft power among Chinese policymakers is that it is a state-driven, centrally organized endeavor. Externally, the concept of soft power has been largely operationalized through the institutions and practices of the party-state's foreign propaganda apparatus (Edney 2012, 905). Put differently, China approaches "soft power from the firm conviction that the task of enhancing national attractiveness is a matter to be orchestrated and directed by the state" (Wilson 2015, 293). Society does not speak for itself in this conception of soft power; rather, the government controls and shapes China's image. Stated more acerbically in relation to public diplomacy, "the Chinese government approaches [it] the same way it constructs high-speed rail or builds infrastructure—by investing money and expecting to see development" (Shambaugh 2015, 107).

Layered on top of soft power is an addition to the Chinese foreign policy lexicon first used officially in 2008, namely "discourse power" (Rolland 2020, 53; see also Zhao 2016). The CCP believes it is in a "discourse war" with the

West (Shambaugh 2015, 103). From this perspective, "China faces a hegemony of discourse" insofar as "Western" ideas and media have excessive sway in the international public sphere and portray China negatively (Wang 2008, 265; Liu 2020, 280–283). The task is to erode or even reverse that hegemony by challenging the superiority and universality of purportedly Western ideas (Pu 2012, 357). The idea behind discourse power, a concept which Xi Jinping stresses repeatedly, is to enhance the Chinese government's ability to communicate internationally and get others to listen (Rolland 2020, 10–12). Sometimes the idea is framed as "speaking rights," suggesting that China needs to increase its right to speak and be heard on the international stage (Rolland 2020, 7; see also Zhao 2016).

Emblematic of the state-centric approach to soft power and discourse power, in 2009 the government put considerable money behind a global propaganda push (Lim and Bergin 2018). Perhaps sensing a moment of opportunity as the United States and much of Europe were dealing with a financial crisis, or perhaps alarmed at how the Tibet Olympic torch protests played out in 2008, the CCP under Hu Jintao devoted an extra 45 billion RMB (about 6–7 billion USD) to revamp its external propaganda system. The idea from the CCP's perspective was to "drown out anti-China forces in the West" (Tsai 2017, 211), with the long-term aim to "wrest global ideological leadership from the hands of the West" (Tsai 2017, 209). Organizationally, the system is broadly led by the CCP Leading Group for Propaganda and Ideology, the CCP Leading Group on Foreign Affairs, and the CCP Central Committee Foreign Propaganda Group (Brady 2015; Tsai 2017). The CCP Central Office of Foreign Propaganda operates under its more anodyne name, the State Council Information Office (SCIO) (Brady 2015, 51). SCIO makes decisions in line with party leadership.

The consumer of China's foreign propaganda confronts content in the form of media outlets like *Xinhua* or *China Daily*, books published by the China Foreign Languages Publishing Administration, or programs on CGTN. It can be difficult for the average end consumer to know that s/he is viewing content overseen by the CCP external propaganda apparatus. Sometimes this is due to lack of knowledge about the Chinese political system or about the relationship between the media and the CCP. At other times, it is because the CCP actively obscures the origins of the content, such as when China Radio International operated stations with pro-Beijing content but with ownership hidden through complex layers of intermediaries (Koh and Shiffman 2015).

While China's external propaganda efforts were clearly on the upswing from 2008, Xi Jinping accelerated the trend after he ascended to power in 2012. In an August 2013 speech at the National Propaganda and Ideology Work Conference, Xi argued that the party should "tell a good Chinese story, and promote China's views internationally" and "should spread new ideas and new perspectives among developing states" (quoted in Brady 2015, 55). From Xi's perspective, it was necessary to "tell China's story well, disseminate China's voice, and enhance its right to speak in the international arena" (quoted in Tsai 2017, 208). This was followed in 2014 with the launching of a new strategy that emphasized the formation of large media conglomerates and integration with social media platforms to promote positive views of China (Brady 2015, 55–56).

In case there was any doubt about the campaign's intentions, on one day in February 2016, Xi visited *Xinhua*, the *People's Daily*, and China Central Television (CCTV, later rebranded as CGTN externally) to remind each that their primary task was to serve the CCP, telling them that "all news media run by the party must work to speak for the party's will and its propositions, and protect the party's authority and unity" (Wong 2016). It was clear that this message was not just meant for China's domestic-facing media. At Xi's CCTV stop, he held a video conference with staff from its US office in Washington, DC, to tell them that he hopes they can "objectively, truly and comprehensively introduce China's social and economic development to the world audience" (CGTN America 2016). As Chapter 4 discussed, registration documents show that Beijing has invested substantial sums of money not only in CGTN in the United States, but also in other propaganda efforts to make China look better to American audiences.

Clearly, a major priority of Beijing is to improve China's image among foreign audiences. In some ways, this is not a new development, as the CCP has always been attuned to managing its image for foreigners. What is new is that China is materially powerful in ways that it has not been since well before the party took power. From the CCP's perspective, normative appeal aids the goal of material dominance (Rolland 2020, 9). The CCP faces new challenges due to its status as an authoritarian global power, but also new opportunities because it has the influence and resources—facilitated in part by communications technology—to aggressively promote its messages and monitor dissent. The following sections illustrate these capabilities in each of the four mechanistic areas proposed in Chapter 3, starting with an analysis of the content of the promotional/diffuse effort to promote the CCP's preferred image to the world.

Development, Harmony, and Shared Destiny: Promotional/Diffuse Narratives

It is clear that Beijing adjusts its message depending on the listener (Brazys and Dukalskis 2020), sometimes preferring to brand itself a great power, sometimes a developing country, sometimes a global leader with a novel model, and sometimes a relativistic transactional partner (Pu 2019). But perhaps the core idea that Beijing wishes to promote abroad is that it will "never seek hegemony" (Shambaugh 2013, 26). It aims to convince other countries that China will not attempt to dominate them in the way that previous colonial empires did, or in the way that, Beijing would argue, the United States does currently. The term has its legacies in the 1960s, when the CCP wanted to underscore its opposition to Soviet expansionist policies (Nathan and Scobell 2012, 28). The underpinnings of anti-hegemony formulations can be found in the 1954 articulation of the "Five Principles of Peaceful Coexistence," namely mutual respect for sovereignty and territorial integrity, mutual non-aggression, non-interference in internal affairs, equality and mutual benefit, and peaceful coexistence (Nathan and Scobell 2012, 27–28). With concepts like this, China's leaders aim to reassure the world that Beijing has benign intentions with its accumulating power.

But the CCP aims to do more than this. Beyond reassurance, the party wishes to articulate an alternative vision of international politics that suits its interests. Especially in the developing world, "China makes great efforts to present its goals, principles, and methods as viable alternatives to American and European policies" (Heilmann and Schmidt 2014, 33). If the Chinese government can alter the terms on which international politics are judged, then it can create for itself more latitude to pursue its interests. Beijing's diplomats often try to change the vocabulary of global norms on issues like human rights or sovereignty in international institutions, most prominently in the United Nations, so that the norms more closely align with its preferred formulations (Nathan 2015, 165–167; Brazys and Dukalskis 2017). The government articulates concepts that simultaneously reassure foreign audiences while also proffering content that emphasizes Beijing's political priorities. Examples include China's "peaceful rise," which was eventually dropped in favor of "peaceful development" (for fear that "rise" sounded too aggressive) and "harmonious world" (Shambaugh 2013, 217–220). The latter emphasized multilateralism, prosperity through cooperation, collective security, and dialogue.

The most recent set of concepts meant to define China's image on the international stage have to do with Xi Jinping's "China Dream" and "Community of Shared Destiny for Mankind." On the former, Xi gave a speech on November 29, 2012, to the incoming top CCP leadership after the group had just viewed the Road of Rejuvenation exhibition at the National Museum of China. The exhibition tells the history of China from an orthodox CCP perspective from the 1840s to the present. In the speech, Xi claimed:

> realizing the great rejuvenation of the Chinese nation is the greatest Chinese dream of the Chinese nation in modern times. Because this dream has concentrated and endowed the long-cherished wish of many generations of Chinese, it reflects the comprehensive interests of the Chinese nation and the Chinese people, and it is a common expectation of all sons and daughters of China.[1]

It is a nationalist legitimation narrative, focused on overcoming what the CCP refers to as the "Century of National Humiliation" (Wang 2012). China was bullied by foreign powers before the CCP's arrival, the narrative goes, and the lesson to be drawn is that China must be strong, prosperous, and retain its Chinese identity to prevent the same from happening again. It also emphasizes material prosperity by presenting an optimistic narrative about the future, with the CCP as the only entity prepared to deliver (Wang 2014, 7).

The China Dream in itself, however, does not offer clear prescriptions or reassuring slogans about China's foreign policy. Indeed, from a certain vantage point, the China Dream may be concerning to foreign audiences because it suggests a return of Chinese power. That return would revive perennial questions about Beijing's intentions, so a soothing companion was necessary. This hints at a larger issue with China's various conceptual formulations for international politics: they seem to lack positive content upon which new international politics can be built. Rolland (2020, 48) puts

---

[1] Full text of translated speech available at: https://chinacopyrightandmedia.wordpress.com/2012/11/29/speech-at-the-road-to-rejuvenation/ (accessed September 1, 2020).

the point more starkly, insofar as such visions are "mostly about inveighing against a Western-dominated liberal order that is deemed threatening to the CCP's survival and about altering the world to make it safer for China's un-impeded rise under the party's continuous rule."

Enter the Community of Shared Destiny for Mankind. Like previous articulations of China's foreign policy principles, this concept is meant to simultaneously reassure foreign audiences, alter the normative vocabulary of international relations, and defend China's interests. In his 2017 report at the 19th National Party Congress, Xi expounded on the idea at length.[2] Presumably to reassure foreign audiences, he emphasized the benign nature of China's power:

> China remains firm in pursuing an independent foreign policy of peace. We respect the right of the people of all countries to choose their own development path. We endeavor to uphold international fairness and justice, and oppose acts that impose one's will on others or interfere in the internal affairs of others as well as the practice of the strong bullying the weak.

He also sought to underscore the need for different governing concepts and normative formulations. The message is relativistic: governments should be left alone to do what they see fit internally. Without naming the United States directly, he indicated Beijing's desire for a different set of rules for an interconnected world:

> We call on the people of all countries to work together to build a community with a shared future for mankind, to build an open, inclusive, clean, and beautiful world that enjoys lasting peace, universal security, and common prosperity. We should respect each other, discuss issues as equals, resolutely reject the Cold War mentality and power politics, and take a new approach to developing state-to-state relations with communication, not confrontation, and with partnership, not alliance. We should commit to settling disputes through dialogue and resolving differences through discussion, coordinate responses to traditional and non-traditional threats, and oppose terrorism in all its forms.

---

[2] Full text of the report available at: https://www.chinadaily.com.cn/china/19thcpcnationalcongress/2017-11/04/content_34115212.htm (accessed September 1, 2020).

But China would not be a push-over. Even amid the soaring rhetoric about peace and cooperation, Xi defended China's right to assert itself:

China will never pursue development at the expense of others' interests, but nor will China ever give up its legitimate rights and interests. No one should expect us to swallow anything that undermines our interests.

Few foreigners (aside from policy analysts and academics) will ever read Xi's report or the party-produced book compiling his ideas on the concept, so the CCP seeks to spread the message via more visible avenues. To popularize the Community of Shared Destiny for Mankind idea, CGTN, for example, produced a four-minute explainer video that reported in glowing terms on Xi's speeches at the United Nations about the concept, and ran opinion pieces extolling its virtues. China's external propaganda apparatus presents the CCP's views on events, processes, and ideas the party deems important. Through media such as CGTN, the *China Daily*, the *People's Daily*, and *Xinhua*, it projects an image of China as peaceful, developing, and technocratic. It often paints "the West" generally, and the United States in particular, as hypocritical, opposed to China, and economically stagnant (Brazys and Dukalskis 2020). These messages are the operational level of the simultaneously lofty but stilted speeches by Xi and other CCP leaders about China's vision of world order.

On paper, the reach of these messages appears considerable. Chapter 4 detailed the financial backing from Beijing that these efforts receive in the United States. But China's efforts extend globally and have been underpinned by a strategy of "localization," using the language of the target audience (Ohlberg 2019). Reflecting the 2014 external propaganda strategy to integrate messages across multiple platforms, *Xinhua*, CGTN, China Radio International, the *Global Times*, and the *China Daily* all have active Twitter, Facebook, and YouTube accounts (Ohlberg 2019). *Xinhua* has accounts in at least 12 languages. The content mixes ordinary news stories, clickbait, positive stories about China, and sometimes directly political posts about China's political system or those of its rivals (Ohlberg 2019). These platforms have millions of followers, although it may be the case that the platforms have artificially boosted their follower counts and engagement metrics (see Zhong et al. 2020). For example, CGTN videos on YouTube about the Community of Shared Destiny for Mankind struggle to crack 1,000 views (as of this writing), even though the network's account ostensibly has more than one million YouTube subscribers.

In terms of print media, the CCP uses a strategy of making print editions of its papers as freely or cheaply and widely available as possible. It promotes *Xinhua* as a wire service to fill content in newspapers and websites around the globe, which helps inject CCP viewpoints into the media content of international readers (Brazys and Dukalskis 2020). Some evidence suggests that the strategy of getting CCP media in front of international eyes is effective (Bailard 2016). Margaret Roberts (2018, 87) describes the strategy aptly:

> China's *Xinhua* news agency's worldwide expansion reflects a strategy to promote China's view of political events in foreign newspapers, as *Xinhua* spins stories quite differently than Western media. In many countries with a small domestic news presence, *Xinhua* is frequently syndicated. By making *Xinhua* stories deliberately cheap, China promotes its perspective on world events, increasing its international audience.

When it cannot disseminate print editions or syndicated copy, the government opts for purchasing space to run propaganda. This is not a new tactic (Wang 2003). During the Mao era, the *Peking Review*, "the stilted international voice of China," was widely promoted and even popular in some circles (Lovell 2019, 14, 125). According to research by Lim and Bergin (2018), newspapers carrying content sponsored by the Chinese state have a collective circulation of over 15 million. This does not include major non-daily publications like *The Economist*, which sometimes carries a sponsored "China Watch" supplement, or many smaller localized papers that have previously carried Chinese state content on an irregular basis, such as the *Irish Independent* or the *Irish Times*. The advertorial strategy seeks out agenda-setting newspapers such as the *Washington Post*, the *Wall Street Journal*, *Le Figaro*, or *El Pais*. The aim is to get China's message in front of influential readers of newspapers that often report critically about China (for evidence on the latter, see Xu and Cao 2019).

Clearly the CCP has views it wants to promote, and it has invested billions in a promotional/diffuse media strategy to disseminate those views. The content changes with the audience (see Pu 2019, 40–49; Brazys and Dukalskis 2020), but the foundations on which any of those messages are built is that the CCP is a positive force, Xi Jinping is a uniquely capable and visionary leader, and China should be welcomed as a constructive force for global improvement.

Friendly Foreign Journalists: Cultivating Promotional Messengers

Beijing takes concrete steps to nurture a positive view among opinion leaders. As Chapter 4 illustrated, in the United States firms hired by the Chinese government try to foster positive images of China among not only legislators and their staff, but also particular groups such as leaders of historically black colleges and universities. The government's Confucius Institutes at foreign universities are meant, in part, to encourage a positive image of China in university communities (Brazys and Dukalskis 2019).

As mentioned briefly in Chapter 5, the Chinese government also tries to foster positive ties with specific foreign journalists so that they report positively about China. In general, the target audience for these promotional/specific efforts are journalists from the developing world. This section will focus on this method, including by drawing on interview data from three journalists who participated in China's efforts to cultivate them as promotional/specific messengers. The interviews reveal that the intent of the programs is clear to their participants, but that the journalists themselves sometimes have mixed feelings about them.

Such programs come in many forms (McCormick 2019). Among the most ambitious is a recurring 10-month program organized by the Ministry of Foreign Affairs that invites about 100 journalists from Africa, Asia, and Latin America, during which time they receive training, privileged access, as well as a stipend and accommodation (Krishnan 2018). Other events might be irregular or more specific, such as the 2018 Zambia Media Think Tank Seminar, which saw the Chinese government host 22 Zambian journalists for discussions about "challenges posed by new technology and economic development" (Reporters Without Borders 2019, 32). Many Belt and Road agreements between China and partner countries include media training provided by the former (Rolland 2020, 41). At other times, embassies abroad may facilitate training of journalists even without travel to China (Rolland 2020, 33). A *China Daily* description of one recent event is illustrative of how promotional/specific image management techniques for foreign journalists operate:

> The 2018 seminar for journalists from Kenya kicked off on Thursday in Beijing, aimed at enlightening the reporters on the development of China's media, Sino-African media cooperation in international news reporting, and China-Africa relations and friendly exchanges.
>
> Additionally, project organizers appointed by the Chinese Ministry of Commerce will invite officials and experts from related departments to brief on China's development, social and economic policies as well as achievements and lessons learned since China's reform and opening up.
>
> Organized by China International Publishing Group (CIPG), the 20-day seminar will also involve study tours to some cities, institutions and companies aimed at offering the journalists a glance at the real and developing China. (Mutethya 2018, n.p.)

The idea is that these journalists can help "tell China's story well" and show how much foreigners admire China. This starts on the trip itself. For example, a story reproduced in several of China's official media platforms headlined "Visiting Journalists Give Glowing Report" summarized the 10-month program and quoted speeches at the closing ceremony.[3] It highlighted two participants—one from Cameroon and one from the Philippines—who both spoke about China in glowing terms, even repeating CCP talking points directly. According to the speakers, the program would help counteract "persistent negative reporting by a section of the international media" and taught journalists that "China is prepared to become a close partner and friend of any country that aspires to economic prosperity for its people."

When the journalists are in China, they produce stories that are then run in their home media outlet. The implication is that these will be positive, or at least anodyne. Returning to the example from Zambia is instructive. The *Zambian Daily Mail* is a partner and its journalists have been participants in these efforts.[4] Stories from its web archive of China-related content are unrelentingly positive, in part because the paper reproduces *Xinhua* stories on a regular basis. However, many of its stories from Zambian journalists in

---

[3] See http://africa.chinadaily.com.cn/weekly/2017-12/08/content_35257660.htm (accessed September 1, 2020).

[4] See http://www.xinhuanet.com/english/2019-12/11/c_138622588.htm (accessed September 1, 2020); see also Reporters Without Borders (2019, 32).

China or about China are propagandistic in tone: "China Living Its Opening Up Dream," "Traversing Beautiful China," "Africa Unites to Stop Anti-China Crusade," "Lessons from China," "China: Reaching out to Africa," and so on.

However, not all journalists who travel on junkets return home as unfailingly pro-CCP. Dorothy Wickham, a journalist from the Solomon Islands, reflected on her sponsored visit to China in *The Guardian* (Wickham 2019). Two months after the country switched its diplomatic recognition from Taiwan to the PRC, the Chinese government sponsored a "look and learn" tour for Solomon Islands journalists. Wickham revealed her complex feelings about the trip. She was impressed with the scale of Chinese development but wary of the fact that the trip was scripted to preclude the possibility of talking about personal rights or everyday life with ordinary people. Mostly she was concerned that her own country was not prepared to deal with China and stood a good chance of getting taken advantage of in this new relationship.

Like Wickham, interviews with three African journalists who participated in Beijing-sponsored programs through the Chinese Ministry of Foreign Affairs between 2017 and 2020 reveal more complex views of China than propagandistic stories suggest. Of course, these are respondents willing to speak with an academic writing about the themes in this book, so they cannot necessarily be considered representative, but their perspectives do reveal that the people who encounter Beijing's journalistic hospitality are sometimes skeptical targets. The interviews were conducted virtually, and to protect anonymity no identifying information will be given here. Because the programs generally select one journalist from each African country, even mentioning the person's country of origin could be identifying, so interviewee characteristics or demographics will not be reported here.[5]

Journalists were recruited for their fellowship via the Chinese embassy in their home country. The programs included training, language instruction, and government-sponsored reporting trips throughout China. The participants filed stories with their home paper about what they were seeing. Respondents reported that there was no coercive censorship pertaining to these trips. The editorial relationship was between the journalist and the home paper, and the journalist was not told overtly to write certain stories (Respondent 3). However, they were aware that they were only being shown a positive side of the country, and they understood implicitly that they were expected to write positive stories. In other words, "they want us to see the

---

[5] The interviews took place between November 2019 and February 2020.

efforts the Chinese government is making, to show Africans the capabilities of China; the program is modelled to change Africans' perception of China—that's the point" (Respondent 2). The idea is to write stories from a "Chinese perspective" and to "report about China differently," which means with an orientation toward improving society and finding solutions: "you have to re-imagine what a story would look like and ask yourself what this would look like from a Chinese perspective" (Respondent 3). The implication is that this perspective stays within the parameters set by the party (Respondent 3).

When writing such stories, one respondent likened it to writing a public relations piece (Respondent 1). While no explicit pre-censorship was re-ported, links to all published pieces are sent to the program organizers, which means that the latter can complain if the content is not suitable from the government's perspective (Respondent 2). As one participant put it, "you could write what you want, but the conditions weren't there to write uncen-sored information" (Respondent 1). Sometimes this was because sources in China were hesitant to speak to foreign journalists, relevant information was not available, or the language barrier was insurmountable, but at other times it was because the journalists felt the pressure to censor themselves.

Indeed, the participants understood that the program was designed to foster self-censorship. They were the guests of the Chinese government, which was supplying them with accommodation, a generous stipend relative to their home salaries, and all-expenses-paid monthly trips throughout China. Says one respondent: "it has an effect on you and you are going to self-censor; it made me feel like I am under threat. Everyone's expectations are that I should write something positive. I am going forward and I don't know what's coming behind me" (Respondent 2). Another pointed out that this is a process of building a relationship with the Chinese partners and so there is a subtle pres-sure to not spoil the relationship by writing negative stories (Respondent 3).

However, promotional/specific programs of authoritarian image manage-ment like this do not have to be effective all the time to benefit the spon-soring government. After all, the positive stories written on the program are still there for all to see in the journalists' home outlet. Some participants, like those who gave speeches at the ceremony described earlier, clearly buy into what the program is offering. Moving forward, if even a few well-placed targets popularize positive images about China, then the resources wasted on the unconvinced may be worth it. If the pro-CCP journalist goes on to a long career writing positive stories about China, then the investment of a junket trip or training program will have paid for itself many times over.

Responding to Criticisms of Repression in Xinjiang

One of the most noteworthy stories about Chinese politics in the Xi Jinping era has been the severe repression of the Uighur minority in the western region of Xinjiang. To be sure, the Chinese government has enacted repressive policies in Xinjiang for decades (Bovingdon 2010). However, more recently Chinese authorities have created, without exaggeration, a totalitarian system of surveillance, control, and propaganda in the region, particularly since 2014. This section will detail the CCP's obstructive/diffuse response to international criticism of its Xinjiang crackdown. This mode was not the only type of response that the CCP mounted. As the AAAD makes clear, the government prosecuted a global campaign of repression against Uighurs. But from an obstructive/diffuse perspective, the strategy was to first deny the existence of the repression, and eventually to respond to criticism through its foreign propaganda outlets, often by distracting from the state's domination and coercion (see Kuo 2018).

Uighurs, predominantly Turkic-speaking Muslims, were about 10 million of the region's 22 million people in the 2010 census. Prior to the 1960s, the percentage of Uighurs relative to Han Chinese was much higher, but Han migration has tilted the region's demographic balance and changed the region's economy in ways largely detrimental to much of the Uighur population (Bovingdon 2010, 54–59; Hunerven 2019). The CCP looks warily on both religion and ethnic diversity, both of which characterize Xinjiang, in part because they are seen as potential threats to state sovereignty (Yeh 2012). The party has long sought to distinguish between "the people" and its enemies in Xinjiang, but the line between them often shifts or is left unclear, such that "many peaceful people cannot help finding themselves on the wrong side" (Bovingdon 2010, 88).

Starting in 2009 the line began to ensnare ever more enemies. A rumor—later found to be untrue by a variety of sources—circulated that Uighurs had raped two Han women at a factory in Guangdong, some 4,000 kilometers away from Urumqi, the capital of Xinjiang (Bovingdon 2010, 167–172; Primiano 2013). This precipitated attacks on Uighur workers at the factory, resulting in at least two deaths and over 100 injuries. News of the attacks spread back to Xinjiang, largely via graphic videos on smartphones, and in July 2009 initially peaceful protests in Urumqi turned into riots in which, according to the CCP media, nearly 200 people were killed and 1,700 were injured, with Han shops also destroyed (Primiano 2013).[6] Revenge killings

---

[6] The extent to which the turn from peaceful protest to riots was driven by police repression is unclear. See Bovingdon (2010, 168) and Roberts (2020, 146).

ensued, with groups of Han Chinese targeting Uighurs (Bovingdon 2010, 169; Roberts 2020, 147). A government clampdown followed, with increased militarization of the region and a months-long blackout on internet-based communications.

In the years that followed, there were violent attacks in Xinjiang and in a few instances in cities elsewhere in China, which the government attributed to Uighur terrorists. It should be stressed that the Chinese government takes an expansive view of terrorism. It views Xinjiang and Uighurs through a securitized lens such that it is prone to label manifestations of dissent as "terrorism" even if they do not meet conventional standards of the term (Tredaniel and Lee 2018; see also Tobin 2020). While much of what the government calls "terrorism" is not actually terrorism, there were in fact serious episodes of violence during this period, such as a 2013 incident in which a Uighur man killed two people and injured 20 others by driving through Tiananmen Square, and a 2014 attack by eight Uighurs on a railway station in Kunming, Yunnan (thousands of kilometers from Xinjiang) which killed 29 people and injured over 140 (Smith-Finley 2019, 2; Greitens, Lee, and Yazici 2020, 22–24). However, it is also important to note that the Chinese government regularly amplifies or downplays the presence of violence in and from Xinjiang for political purposes. After analyzing protest events and instances of violence in Xinjiang from 2001 to 2009 alongside government portrayals of the same time period, Bovingdon (2010, 106) concluded that "there is no obvious relationship between official depictions of the threat and the actual trends revealed by the independently compiled record of public protests."

Regardless, starting in 2014, the government's security measures in Xinjiang were initially heavy-handed but evolved into draconian by about 2017 (S. Roberts 2018, 245–252). The party, in part by contracting with private technology firms, built a formidable surveillance system to monitor Xinjiang's Uighur minority, which resulted in daunting barriers to dissenting collective action (Leibold 2020). It began to gather more information on the population for signs of "extremism" in 2014 and 2015 and started to rank individuals by their levels of trustworthiness in 2017 (Smith-Finley 2019, 3–4). Starting in 2014 and continuing thereafter, the government organized campaigns that saw party members and civil servants sent to Uighur homes—sometimes for weeks at a time in the form of an involuntary homestay—to bring party propaganda and to monitor the population for its loyalty (Byler 2018).

Beginning in spring of 2017, the government escalated these policies into a mass internment and re-education program in which Uighurs were forced to learn Mandarin, study party ideology, and rid themselves of their ostensibly extremist views (Zenz 2019). The behaviors that could lead one to being incarcerated were expansive, ranging from ordinary expressions of the Islamic faith to studying abroad to having family abroad to possessing religious digital content (Smith-Finley 2019, 5–6). Reports stemming from the Chinese government itself indicate that over 1 million people were interned (Zenz 2019).

Foreign journalists had been reporting on the campaign as it unfolded, but in November 2019 the issue garnered newfound attention. Two major leaks of CCP documents to foreign news outlets revealed new evidence of the party's campaign against the Uighurs. The *New York Times* published over 400 pages of leaked documents, known as the Xinjiang Papers, detailing the parameters of the crackdown (Ramzy and Buckley 2019). Included are internal speeches by Xi Jinping in which he advises in 2014 that there should be "absolutely no mercy" in dealing with Xinjiang and that the "full organs of dictatorship" should be marshalled to fight against terrorism and separatism. Other documents showed a guide for officials containing answers to questions from children of parents who had been interned. A second leak, this time to the International Consortium of Investigative Journalists, was reported simultaneously in more than a dozen newspapers throughout the world and dubbed the China Cables (Allen-Ebrahimian 2019). This leak featured different documents and shed light on repression in the camps and the program of re-education. Inmates were required to attain a certain number of points to be eligible to talk to their family or get released. Points were earned for high marks studying Mandarin and ideology. The general thrust of the China Cables is that the camps are clearly prison-like re-education facilities, not voluntary boarding schools as the Chinese government claims.

The repression in Xinjiang has led to widespread criticism in foreign media, academia, and political circles. In addition to the targeting of activists abroad and their families still in China detailed in the following and in the AAAD, the party-state media mounted an external obstructive/diffuse propaganda campaign to deflect criticism of its policies. The contours of this campaign continue to unfold as of this writing, but patterns from 2014 through 2019 are apparent. First came the silence, then the misidentification of the camps as vocational centers as evidence of their existence accumulated; then after the leaks, the strategy shifted to highlighting the carnage wrought by terrorism as a justification for the camps, along with accusing the accusers of hypocrisy. These efforts are part of the Chinese government's broader aim to "persuade the world of its own view of politics in Xinjiang" (Bovingdon 2010, 136).

We can trace Beijing's obstructive/diffuse response to criticism of its Xinjiang record by analyzing the content of CGTN. The network is the flag-ship foreign-facing TV channel telling the CCP's side of the story, so it is worthy of attention when thinking about China's diffuse messaging. To select videos to analyze, the CGTN YouTube channel was used. As of this writing the channel has over 77,000 videos going back to 2013, in addition to those it posts on its more specifically branded channels such as CGTN America, CGTN Africa, or CGTN Arabic. The channel mixes together short news videos with longer documentaries and news commentary shows in which analysts develop points in more detail.

Early videos in the collection generally take two approaches to Xinjiang. Some emphasize ostensibly harmonious cultural relations and develop-ment. For example, a two-and-a-half-minute video from December 31, 2013, titled "Xinjiang ethnic groups celebrate in downtown Urumqi," shows scenes from a pop concert and interviews about people's aspirations for the new year. A local official stresses "ethnic unity" and the corre-spondent closes the segment by mentioning that despite terrorist attacks, people in Xinjiang "are hoping for a better, safer, and more stable year in which they can continue to enjoy the fruits of ethnic unity and develop-ment."[7] The implication is clear: a strong government presence is necessary to provide those goods.

Other videos from the early days of CGTN's web presence more di-rectly highlight terrorist attacks and the threat of terrorism, as well as the government's response. On the former, an example is a video uploaded on August 2, 2014, titled "Xinjiang violence: 37 killed, 13 injured," that details an attack on police stations and government offices in Shache/Yarkant county.[8] In these early videos one can detect the emergence of what was to become Beijing's comprehensive crackdown in Xinjiang. Indeed, a few months prior, on May 23, 2014, viewers could see a one-minute report called "Xinjiang launches 1 year crackdown on terrorism."[9] Three days later, a one-minute report called "Xi Jinping urges stability in Xinjiang" outlined the necessity

---

[7] https://www.youtube.com/watch?v=k0ads3H4p1g (accessed December 13, 2019).
[8] https://www.youtube.com/watch?v=18jxMq3w6Us (accessed December 13, 2019). Fifty-nine people were shot dead by police and 215 were arrested. The incident was apparently triggered by two Uighur men being sentenced to death (Demick 2014).
[9] https://www.youtube.com/watch?v=9wPabkT9dQc (accessed December 13, 2019).

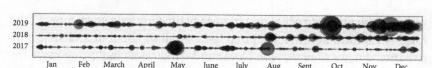

Figure 6.1. Frequency of "Xinjiang" in global media (GDELT).

to "crack down on terrorism, unite all ethnic groups, promote religious harmony, solve employment issues, improve living standards, and promote education."[10] A May 29, 2014, video called "Chinese President calls for anti-terrorism 'nets' in Xinjiang" further publicized this approach.[11]

The dates of these May 2014 reports are significant because they coincided with private speeches that Xi gave to other CCP leaders after he visited Xinjiang in April 2014 in which he called for a full-scale repressive campaign (Ramzy and Buckley 2019). Shortly after his visit, there was a bomb and knife attack at a train station in Urumqi (BBC 2014), news of which was initially censored in China (Shao 2014). Overall, however, there are not many early videos about Xinjiang and very few (if any) in-depth documentaries or talk shows about it during the early years of the crackdown.

This changed as the issue became more salient internationally. As repression in Xinjiang became a bigger story, and particularly as reports of forced re-education camps started to percolate out of China, the CCP changed its strategy. Prior to 2019, little mention was made of the camps in CGTN content. Throughout 2018 and early 2019, several major stories in international media began to detail the scope and purpose of the camps. In August 2018, the United Nations Committee on the Elimination of Racial Discrimination indicated that it had received credible reports of Uighurs being held in secret internment camps (Nebehay 2018). It seems that China's external propaganda apparatus could no longer ignore the story and felt compelled to respond.[12]

Figure 6.1 shows data on the frequency of articles mentioning Xinjiang from the Global Database of Events, Language, and Tone (GDELT). GDELT covers over 100 international news sources in several languages. The data for this figure come from GDELT's Global Knowledge Graph analysis service,

---

[10] https://www.youtube.com/watch?v=cMpqt2BR4f4 (accessed December 13, 2019).

[11] https://www.youtube.com/watch?v=BLLL3flL2RQ (accessed December 13, 2019).

[12] After August 2018, articles in *Xinhua* about Xinjiang became markedly more positive from an already high floor, highlighting peace, culture, and development in the region, ostensibly to distract from repression. See Brazys and Dukalskis (2020).

which enables users to generate a frequency timeline for a given topic.[13] This roughly captures how much a given issue is talked about in a variety of international news sources, with bigger and darker dots indicating more frequency. The data show that, aside from a few exceptions, until the second half of 2018 Xinjiang was not the major news story internationally that it would later become.

However, coinciding with the UN statement mentioned earlier, from August 2018 onward the story became more frequent and remained on the agenda at a relatively stable level until around October 2019, when coverage increased dramatically. In September and October 2019, the US government became more vocal about the issue, with a bill being debated in the House of Representatives at the time and some sanctions being imposed on entities contributing to the repression. During this time, the European Parliament also awarded its annual Sakharov Prize for Freedom of Thought to Ilham Tohti, an imprisoned Uighur scholar. In November 2019, both document leaks about the crackdown hit the headlines. These data are only a bird's eye view of global coverage on Xinjiang, but they do illustrate the increased salience of Xinjiang in the international press from late 2018 onward, and especially from late 2019.

The response as indicated by CGTN content in late 2018 and early 2019 was to argue that the camps were in fact voluntary re-education facilities. In November 2018, a group of 15 ambassadors to China sent an open letter expressing their concern about Xinjiang and asking for a meeting (Wen, Martina, and Blanchard 2018). CGTN a day later ran a video calling the letter "rude and unacceptable" and stating that "Xinjiang is an open region that welcomes those who go there with goodwill. Anyone harboring malicious intentions and prejudices and seeking to interfere in China's internal affairs will be firmly rejected."[14] Six weeks later, CGTN ran a short video about a group of foreign diplomats visiting Xinjiang, including the "vocational training centers." Although no details were given about who the diplomats were, the video featured only positive descriptions of Xinjiang's development.[15]

Over the course of 2019, CGTN content emphasized the ostensibly positive aspects of the "vocational training centers" and the government's role in Xinjiang more generally. A video called "A look at vocational education and training programs in Xinjiang" stresses that the programs are voluntary and claims that

---

[13] Available at: http://analysis.gdeltproject.org/module-gkg-timeline.html (accessed September 1, 2020).

[14] https://www.youtube.com/watch?v=GhJjnNfbw-Y (accessed December 16, 2019).

[15] https://www.youtube.com/watch?v=_3N04TYE_Ho (accessed December 16, 2019).

"most of the attendees are influenced by terrorism and extremist thoughts."[16] In a brief March 15, 2019, video called " 'Campus, not camps': China defends Xinjiang policies at UN," the vice foreign minister claims that the "training centers" were akin to voluntary boarding schools.[17] A few days later, the network ran a 15-minute discussion about the government's new white paper on Xinjiang that developed the argument that terrorism plagued Xinjiang, that Beijing's response is necessary, but that it is being mischaracterized by the "mainstream Western media."[18] The discussion is an uncritical and supportive elaboration of the government's policies; however, it does make an attempt to respond to common criticisms of the camps.

In late 2019, the obstructive/diffuse CGTN response went into overdrive, presumably in response to the two document leak stories in November of that year, US government attention to the repression, and the corresponding increase in international news coverage. CGTN released a 50-minute documentary on December 11, 2019, called "Fighting Terrorism in Xinjiang."[19] The video details several attacks over the years, showcasing statements (likely under threat of reprisal unless they complied) of family members of victims and several perpetrators that offer depictions of their violence. The piece features commentary from various people, including the head of the Xinjiang Islamic Institute, which is a common "model" location to which foreign reporters and ambassadors are taken. After about 45 minutes of such content, the documentary moves on to explain the government's solution, namely the "Three Studies and One Elimination" campaign. According to the documentary, this program sees people in the "vocational training centers" studying ideology, vocational training, and Mandarin Chinese. The target for elimination is "thoughts of extremism." The documentary was the subject of numerous CGTN talk shows and video segments after it was released, as well as amplified through China's other external propaganda outlets. CGTN released a companion documentary alleging ties between terrorist groups in Xinjiang and those abroad (on the evidence for these alleged ties, see Roberts 2012; Greitens et al. 2020, 28–37 Roberts 2020).[20]

When it comes to Xinjiang, the Chinese externally oriented media frequently claim that "the Western media" are biased against China or do not tell the truth about Xinjiang. Regarding the documentary, CGTN, Chinese

[16] https://www.youtube.com/watch?v=Hb4v7g6yM0Y (accessed December 16, 2019).
[17] https://www.youtube.com/watch?v=02RXDeTDrg0 (accessed December 16, 2019).
[18] https://www.youtube.com/watch?v=FLxdJ6XeLSw (accessed December 16, 2019).
[19] https://www.youtube.com/watch?v=u4cYE6E27_g (accessed December 16, 2019).
[20] https://www.youtube.com/watch?v=6lXr4a113sU (accessed December 16, 2019).

diplomats on Twitter, the *Global Times*, and other outlets all pushed the same narrative: that Western news outlets are ignoring the documentaries. CGTN ran a video on December 11, 2019 (the same day the original documentary was released), called "We showed the truth about Xinjiang, but Western media ignored it."[21] The video features a scolding from the Ministry of Foreign Affairs spokeswoman to foreign journalists, claiming they are not interested in the facts about Xinjiang. It claims that the documentaries have been a "smash hit on the internet," with 67 million views on unspecified platforms (on YouTube there were only about 150,000 views as of this writing). The video details and advertises the documentaries. It claims to expose the unfairness of foreign media by showing that were one to search "Xinjiang" on Google, one would receive stories from the *New York Times* or BBC, noting that "people who are not clear about what has happened in Xinjiang might believe such stories are reliable, but we hardly see in-depth coverage of the terrorism in Xinjiang from Western media." It ends by providing clickable links to each documentary.

This case study of obstructive/diffuse CGTN coverage about Xinjiang shows how the strategy shifted from one of studiously ignoring criticisms of repression while highlighting the threat of terrorism to responding to criticisms of the repression while accusing the accusers of bias. At first the response was to suggest that the camps are not what foreign observers think they are. This was the "campus, not camps" argument, highlighting positive aspects of Xinjiang. In late 2019, as criticism of Beijing's Xinjiang policy accelerated, the response shifted to emphasize that this was a response to terrorism and that at any rate "the West" and its media are hypocritical. Perhaps more importantly, the volume of content increased dramatically as the foreign-facing Chinese media apparently felt that they had to respond directly rather than let criticism go unanswered.

Repressing Citizens Abroad: Obstructive/Specific Silencing

The CCP works to silence its critics abroad. Despite its attempt to control foreign correspondents detailed in the previous chapter, promotional messages and narratives about China enter a global public sphere in which they must compete with other content for validity. The CCP cannot control discourse

---

[21] https://www.youtube.com/watch?v=smxScIJ-CP4 (accessed December 16, 2019).

internationally to the extent that it does domestically. It does not have the opportunity to socialize its international viewers via the Chinese school system, nor can it censor undesirable content in foreign markets the way it does domestically. Likewise, the tools available to it to repress critical messengers are less varied and effective.

Nevertheless, the party does target critics abroad for extraterritorial repression. These are people who would undermine the CCP's sanitized narrative about China by speaking out about causes the government euphemizes as "sensitive." The AAAD, explained in Chapter 4 and Appendix 2, documents 167 cases, based only on publicly reported incidents in which the Chinese government threatened, abducted, arrested, extradited, or threatened the family of exiles whom it saw as threats to its image and thus security. The true number of such incidents is undoubtedly much higher, and because some of those 167 cases involve multiple individuals, the number of people affected is more numerous. Indeed, those 167 cases for which information is available publicly involve at least 700 individuals (in one case the number of people is unknown). Recall that these data do not include most anti-corruption cases unless it was clear that corruption was an obvious pretext to mask political motives.

Over 44% of the incidents—74 out of 167—are of Chinese authorities threatening the families of Chinese nationals residing abroad. The tactic is meant to silence the exiled critic. Many of the recorded cases come from Beijing's crackdown on Xinjiang since 2014. More than half of the cases feature ordinary citizens as targets. The simple act of being a Uighur abroad invites suspicion from the Chinese authorities. For example, students in France reported being monitored and pressured via WeChat for information. One student in Paris reported that "they want to know where I live, what I do, how I spend the weekend. They want me to give them information about Uighurs here. They threaten my family who beg me to do what they ask" (AFP 2018).

Sometimes entire groups of Uighurs are targeted abroad. In 2015, Thai authorities repatriated 109 Uighurs back to China despite condemnation from Turkey, the United States, and parts of the United Nations (Campbell 2015). Thailand was not the only willing partner. Egyptian authorities detained hundreds of students, many of them studying at Al Azhar Mosque and University, and deported many of them back to China (Youssef 2017). The fate of those who were returned is unknown, but according to the China Cables leaks, the government views Uighurs abroad or those who have connections abroad as special targets in need of surveillance and re-education (Allen-Ebrahimian 2019).

The state targets Uighurs even more fiercely if they speak out. For example, Guly Mahsut, who fled to Canada and became an activist, received messages from security operatives such as: "You should have been more cooperative. Don't become the source of misfortune for your relatives and family in Toksun. You should be more considerate of your family" (Straits Times 2019). She would also receive messages from her relatives encouraging her to stop her activism. This tactic is a commonplace form of obstructive/specific authoritarian image management for China. It attempts to stop Uighurs abroad from engaging in criticism or activism without the authorities having to physically leave Xinjiang.

While the extraterritorial repression of Uighurs comprises many of the China-related data points in the AAAD, this is not the only category of people that the state targets. There have been several dramatic cases of abduction of critics abroad, ostensibly by people acting on behalf of the Chinese authorities. The targets were people critical of the CCP and supportive of freedom of expression and political reforms. In 2002, three dissident activists were abducted in Vietnam and repatriated to China (BBC 2002). One of them, Wang Bingzhang, remains in prison in China as of this writing after having been found guilty in a closed trial of espionage and terrorism. His two associates were not convicted. The three had been networking with other democracy advocates and holding a meeting with them in Vietnam.

More recently, Chinese authorities have been seeking dissidents in Thailand and attempting to repatriate them to China. Thailand had become a destination for activists fleeing persecution in China, but the authoritarian turn within Thailand itself made it a more perilous locale. In 2016, Li Xin, a journalist and activist, was abducted from a train in Thailand and resurfaced the next month in China (Phillips and Holmes 2016). He could speak from prison with his wife, who had remained in China, and told her that he had returned voluntarily to assist the police in their investigations. Li had been a pro-democracy advocate and had leaked CCP documents about the party's propaganda apparatus. As of this writing, it appears that he is still detained, but little information is available about his case.

Thai immigration authorities detained two other pro-democracy activists, Dong Guangping and Jiang Yefei, in October 2015 (Front Line Defenders 2020). Both had been granted refugee status by the UN High Commissioner for Refugees, but were nonetheless deported to China the next month. After being detained in China for over two years, both were tried. Chinese authorities sentenced Jiang to six and a half years in prison for "subverting state power" and "illegally crossing a national border." Dong was given three and a half years for "inciting subversion of state power" and illegal border crossing. Both remain in prison as of this writing.

The CCP fears the messages of those activists in Thailand influencing politics within China itself. The relatively freer information environment in Thailand allows dissidents to publicize human rights abuses, advocate for their causes, and network with like-minded people. The CCP sees this as a threat to China's image abroad and, by extension, the party's political power at home. A more willing Thai government after a coup in 2014 saw closer cooperation between Bangkok and Beijing on the former deporting dissidents to the latter. Indeed, all 18 recorded cases in the AAAD with China as the origin country and Thailand as the target country happened from 2015 onward. From the CCP's perspective, the politically threatening extraterritorial space of Thailand is something to be tamed, with the Thai government an apparently willing partner.

These cases provide just a glimpse into the extraterritorial dimension of China's repression. Due to the shadowy nature of extraterritorial repression, the reality is likely much more expansive than the AAAD data reveal. The international elements of the crackdown in Xinjiang, for example, are multidimensional and broad (Greitens, Lee, and Yazici 2020, 20). They are also intentionally secretive. Nonetheless, publicly available data show that the Chinese government actively hunts down its critics (or those damaging to its image) overseas with the aim to silence them.

Conclusion: A Perpetual, Global, and Multidimensional Image Management Campaign

Chinese soft power and public diplomacy rightly receive sustained scholarly attention (e.g. Edney, Rosen, and Zhu 2020). Beijing has clearly invested in these areas and expects to see its image improved. The visibility of these initiatives also makes them easier to study than more covert forms of authoritarian image management. Clearly, the Chinese government prioritizes getting its message heard by broad audiences through familiar means of external propaganda (Brazys and Dukalskis 2020). And yet, the traditional promotional/diffuse mode of image management is only one type of tactic that the CCP employs.

To make its world safe for its dictatorship, the CCP's approach is much more multidimensional. This chapter has outlined how the Chinese government attempts to cultivate friendly journalists to tell its story for it. With some notable exceptions (Brady 2003, 2008), promotional/specific tactics like this have not typically attracted the attention of scholars in systematic ways. Yet the tactic may be even more effective than outright external propaganda because it appears more genuine. The journalists writing such stories are not CCP propaganda workers or necessarily publishing in CCP outlets, both of which would immediately raise skepticism. Instead, this is a form of embedded propaganda in which foreign journalists "tell China's story well" in their own words and in their own outlets.

If arguments circulate in international media to which the CCP objects, it uses its external propaganda outlets to respond to them or deflect from them. The party would undoubtedly prefer to avoid using obstructive/diffuse tactics because their necessity indicates that arguments critical of the CCP are gaining prominence. However, this chapter has showed that as the repression of Uighurs in Xinjiang became more internationally salient, the CCP went all-out to counter the criticism. Across multiple platforms, it advanced the argument that what was happening in Xinjiang was a rational response to terrorism, that Uighurs were happy under CCP rule, that the re-education camps were voluntary, and that Western critics were hypocritical or lacked credibility.

But Chinese authorities do not stop there. In some cases, they engage in obstructive/specific tactics that repress carriers of messages critical of the CCP. Sometimes these are activists, such as those in Thailand working for democratic reform in China. At other times, they are ordinary citizens abroad for non-political reasons who are pressured to keep silent about China's domestic repression. The idea is to keep news stories about internal repression from featuring in the international press and tarnishing China's image.

As the largest and most powerful authoritarian state in the world, China is actively using all four mechanisms of authoritarian image management globally to craft a more positive image of itself and to silence criticism. Its government uses multiple methods to propagate its preferred image and to inhibit dissent around the world. The overarching objective is to enhance its internal and external security—to make its world safe for dictatorship—so that it can continue to rule without serious challenge.

7

Projecting Peace and Prosperity

Authoritarian Image Management and RPF Rwanda

After the Rwandan genocide in 1994, Paul Kagame, the leader of the Rwandan Patriotic Front (RPF) that drove the genocidaires from power, assumed authority, first from within a transitional government and later as president, and as of this writing has not relinquished it. While he was vice president from 1994 to 2000, Kagame was "the real power holder" even then (Reyntjens 2013, 2). In his last election in 2017, Kagame ostensibly earned the support of 98.79% of voters, a nearly Soviet-level electoral mandate. Throughout his rule, Rwanda has had image problems insofar as it was often perceived abroad as unstable and violent, especially in the early days, or in more recent years as an increasingly authoritarian state because of the RPF's tightening grip on power. The RPF had for some time taken steps to manage its image for foreign audiences, but especially since 2003 its efforts expanded, including with the use of PR firms to shape the country's image abroad.

For example, the Rwandan government retained the PR firm Racepoint Group for $50,000/month (York 2012). A remarkable 2009 memo published by the US Department of Justice pursuant to the Foreign Agents Registration Act (FARA) reveals Racepoint's suggested plan to remake Rwanda's reputation.[1] It proposed improving Rwanda's image among "key political elites in global capitals" and negating "the misinformation being pedaled by expats, NGOs and others with a vested interest in creating an image of Rwanda as a failed state." The strategy involved cultivating elected officials, their staffers, business elites, and journalists in influential outlets such as the *New York Times* and *The Economist*. Although the memo notes that Beijing is a key audience for Rwanda, it concludes that "this particular capital can be reached through other means and methods" and that China will therefore not be

---

[1] https://efile.fara.gov/docs/6055-Exhibit-AB-20110812-1.pdf#page=17 (accessed September 1, 2020).

Making the World Safe for Dictatorship, Alexander Dukalskis, Oxford University Press (2021). © Oxford University Press.
DOI: 10.1093/oso/9780197520130.003.0007

included in the plan. The campaign was to proceed in stages by first crafting an appealing narrative, finding a small number of key opinion leaders to pedal it, protecting the narrative from criticism, and then building on that foundation by engaging in a wider public-facing effort. Inherent in this plan was the need to present Kagame as a democratic and visionary leader to reinforce his legitimacy with international audiences.

The memo is a small but telling glimpse of RPF Rwanda's authoritarian image management activities insofar as it shows a multidimensional effort to remake Rwanda's reputation with the aim of enhancing regime security. The strategy ranges from relatively innocuous efforts like sponsoring a "Visit Rwanda" badge on the jerseys of the Arsenal Football Club to rhetorically aggressive tactics like undermining critics as genocide deniers to violently repressive actions like assassinating exiled critics. Of the three cases examined in detail in this book, Rwanda may be the most successful. Any other small state that had the same authoritarian leader for decades, which had sponsored militias leading to brutal wars in neighboring states, and which had assassinated its critics abroad, would stand a good chance of being isolated, sanctioned, and branded a dictatorship. Yet, despite some criticisms and diplomatic battles, with France in particular, Rwanda still receives high levels of aid and faces no serious pressure from external actors to democratize (on aid, see Desrosiers and Swedlund 2019). This mix of authoritarianism at home, military forays abroad, and aid dependence has prompted scholars to note that "image management abroad is central to the Kagame regime" (Desrosiers and Thomson 2011, 446; see also Matfess 2015, 197). Indeed, it "has been extremely successful in projecting an image of morality, vision, and success" (Reyntjens 2013, 187).

This chapter will unpack and assess the RPF's efforts. It will first present a brief contextual background of the RPF's authoritarian consolidation. The subsequent section will establish how the RPF first tried to create a foundation on which to build its promotional image management efforts. This is similar to the argument elaborated in Chapter 5 about China's limitations on foreign journalists. By limiting, through obstructive tactics, the information available to outsiders, the government frees up space on which to paint its preferred image. The third section will describe Rwanda's PR efforts in the Kagame era by analyzing its FARA filings in the United States and presenting some of the results of those contracts. Fourth, the chapter will turn to the most brazen element of the RPF's image management, namely the intimidation and repression of critics abroad. Finally, concluding remarks will discuss why the RPF has been an unusually successful authoritarian image manager in enhancing regime security.

Autocracy, Aid Dependence, and the Importance of Image

Scholars of Rwanda frequently note that there are two prevalent visions of the RPF-led state (e.g., Longman 2017, 27–32). Some emphasize the RPF's sponsorship of militias in neighboring Democratic Republic of Congo (DRC), and/or its dictatorial practices at home, such as its assassinations of opponents, restrictions on free speech, manipulation of electoral processes, and the long tenure of Paul Kagame as the country's president. Others stress the RPF's developmental prowess, pointing to Rwanda's sustained economic growth in the wake of tragedy, its competent bureaucracy, relative lack of corruption, and its commitment to including women in the government. To paraphrase Jones (2012), some view RPF-led Rwanda as closer to North Korea, a violent dictatorship with totalitarian ambitions, while others view it as more like Singapore, a relatively benign and developmentalist authoritarian regime.

Clearly, the RPF wants Rwanda to be viewed more like Singapore. In fact, Kagame has invoked the comparison himself on occasion (Longman 2017, 174). The intent of this section is not to adjudicate between these visions, but rather to demonstrate that because RPF-led Rwanda has taken an authoritarian turn while also receiving relatively high levels of foreign aid, the government has clear incentives to downplay its authoritarianism and amplify its development credentials. This is not a unique set of circumstances, but it is exaggerated in the Rwandan case given the extreme violence of the genocide, the foreign aid sustaining the government's general budget for much of this period, and the RPF's undeniable authoritarianism, mixed with Rwanda's relatively successful economic track record under its rule. Authoritarian image management is key to the RPF's internal and external security.

In 1994, Rwanda was destroyed. Setting aside the obvious human tragedy of the genocide and war, Jones (2012, 230) summarizes the challenges that would have confronted any government trying to rebuild: about 40% of the population was dead or had fled abroad, including about three out of every four government employees, infrastructure was decimated, there were about 500,000 orphans, businesses and houses were looted, and internally displaced persons were too scared to return home. The fact that Jones (2012, 228) could write less than 20 years later that "the Rwandan state functions beyond the dreams of most contemporary African state-builders" is a testament to the RPF's organizational competence. Since the release of the government's economic plan Vision 2020 in the year 2000, the country enjoyed 20 straight years of GDP growth. Its per capita GDP nearly tripled between 1995 and 2019. This has happened on the RPF's watch, and while there are critics of Rwanda's economic policies, particularly as they pertain to inequality, the party clearly wishes to take credit for creating the "Singapore of Africa."

The RPF was initially part of a power-sharing government ruling Rwanda. Some greeted this as an impressive measure of the RPF's restraint and commitment to democracy. The RPF could have taken full control as the military victor in the war and ousted its enemies, the argument goes, but chose instead the path of power-sharing. But already in 1995 and 1996, it was beginning to purge the government of its critics (Reyntjens 2013, 8–11). Especially from 1998, the RPF became increasingly unsatisfied with ruling as part of a coalition (Longman 2017, 152).

The year 2000 is often identified as a turning point, as the RPF took full and overt control of all political institutions in the state (Longman 2017, 151; Thompson 2018, 134). Local elections in 1999, meant to be a practice run for the 2003 national elections, were heavily manipulated by the RPF (Reyntjens 2013, 34–37). To control avenues for political decision-making, the government set up the Forum of Political Parties, which among other powers has the right to vet, veto, and dismiss parliamentary candidates, and which is dominated by the RPF (Jones 2016, 347; Longman 2017, 152; Thomson 2018, 133–134). By 2000, Longman (2017, 152) observes, Rwanda was a "de facto one-party state." Elections in 2003 saw Kagame ostensibly win with 95.05% of the vote (Reyntjens 2013, 37), with results in 2010 giving him 93.08% of the vote with 98% voter turnout (Reyntjens 2013, 52). A 2015 referendum on constitutional changes that would allow Kagame to rule until 2034 officially earned 98% support, while the 2017 presidential elections saw Kagame claim victory with 98.79% support (Baddorf 2017).

Beyond the electoral sphere, the RPF has penetrated and permeated society, which allows it to exert control at the local level. It oversaw an ambitious transitional justice initiative that featured local trials, and which helped the party consolidate political control and propagate its narrative of the 1994 genocide (Longman 2017; Loyle 2018). Ethnic distinctions are officially suppressed (except in genocide commemorations or remembrance events) with an enforced ideology of "Rwandanness" or "Rwandanicity," mandating that "we are all Rwandans" (Beresford, Brady, and Mann 2018, 1238). In a form reminiscent of Leninist political control, the state's organizational structure is mimicked at every level by the RPF (Purdekova 2011, 480, 489; on Lenin and Mao as inspirations for the RPF, see Longman 2017, 137–139). Local officials ceremonially sign on to meet goals in a "localized public pledge of compliance with national policies" (Purdekova 2011, 484). The military, which controls substantial economic interests (Behuria 2016), implements local policies and is extolled as a model of sacrifice and loyalty, in part because Rwanda is a major contributor to UN peacekeeping initiatives abroad (Jones 2012; Purdekova, Reyntjens, and Wilen 2018).

Surveillance and informers regulate public political life, and even where spies are not present, "the perception nonetheless remains that surveillance and locally traced intelligence are ubiquitous, and the effects of this behavior are very real" (Purdekova 2011, 489). These modes of control help the RPF mobilize the population to participate in its programs. They also provide the institutional foundation from which the RPF can marginalize real or potential enemies (see Beresford, Brady, and Mann 2018, 1240–1243). The RPF takes an "if you aren't with us you're against us" attitude to civil society (Gready 2010) and has "accentuated the continuous need to combat internal and external enemies, maintaining a simultaneous sense of insecurity, need for securitization and call for alertness among the population" (Purdekova, Reyntjens, and Wilen 2018).

Amidst all these developments, the Rwandan government remained heavily aid-dependent. As of 2008, roughly half of the government's budget came from aid, and in any given year in the decade after 2000, Rwanda received aid equivalent to about 20% of its gross national income (see Zorbas 2011, 103–104). In subsequent years, the government's dependence on aid for its operating budget decreased, although there were debates about this and about the government's borrowing. The general level of aid dependence remained high, although by no means extraordinary or unheard of, and Rwanda's aid dependence before the genocide under the previous regime was also high (Desrosiers and Swedlund 2019).

Aid reliance plus authoritarianism means that the RPF has clear incentives to present itself as stable, responsible, and even democratic. As noted at the outset of this chapter, scholars of Rwanda agree that image management is key to the RPF's regime stability. It works to present itself as the "voice of the 'new Africa'" (Desrosiers and Thomson 2011, 446). The strategy largely works: "Rwanda has been heralded as a success story; the nation's transformation from a war-torn state into an economic dynamo is all the more striking when the instability of its surroundings are taken into account" (Matfess 2015, 197). Respect for Rwanda abroad also helps feed back into domestic legitimation messages insofar as Rwandans can take pride in being lauded as a model (Thomson 2018, 178).

Building a Foundation: Obstructing Negative Information

As with other authoritarian states, limiting negative information circulating abroad facilitates the government's efforts to portray a positive image. Keeping the violence, repression, and information manipulation that sustains dictatorship out of view is beneficial for the image of the leadership. This obstructive approach sometimes involves targeting specific actors, such as limiting access for journalists or researchers, and sometimes is more diffuse, such as responding to criticism or attempting to minimize a topic in international discourse. The RPF has well-developed strategies to police its image abroad by limiting and shaping the information that leaves Rwanda and attacking those who challenge it (Reyntjens 2015, 637).

The RPF has long attempted to limit what it perceives as damaging information about it from escaping, and to shape and preemptively interpret information for foreign analysts. The RPF has a narrative that it wishes to promote about Rwanda's past and the RPF's role in its recent history (Longman 2017, 46–60). Not surprisingly, the RPF is portrayed in glowing terms according to this account, which means that RPF abuses or shortcomings can potentially undermine the regime's image and therefore its security. Longman (2017, 87–88) summarizes the RPF's preferred narrative:

> Rwanda's people historically got along, colonialism divided the country by creating the division between Hutu, Tutsi, and Twa, the post-colonial national leaders bought into the colonial definition of ethnicity and betrayed the interests of the Rwandan people, and the RPF waged war only reluctantly and with the noblest of intentions.

The narrative is clear and easy to retain, but leaves out or mischaracterizes a great deal (Pottier 2002, 51). It is clear that the narrative omits war crimes, crimes against humanity, violent repression, and authoritarian practices of the RPF. The RPF killed civilians and engaged in massacres as it took control of the country in the early days from 1994 to 1996 (Human Rights Watch 1995; Reyntjens 2013, 98–109; Thomson 2018, 85–87). Those who raise these points and/or call for RPF accountability are often called genocide deniers or espousers of "genocide ideology." The ostensible logic is that raising these points equates RPF killings with the horrors of the genocide and thus minimizes the latter. The RPF and its proxies also committed atrocities in Zaire (later the DRC) for several years from 1996, as well as in a domestic counterinsurgency particularly in northwest Rwanda in 1997 and 1998 (Reyntjens 2013, 110–119).

To limit information about these abuses from reaching international audiences, the RPF restricted access available to foreign journalists, researchers, and officials and denied that the RPF did anything wrong (Pottier 2002, 58). Even today, foreign researchers and development workers perceive themselves to be under surveillance while in Rwanda (Thomson 2018, 185). Des Forges (1999, n.p.) explained the RPF's information control in the mid-1990s:

> The RPF established close control over foreigners working or traveling in areas under its authority. Information and liaison officers worked hard at shaping the ideas of outsiders while persons employed by foreigners were ordered to report on their activities and conversations. Ordinarily journalists and aid workers were allowed to travel in RPF territory only in the company of officially designated "guides" who sought to ensure that they travel just to approved areas, usually via the main roads. The RPF closed whole regions to UNAMIR [United Nations Assistance Mission for Rwanda] and other foreign observers for weeks at a time.

The most well-known example of this strategy took place in April 1995 in Kibeho in southern Rwanda (Pottier 2002, 160–164). Between 90,000 and 120,000 internally displaced persons (IDPs) had been taking refuge on a large hilltop for months (for background, see Reyntjens 2013, 105–109; Thomson 2018, 88–94). Local authorities ordered that IDP camps be closed, but residents were fearful of returning to their villages. Between April 18 and April 22, the Rwandan army killed between 1,000 and 4,000 people by shooting into crowds and firing mortars into the camp. Local authorities stopped bodies from being counted, so the death toll may be higher. The RPF admitted to 338 deaths, but argued that the killings were an unfortunate consequence of genocidaires using the camp as cover to regroup (Prunier 2009, 41; Reyntjens 2013, 106).

The Rwandan army quickly required all foreign organizations to leave Kibeho (Pottier 2002, 164–165). Even Interior Minister Seth Sendashonga was refused access to the scene on April 23 by the military (Reyntjens 2013, 106; Thomson 2018, 90). An international commission of inquiry, the terms of reference for which were drafted by the Rwandan prime minister's office (Thomson 2018, 92), arrived at conclusions that echoed the RPF's narrative. This gave credibility to the RPF's claims and gave the government's international supporters political cover to consider the case closed so that the aid which had been partially suspended could be reinstated (Pottier 2002, 168). By limiting access to the site, sticking to one explanation, and denying wrongdoing, "the RPF controlled the narrative of the Kibeho massacre" and "effectively managed information flows about what happened, and to whom" (Thomson 2018, 93). Media outlets that questioned the death toll or RPF culpability were accused of spreading disinformation as part of an anti-Rwandan conspiracy (Pottier 2002, 164).

Aid dependence would have seemed to provide an incentive for the RPF to respond to criticism from abroad with caution, yet it takes precisely the opposite approach by responding stridently (Reyntjens 2011). The party's ideology has long stressed self-reliance and skepticism of Western powers (Reyntjens 2016; Chemouni and Mugiraneza 2020). The RPF, in this view, is the savior of Rwanda, including from the meddling of foreign powers (Longman 2017, 56–60). As a result, it has shown little appetite to take seriously criticisms of its governance from abroad. Rather, "even moderately formulated criticism by international partners, among them some of the main donors, [is] treated furiously and with disdain," an approach that has largely been effective in casting doubt on or deflecting the criticisms (Reyntjens 2013, 159).

When material critical of the RPF is published, the government often responds to it by attempting to discredit the authors and/or their institutional affiliations. It targets foreign academics and journalists it views as too critical by denying them access to the country and trying to impugn their reputations (Reyntjens 2011, 4–5). Foreign critics are either responsible for the genocide or genocide deniers; they are focused on undermining the unity of Rwanda; they are biased liars with ulterior motives; their research is shoddy and baseless; and so on. When foreign states or organizations question the positive image projected by the RPF, the regime and its spokespeople remind them of the international community's role in letting the genocide happen, the RPF's role in stopping it, double standards and hypocrisy of the critics, and the visionary leadership of Kagame (Desrosiers and Thomson 2011). These obstructive/specific authoritarian image management efforts are meant to discredit carriers of critical messages about the RPF so that the messages themselves are cast aside.

Indeed, "the Rwandan government is renowned for its outspoken responses to criticism, especially on issues that touch upon questions of national security and governance" (Hayman 2011, 125). After reviewing several instances of the Rwandan government confronted with criticism from foreign sources, Reyntjens (2013, 133) concluded that the approach was systematic and that instead of ignoring or engaging with critics, "it vehemently denounced them, accused them of acting in bad faith, practiced character assassination, and systematically avoided debate" (see also Thomson 2018, 195–196). A search of the website of the state-controlled Rwandan paper *The New Times* reveals more than 40 articles casting the scholars cited in this chapter negatively, *not including* the eight pages of search results with roughly 80 articles containing negative statements about Filip Reyntjens alone.[2]

The 2011 edited volume *Remaking Rwanda: State Building and Human Rights after Mass Violence* seemed to especially perturb the government. One of the contributors, Timothy Longman, notes that when he presented a draft of his chapter at Harvard University in 2009, the Rwandan ambassador to the United States came and challenged his findings (Longman 2011, 43). After publication, a website was set up to undermine the book. Ostensibly launched by the government (Reyntjens 2015, 638), the blog features contributions by reporters from *The New Times*, Rwandan diplomats, and presidential advisors. Some of the content is almost cartoonish in its character assassination.[3] Scott Strauss from the University of Wisconsin and Lars Waldorf from Essex University, the landing page claims, are apparently so discredited that "in a last-ditch effort, they've drawn together a whooping [*sic*] 26 fellow 'experts' so that together they can salvage their withering legitimacy." The contributors are apparently a "scattering of shady individuals" who are variously "fraud Ph.D.s," have a "pathological hatred of Rwanda," are "unprofessional and unethical researchers," and are "stuck with the old lenses." A few of the seven posts on the site do engage with interpretations of facts, but the rhetorical approach of ad hominem attacks is prevalent.

[2] The search was completed in April 2020.
[3] The blog can be seen at: http://theremakingrwanda.blogspot.com/2011/04/remaking-rwanda-or-wishing-to.html (accessed April 15, 2020).

Obstructive tactics of information denial and discrediting critics help to lay the groundwork for the government's efforts to portray itself positively. Doubt is cast on information about RPF misdeeds because those documenting them have restricted access to the country. This means that the information used by critics must be unreliable, so their usage of it is unethical and, by extension, must be driven by hidden anti-Rwanda motives. Critics are portrayed as hysterical and/or single-minded in their ill intentions, while the RPF is responsible, sober, and has the best interests of all Rwandans at heart. Marginalizing foreign critics and/or restricting them from entering the country helps shape the environment into which the government's efforts to portray itself positively are disseminated. If potential critics cannot access information, then their research is more difficult and costly, and if they know they may be slandered by a government or denied access, then they may be less critical.

Building a Positive Image (with an Eye on Its Critics): Rwanda's PR Efforts

The RPF presents an image of itself as competent and democratic. It wishes to be considered forward-looking and visionary, even as it looks backward to make the genocide central to Rwanda's narrative (Longman 2017, 52–56). Given that aid dependence makes good relations with certain foreign actors crucial to its stability (Desrosiers and Thomson 2011, 438), the RPF has powerful incentives to not only limit damaging information from leaving Rwanda, but also promote a positive image of itself.

In the early days of its power consolidation, "the regime befriended international opinion makers who were cowed into believing some easy-to-grasp narratives regarding Central Africa's crises and solutions; narratives so seductively simple that no one new to the region thought of asking about their ideological underpinnings" (Pottier 2002, 4). In the logic of the promotional/specific mechanism of authoritarian image management, the RPF amplified the voices and granted access to supportive journalists and public opinion leaders (Pottier 2002, 109–129). *New Yorker* writer and author Philip Gourevich, for example, often comes in for critique by some Rwanda-focused scholars for portraying Kagame and the RPF in uncritical terms (e.g., Pottier 2002, 56–57, 168–169; Longman 2011, 25–26; Peskin 2011, 175; Reyntjens 2013, 189–190). Positive portrayals by influential journalists, writers, public figures, and businesspersons helped frame post-genocide RPF Rwanda as a success story (Straus and Waldorf 2011, 6). This does not impugn the motives of those who portray Rwanda positively, but only suggests that the RPF has worked hard to get its preferred story told in the international press.

Analysis of FARA documents filed with the US DoJ reveal that especially in the first few years after 2003, the Rwandan government invested in lobbying and public relations. The timing coincides with the RPF's consolidation of single-party rule and the 2003 elections that ratified Kagame's power, as well as an official visit to the United States in March 2003. The Rwandan government contracted with Fleischman-Hillard for $45,000 plus expenses for a two-week period in which the firm "prepared media alerts, press releases, media list and press packets . . . contacted domestic and international media to alert them of President Kagame's visit," reviewed media materials produced by the Rwandan government, and organized a press pool to follow Kagame around on his US visit.[4] Following that visit, the Rwandan president's office retained Jefferson Waterman International starting in September 2003 on an annual $300,000 contract plus expenses for media outreach and lobbying.[5] Two contracts with GoodWorks International filed in 2005 and 2006 totaled $350,000 plus expenses,[6] and the next available registration is the well-known Racepoint agreement described at the outset of this chapter. Several subsequent contracts total more than $1 million in fees. Nearly all feature lobbying and building good relations with members of the US government as well as diffuse public relations.

FARA filings are often vague, but sometimes they are specific and illuminating. Two examples from the Rwanda filings stand out because they show how consultants can be used for both promotional and obstructive authoritarian image management tactics. The first example involves a television show about Rwanda and illustrates well the promotional/diffuse dimension of authoritarian image management. Peter Greenberg's *The Royal Tour* is a travel show in which Greenberg is shown a guided tour of the country by its head of state. Mercury Public Affairs was paid $80,000 including expenses to subcontract for Greenberg's company for the benefit of the Rwanda Development Board to help organize media outreach and events surrounding the premier

---

[4] https://efile.fara.gov/docs/3774-Exhibit-AB-20030922-HOYTER03.pdf (all FARA filings in this section last accessed September 1, 2020).

[5] https://efile.fara.gov/docs/4990-Exhibit-AB-20030925-HPA7SI03.pdf.

[6] https://efile.fara.gov/docs/5414-Exhibit-AB-20050304-9.pdf and https://efile.fara.gov/docs/5414-Exhibit-AB-20061204-12.pdf.

of the episode in April 2018.[7] This included a launch event with Greenberg and Kagame in which the latter was asked obsequious questions by audience members, mostly from the tourist industry.[8]

While this is an example about tourism, the project foregrounds politics. The promotional materials and the video itself present Kagame in a flattering light as a freedom fighter, a military genius, and a "wonkish technocrat." The first roughly 14 minutes of the 55-minute video explain Rwandan history and politics from an uncritical RPF perspective, interspersing an interview with Kagame with other footage. After two mildly critical questions at the end of the segment are quickly dispensed with, it's off to explore Rwanda's tourist sites. The trailer gives a flavor of the political content as it pairs dramatic shots of Kagame on the patio of a skyscraper in Kigali with a voiceover that says the following:

> And our guide on this special journey is a man who knows this country perhaps better than anyone. He was born here, then forced to flee, only to have to fight his way back in to bring stability, justice, and reconciliation to this once very troubled land. His name is Paul Kagame and he is the president of Rwanda.[9]

One can hardly imagine a more RPF-friendly introduction to Rwanda's president. This kind of public outreach and image crafting is meant for those unfamiliar with Rwanda's politics, or perhaps those who only know it as a place where genocide was perpetrated. It helps to present a positive image to a diffuse audience, ideally with the result of drumming up tourist business. For example, the Rwandan Development Board organized a screening of the film in London for travel agents (Ngabonziza 2019). Documentaries like this also have a domestic legitimation function insofar as they are evidence for Rwandans that the country and its leader are respected abroad. Likely for this reason, the film was screened in Kigali and received extensive positive coverage in *The New Times*. The FARA filing and the documentary reveal a straightforward case of promotional/diffuse authoritarian image management.

---

[7] https://efile.fara.gov/docs/6170-Exhibit-AB-20180515-43.pdf.

[8] A video of the session is available at: https://www.youtube.com/watch?v=0sI33ufC29M (accessed April 28, 2020).

[9] Trailer available at: https://petergreenberg.com/2018/04/26/rwanda-royal-tour/ (accessed April 28, 2020).

The second case illuminates obstructive authoritarian image management tactics. It stems from a June 2013 filing listing an agreement with a monthly fee of $5,000 between the Rwandan Ministry of Foreign Affairs and an American academic.[10] The agreement lays out a seven-point research agenda that focused on mapping the online engagement and organizational networks of the Rwandan "negative" diaspora (see next section for more on this term) and documenting what the contract calls "propaganda dissemination involving genocide ideology, negation, and trivialization." The contract stipulates that the consultant will "establish a publishing record . . . relating to the above-referenced dynamics, both within the popular press as well as within scholarly publications." It is worth recalling that while there are still genocidaires at large and that actual genocide deniers exist, the accusation that one is a genocide denier or harbors genocide ideology is often used indiscriminately against those who do not actually support or minimize genocide, in order to discredit political opponents (Waldorf 2011).

Regardless, it is not clear now effective this agreement was from the RPF's perspective. Subsequent amendments show that the contract was renewed for a six-month period but that the scope of the agreement was narrowed.[11] Ultimately the government received a review of scholarly literature[12] and one media interview done by the consultant.[13] The agreement was terminated in March 2014.[14] The academic publishing record by the author as it pertains to Rwanda has not made a discernible impact, with only two Google Scholar citations to relevant work as of November 2020, and it is difficult to find any notable media that feature the academic's views on Rwanda or the RPF. Taken together, the case reveals, importantly, that the RPF was interested in the theory and empirics of tracking and discrediting its opponents abroad and in establishing a scholarly literature to that effect, but also that the publicly discernible substantive result of the endeavor has been thus far minimal. Although this effort may not have yielded obvious results, it is an indication that the RPF emphasizes obstructive/specific authoritarian image management to a remarkable degree.

[10] https://efile.fara.gov/docs/6175-Exhibit-AB-20130612-1.pdf.
[11] See amendment at https://efile.fara.gov/docs/6175-Amendment-20131230-1.pdf.
[12] https://efile.fara.gov/docs/6175-Supplemental-Statement-20131230-1.pdf.
[13] https://efile.fara.gov/docs/6175-Supplemental-Statement-20131230-1.pdf.
[14] https://efile.fara.gov/docs/6175-Amendment-20140707-2.pdf.

Preempting, Discrediting, and Repressing Exiled Critics

As the political environment domestically developed into a one-party state, particularly since the late 1990s (Longman 2017, 152), it has become ever more difficult to effectively challenge the RPF from within Rwanda. As opposition parties met with increasing obstacles to organizing domestically and as RPF elites who defected from the ruling party found their lives in danger, the Rwandan diaspora abroad became a locus of oppositional politics. In addition to domestic challengers, political threats to RPF rule were now perceived to come from exile groups in Kampala, Brussels, Paris, Washington, London, and Johannesburg. Exiled opponents face barriers in challenging authoritarian states insofar as being located abroad makes it more difficult to build networks, maintain credibility, and gather information about conditions in the country, but such groups still try to confront the RPF (Jones 2016).

The discrediting of foreign journalists or scholars who criticize Rwanda was discussed earlier, but this section focuses on the Rwandan diaspora. The RPF appears to take a three-stage approach by first attempting to preempt oppositional mobilization in the diaspora. If that fails, it adopts a second tactic by discrediting those intent on vocally criticizing or challenging the RPF abroad. Third, if those steps fail, the government represses its critics abroad, even going so far as to assassinate prominent exiled challengers.

Preempting

To preempt threats to its image from abroad, the Rwandan government "reaches out into the diaspora and actively shapes its character" (Betts and Jones 2016, 156). Even though it is diverse and politically divided, the RPF would prefer an image of the Rwandan diaspora that is "unified, pro-regime, industriously developmentalist, but largely apolitical beyond their patriotism, and unthreatening" (Betts and Jones 2016, 156). The government tries to create a positive image of the diaspora as supportive and depoliticized, both to bring it under control and to mobilize resources from it for development at home (Turner 2013, 265–268). In 2008, the government formalized its engagement by creating the Diaspora General Directorate to unite Rwandans abroad to work for the government's aims and to sideline challengers (Turner 2013). The state facilitates a "calendar of diasporic activity" such as cultural, business, and sporting events to help bind the diaspora closer to the RPF's de-politicized, patriotic, and developmentalist vision for it (Betts and Jones 2016, 183–184).

Discrediting

However, the government's strategy for the diaspora is not all anodyne cultural celebrations and festivals. Turner (2013, 266) finds that the state classifies the diaspora into three categories: positive, skeptical, and hostile. Those defined as positive support the state. The skeptics may be won over through persuasion and become incorporated into the positive category, or failing that, at least may be convinced to keep their criticisms to themselves due to the threat of social exclusion or violence (Turner 2013, 277). Persuasion may be done through, for example, "come and see" tours so that diaspora members can visit Rwanda and acquaint themselves with the country's advances (Turner 2013; Betts and Jones 2016, 169–170). The hostile group is unconvertible and instead must be targeted and controlled (Turner 2013, 80).

The "hostile" designation overlaps with the label "negative forces" or "negative diaspora" that the government often uses to describe exiles who take an oppositional stance (Betts and Jones 2016, 117). This is the category that the government was willing to pay $5,000 per month to a foreign academic to analyze. Furthermore, to differentiate between the hostile/negative category and the positive or skeptical ones, there is some evidence that the government spies on exiles through a network of informants (Turner 2013, 278) or directly by security operatives (Jones 2016, 359; Thomson 2018, 184). Reflecting its domestic analogue, regardless of the actual extent of the surveillance, there is clearly the perception among the Rwandan oppositional diaspora that they are being spied upon, monitored, and infiltrated, which helps sow distrust and paranoia that undermines oppositional solidarity and functionality (Betts and Jones 2016, 148).

The RPF argues that the "negative forces" mislead Rwandans abroad and the international community (Turner 2013, 277; Betts and Jones 2016, 122). Some of these RPF critics are themselves former insiders who defected and fled the country. When they speak out, the Rwandan government attempts to discredit them. In August 2010, four prominent former RPF figures started a political party and issued a 57-page document called "Rwanda Briefing" that was highly critical of the RPF and Kagame in particular (Nyamwasa et al. 2010). It characterized Rwanda as a one-party state, with Kagame as its power-hungry leader, that frequently violates human rights at home and abroad. The document attempts to refute what it calls three "myths" about Kagame: that he is a strategic and visionary thinker, that he is incorruptible and austere, and that he is a reformist and unifying leader.

The RPF response was to counterpunch by engaging in what one observer called a "smear campaign" against the authors (Thomson 2018, 226). The RPF had to be careful because as former insiders in the areas of military, security, and justice, the authors may have been privy to information that the party preferred to keep secret (Thomson 2018, 226–227). The response was twofold.

First, through an advisor and a spokesperson, the government issued a document called "Response to Allegations by Four Renegades" (Rutatina and Rutaremara 2010). While the tract does engage with some of the substance of the argument laid out in "Rwanda Briefing," the first two and a half pages of the 14-page document focus on discrediting the authors. Perhaps most notably, it accuses the authors of being "proselytes of genocide ideology." The government made genocide ideology a crime in 2008, but in practice the RPF has defined the term so widely that it has come to include a variety of criticisms of the Rwandan government. As briefly noted earlier, and as Waldorf (2011, 57) puts it, "the government uses sweeping accusations of genocide ideology to intimidate or silence its critics." Calls for the RPF to be held accountable for war crimes, for example, are often met with accusations of genocide denial (Peskin 2011, 174). The strategy is to connect critics to the tragedy of the genocide to discredit them as messengers and, by extension, their messages.

Second, the Rwandan government staged a trial in absentia in January 2011. All four defendants were found guilty and sentenced to between 20 and 24 years in prison (Thomson 2018, 227). Their crimes were apparently "disturbing public order, threatening state security, making insulting and defamatory remarks, sectarianism and criminal conspiracy" (Daily Nation 2011). The ruling thus diminished the ability of the authors, and the oppositional group that they founded, to get their message heard and to gain supporters within Rwanda, as they were now enemies of a state that closely polices public discourse and political loyalties (Thomson 2018, 229).

Repressing

Eventually, one of the authors of the "Rwanda Briefing," Patrick Karegeya, was killed in his hotel room in South Africa in January 2014 (Wrong 2019). As discussed in Chapter 4, it is often difficult to determine responsibility in cases of possible extraterritorial repression, but a South African investigation into his death found that those who killed him had links to the Rwandan government (York 2019). Kagame officially denied that the Rwandan government had ordered the assassination, but two weeks after the murder he told a prayer breakfast of Rwandan elites in Kigali that "whoever betrays the country will pay the price, I assure you. Any person still alive who may be plotting against Rwanda, whoever they are, will pay the price. Whoever it is, it is a matter of time" (Wrong 2019, n.p.).

Karegeya is not the only victim of Rwanda's extraterritorial repression. As the data in the AAAD presented in Chapter 4 reveals, the Rwandan government frequently goes far beyond rhetorically attacking or even spying on its enemies abroad. The AAAD records 34 cases of the Rwandan state threatening or repressing critics abroad. To reiterate, this data should be viewed as an extremely conservative estimate of authoritarian extraterritorial repression given the secretive nature of the subject matter, the inherent deniability of many of the actions, and the fact that the database relies on publicly available sources only.[15]

Nevertheless, despite being one of the least populated countries in the database, Rwanda accounts for 11.5% of the assassinations and nearly 17% of the attempted but ultimately unsuccessful assassinations. Overall, in the AAAD, assassinations and attempted assassinations together account for only about 7% of all actions. Rwanda's strategy appears more violent and brazen than the norm, as nearly one-third of all recorded actions by the country in the database are either assassinations or attempted assassinations. When the RPF wants to silence one of its exiles, it has the capacity and willingness to go to extremes.

Four of the six assassination victims, including Karegeya, were former government officials. Perhaps the most well-known was Seth Sendashonga. A former minister of the interior in the post-genocide government, Sendashonga resigned and fled to Kenya in 1995. After a failed assassination

---

[15] As explained in Chapter 4 and Appendix 2, these cases do not include actions against violent or demonstrably criminal actors, such as anti-RPF militias or genocidaires.

attempt in February 1996, he was ultimately murdered in Nairobi in May 1998 (Human Rights Watch 2014). Sendashonga had set up a political party, along with former prime minister Faustin Twagiramungu, that was nonviolent and that espoused, in the estimation of two observers, "a sophisticated discourse of democratic pluralism, liberal constitutionalism, and ethnic reconciliation" (Betts and Jones 2016, 128). He also, perhaps crucially, had been present in the aftermath of the aforementioned Kibeho massacre by the RPF in April 1995 and so was in a position to challenge the government's version of those events (Prunier 2009, 37–41; Thomson 2018, 90–91).

Former government officials constitute the biggest category of cases involving Rwanda in the AAAD. Sixteen of the 34 cases, or 47% of Rwanda's authoritarian actions abroad, target former government officials. Of all 1,177 incidents involving all countries in the AAAD, only about 9.5% have former government officials as their targets. It seems clear that the RPF wishes to deter defection from its ranks and to enforce silence from those who do ultimately defect. Although difficult to verify, it may be the case that one reason for this is that it does not want its dirty laundry aired publicly.

However, former government officials are not the only targets of the RPF abroad. Exiled journalists have been threatened or attacked abroad in Uganda and Sweden. Charles Ingabire, who ran an oppositional newspaper and website in Uganda, was assassinated in Kampala in November 2011 (Human Rights Watch 2014). The month prior, two attackers beat him, took his computer, and told him to shutter his website (Meldrum 2011). From the RPF's perspective, people like Ingabire are a potential threat. In 2003, a different Kampala-based newspaper, Umuseso, exposed internal rifts in the RPF and published leaked documents exposing possible corruption, all of which helped trigger "the first serious crisis within the RPF" (Betts and Jones 2016, 137). For a government that closely guards its secrets and is intent on maintaining an image of unity, independent journalism that exposes divisions undermines its image and thereby threatens its internal security.

Ultimately, the RPF wishes to tame opposition not only domestically, but also abroad, at least in part because of the information its exiles can reveal. Given tight restrictions on challenging the RPF domestically, serious critics of the Kagame government often conclude that they will be heard more effectively abroad. Thus far the RPF has not been seriously threatened by any exiled political party and has met perceived threats through a strategy of preempting, discrediting, and repressing.

Conclusion: Rwanda's Successful Authoritarian Image Management

Rwanda is perhaps the most successful example of authoritarian image management in the contemporary world. Since the RPF has taken power, it has engaged in military actions twice in a neighboring state, both of which resulted in grave humanitarian and human rights catastrophes. It has assassinated its political opponents in foreign countries, temporarily severed diplomatic relations with a permanent member of the UN Security Council, and feuded with the United Nations. Domestically, it has overseen a violent autocratization of politics, with critics imprisoned, assassinated, or forced to flee.

And yet despite these transgressions, Rwanda is not generally thought of as a rogue dictatorship by most observers. In fact, it is feted as a developmental and/or peacebuilding model by some powerful actors (see Storey 2012, 23–27). Not only is Rwanda not sanctioned, but countries like the United States, Canada, the Netherlands, the United Kingdom, Belgium, Japan, South Korea, and Germany all willingly give money to the country through its government. That the RPF has escaped not only accountability, but even much rhetorical criticism, is made all the more remarkable by the fact that it has no natural resources on which external powers rely, and as a small country with only about 12 million inhabitants it has little leverage over most powerful external actors. The RPF's authoritarian image management strategy works.

To help explain this, some analysts point to the RPF's skillful use of the memory of the 1994 genocide (e.g., Pottier 2002, 156; Reyntjens 2015, 637). The argument is that the RPF can play on the guilt of international critics for failing to stop the genocide so that they appear hypocritical for criticizing the RPF. The government "displays exceptional skill at converting international feelings of guilt and ineptitude into admissions that the Front deserves to have the monopoly on knowledge construction" (Pottier 2002, 202). From this perspective, the RPF's actions to rebuild Rwanda since the genocide are beyond reproach by international critics. There is something to this, but it does not explain entirely the mismatch between the RPF's image and its actions, particularly as time moves forward. Virtually all dictatorships point to the hypocrisy of international critics, and while the genocide is an extreme case, if accusing the accusers were such an all-powerful rhetorical weapon, then most authoritarians would enjoy better reputations.

Two further speculative explanations can be offered for the success of Rwanda's authoritarian image management. The first is that the RPF clearly prioritizes it. It pays attention to discourse about Rwanda abroad, sometimes even at a granular level. The strategy is multidimensional, covering all four quadrants of the audience/form heuristic in comprehensive ways. As the FARA filings reveal, it advances its narrative but also tracks and responds to criticisms in detail. And, as the AAAD reveals, the possibility of extreme violence casts a shadow on real or would-be critical messengers, protecting the RPF's secrets and its narrative. Authoritarian image management is a conscious part of the RPF's strategy due to its authoritarianism and aid dependence. The evidence in this chapter suggests that it not only responds to those incentives, but is reasonably successful in doing so.

A second reason for its success is that the RPF has delivered in meaningful ways. It has a good story to tell, even if it must obscure a lot to make it entirely convincing. Like Singapore, or Vietnam, it can point to its record of building a competent state in the aftermath of violence and overseeing sustained economic growth. Its narrative can be shaped in even more remarkable ways given the country's recovery from the genocide. The objective successes of the regime in some areas, combined with the RPF's skilled authoritarian image management, together contribute to the Rwandan government's image being more positive than it otherwise would be given its record of transgressions against democracy and human rights.

8

Coping with a Post-Communist World

North Korea

North Korea is seen by some as an anachronistic dictatorship stuck in the Cold War. In this view, it is isolated and fundamentally inward-looking. Its people know little about the outside world, and the government steadfastly refuses to engage in meaningful international relationships. The leadership participates in strange publicity endeavors, like hosting flamboyant American former basketball star Dennis Rodman or publishing strident editorials insulting foreign leaders by calling them "dotards" (Donald Trump), "crafty prostitutes" (Park Geun-hye), or racist epithets (Barack Obama). On this account, it is a leadership that seemingly does not care what people think of it and revels in thumbing its nose at conventional standards of diplomacy. It is stubbornly sticking to its Stalinist ways, despite its knowledge that reform would likely improve the livelihood of its people. Partly as a result of these caricatures, North Korea is often framed in international discourse as either a weak and fragile state about to collapse, or a menacing military power ready to attack its enemies at any minute (Shim and Nabers 2013).

There are grains of truth to this caricature, but it ignores and misrepresents a great deal. It obscures the social changes that have occurred in North Korea during the past 30 years (see Dukalskis and Joo 2020), treats the North Korean population as lacking agency or sometimes even humanity, and glosses over the reasons why Pyongyang may think it needs to act as it does. For the purposes of this book, the view of North Korea as a menacing but weak oddball ignores the serious and sustained efforts that the government has long made to shape the way it is seen abroad.

North Korea has worked to craft its image since its earliest days as a state. It engaged in public diplomacy projects with other communist and post-colonial states throughout the Cold War and tried to manufacture an image of itself as a modern socialist state worthy of emulation. It promoted its leader Kim Il Sung as a cutting-edge revolutionary ideologist. Aside from

Making the World Safe for Dictatorship, Alexander Dukalskis, Oxford University Press (2021). © Oxford University Press. DOI: 10.1093/oso/9780197520130.003.0008

South Korea, it did not have serious ambitions to export its political system, but it did want that system to be seen positively abroad. Always a fiercely independent state, North Korea became more inward-looking as the global communist movement all but vanished and as China and Russia established diplomatic relations with South Korea. North Korea's authoritarian image management portfolio is more limited in scope and ambition than an aspiring great power like China and less successful than an analogous regional power like Rwanda.

Nonetheless, it maintains a multidimensional image management strategy. This includes a network of schools, universities, and media among Chongryon, its representative group in Japan, a network of sympathizer groups around the world, efforts at attracting foreign tourists to whom the state can show a positive image, and externally facing media like the Korea Central News Agency and YouTube channels. There is, of course, also a darker side to these efforts. As discussed in Chapter 4, the North Korean government has threatened and assassinated exiled opponents and former regime insiders abroad. It attempts to silence critics in Japan and South Korea by intimidating their families remaining in the North. Defectors who speak out and gain notoriety abroad are mocked and maligned by the state's propaganda apparatus.

After providing a conceptual historical overview, the chapter analyzes two specific instances of North Korea's authoritarian image management spanning both the Cold War and post–Cold War eras, namely its Japan-based efforts to craft an appealing image among Koreans there, and the loose organizational network of North Korea sympathizer associations around the world. The chapter draws on secondary sources, primary North Korean media sources, online evidence of friendship group activities, and fieldwork conducted about Chongryon in Japan in 2019. The main argument is that North Korea's image management efforts have been effective in some respects, but they appear outdated and ill-suited to the contemporary world because the country was slow and hesitant to adapt to new realities. The system was designed for a context of party-to-party relations and Third World solidarity initiatives that faded in relevance as international politics evolved. The domestic realities of North Korea—its repression, lack of basic political rights, and humanitarian struggles—mean that a highly coordinated and professional image management effort would be required to make the country appear broadly attractive to foreign audiences. The DPRK's efforts have not thus far succeeded in that regard.

Shaping North Korea's Image Abroad: An Overview

North Korea's efforts at improving its image can be found at the very origins of the state. After Korea was divided into Soviet and American zones at the 38th Parallel at the conclusion of World War II, a communist system developed in the north, and in 1948 the Democratic People's Republic of Korea (DPRK) was established. From the very beginning, North Korea found itself in an ideological and propaganda competition with its southern neighbor and sought to portray itself as a modern and progressive alternative to the corrupt and repressive south (Scalapino and Lee 1972, 360, 461).

The Korean War from 1950 to 1953 accelerated the importance of winning the global propaganda battle as the state's very survival was at stake. During the war, North Korea's official media sought to get its narrative heard by frequently attacking the United States, praising the Soviet Union and China, and highlighting the international support it received (Scalapino and Lee 1972, 415). Cultural projects were used to win support. North Korean performers went on a tour of Europe to raise funds for the war and win supporters for its cause. As Cathcart and Denney (2013, 32) put it, commenting on a time when the North Korean state was in its infancy, "even in the 1950s the North Koreans were gaining understanding and experience in conducting international tours and projecting a national identity into the international sphere."

De-Stalinization in much of the rest of the communist world presented a problem for North Korea's legitimation foundations and image abroad (Scalapino and Lee 1972, 504–505). As the Soviet Union distanced itself from personalist rule after Nikita Khrushchev's "Secret Speech," communist parties around the world had to wrestle with their legacies and futures (Brown 2009, 227–292; Radchenko 2014; McAdams 2017, 290). The DPRK was among the states that remained steadfast in its commitment to personalist politics, finishing the 1950s with a major purge of the party ranks to ensure loyalty to Kim Il Sung (Lankov 2002). After this time, North Korea's ideology and propaganda took an inward turn, emphasizing the creative application of socialism to the North Korean context under Kim's leadership (Shin 2006, 87–95; Smith 2015, 120–126). The justification, both internally and externally, was the wisdom and unique characteristics of the leader and the mutable ideological slogan of "Juche," or self-reliance.

North Korea's image during the 1960s and into the 1970s was somewhat easier to manage externally because of the condition of South Korea. South Korea was not the wealthy democracy observers are familiar with today.

Instead, it was ruled by the US-backed autocratic leader Syngman Rhee from 1948 to 1960, and after a coup in 1961 Park Chung Hee presided over a military dictatorship until his assassination in 1979 (Cumings 2005, 309–314; on the Park era, see Kim and Vogel 2011). During this period, to outside observers South Korean looked like an impoverished, corrupt, and autocratic country, controlled in important ways by the United States. Indeed, North Korean propaganda was perceived as threatening enough by South Korean leaders themselves that they cast a wide net in banning it, along with other expressions of support for communist positions and left-leaning literature, under the sweeping National Security Law.

North Korea's authoritarian image management endeavors during this period included efforts designed to cultivate an image of legitimacy abroad and build relations beyond the communist world. To some on the political left, North Korea appeared to be the more appealing Korea, and the DPRK actively sought ties with sympathetic groups in both the developing world and the West (Gauthier 2014; Young 2015). Juche Idea Study Groups and other friendship societies began to be set up abroad from the late 1960s onward (Cathcart and Denney 2013; Young 2015, 112). North Korea ultimately financed and/or facilitated about 200 such groups in dozens of countries, including a New York–based organization called the American-Korean Friendship and Information Center from 1971 to 1976 with the aim to cultivate support in the United States for the withdrawal of American troops from South Korea (Gauthier 2014). These groups held events and meetings to support North Korea's positions on various matters, which would then be reported back to the North Korean population via the state media. State-funded trips aimed to showcase the best of North Korea to potentially influential allies from abroad (Young 2015, 114). This arrangement built North Korea's contacts abroad while allowing it to use the ostensible praise it received in the international sphere for its domestic legitimation purposes.

Starting in the early 1970s, North Korea also began to send gymnastic advisors to Third World states to train them in organizing DPRK-style Mass Games (Young 2020). The Mass Games is an enormous event featuring choreographed gymnastic, dance, and visual routines using painted cards that together create animation-like images on a grand scale. The messages are historical and political and are meant to provide "a succinct, exemplary narrative of North Korea's past and future that the state wishes to convey to its people and to the outside world at a given historical moment" (Kwon and Chung 2012, 130). North Korea supplied its expertise in organizing these events to build better relations with developing states, starting with Somalia in 1973, Uganda and Burundi in 1974, Rwanda in 1975, and several other states, including Ghana in 1984 and Nigeria in 1996 (Young 2020). Trainers were provided free of charge to the host governments and helped to bolster North Korea's image abroad in its larger diplomatic and legitimation struggle with South Korea (Young 2020).

Ultimately, by the 1980s many of North Korea's image management activities abroad faded (Gauthier 2014, 162). The subsequent collapse of European and Central Asian communist states in the late 1980s and early 1990s had a well-documented and catastrophic effect on North Korea's population, economy, and state (Haggard and Noland 2007; Smith 2015, 188–208; Fahy 2015). North Korea entered a period of economic crisis that resulted in a punishing famine and state breakdown that severely tested the regime's capacity to survive. Kim Il Sung died in 1994 and his son Kim Jong Il took over during this challenging period. His plan for survival and recovery, in a policy called *Songun*, or "Military First," was to emphasize the military as a vanguard of the revolution and protector of the Korean people (Suh 2002). At around this time, North Korea accelerated its nuclear weapons and missile programs, which resulted in a prolonged dispute with the United States and other international actors wishing to halt the DPRK's capabilities (Howell 2020). North Korea's military posture, combined with its post-famine poverty and persistent human rights abuses, help explain why it is perceived among many abroad as simultaneously weak and menacing (Shim and Nabers 2013).

After Kim Jong Un assumed power upon his father's death in December 2011, some international observers had hope that he would cautiously liberalize North Korea because he had been educated in Switzerland and seemed positively disposed to some Western habits and technologies (Harlan 2012; Lorenz 2012; for biographies of Kim Jong Un, see Fifield 2019; Pak 2020). Purveyors of this argument were of course disappointed. While some economic reforms helped raise the livelihood of some of the population, the basic structure of North Korea's political system remained intact, and North Korea's international relations continued to oscillate between ratcheting up tension and taking conciliatory measures. The third Kim proved to be just as committed as his father and grandfather to preserving the political structure. However, public diplomacy initiatives, like concert tours and media partnerships, continued to be used to gain sympathizers, foster hopes for reform and engagement, and as material that can be fed back into domestic propaganda to show that North Korea is internationally respected (Cathcart and Denney 2013).

North Korea's authoritarian image management toolkit, however, extends well beyond disseminating positive messages via state media or sending artistic troupes abroad. It is much more extreme than China and Rwanda in building its obstructive foundation, insofar as it allows virtually no foreign journalists or researchers to work independently in the country, aiming to create unspoiled ground on which it can build its preferred narrative. As detailed in Chapter 4, the North Korean government attempts to repress or discredit defectors abroad who criticize the state. As Fahy (2019, 4) puts it, "the state's memory is long, and its reach is global." The very act of defection is threatening to North Korea's image, and "the defectors' ability to tell about the life of the North Korean collective to the international community is what the state seeks to silence" (Fahy 2019, 4). The government produces documentaries to try to discredit prominent defectors (Fahy 2019, 18–19). The AAAD documents 156 instances in which the DPRK threatened, detained, abducted, attempted or successfully extradited, or even assassinated its defector critics abroad. Because they are only from publicly available sources, these numbers likely underestimate North Korea's extraterritorial repression. Furthermore, they do not include the country's "anchor" system for citizens officially sent abroad, which ensures that at least one family member remains in North Korea as leverage to prevent the person abroad from criticizing the state (Fahy 2019, 93). Although less systematically studied than North Korea's diffuse external messaging (e.g., Whang, Lammbrau, and Joo 2017), the obstructive/specific mechanisms of North Korea's authoritarian image management are robust and have been developed over a long period of time.

When faced with criticism, North Korea generally resorts to the rhetorical tactic of "whataboutism," or accusing the accusers (Fahy 2019, 203). For example, in 2014 the United Nations completed its Commission of Inquiry on Human Rights in the Democratic People's Republic of Korea (hereafter COI), which documented the human rights abuses perpetrated by the DPRK (UNHCR 2014). The government's response was to impugn the motives of the commission, point to human rights abuses in the United States, South Korea, and Japan to suggest that they are not fit judges, slander the individual members of the commission, claim that nobody had seen the situation in North Korea firsthand, and try to discredit defectors who gave testimony about their experiences. During hearings and press events relevant to the COI in New York, it sent diplomats to read prepared statements rehashing these talking points (Fahy 2019, 215–220). It also released its own human rights report via the state-controlled DPRK Association for Human Rights Studies, which proceeded along familiar lines: the situation in North Korea is good and the United States and "anti-DPRK hostile forces" are just attacking the country under the guise of human rights (Fahy 2019, 222–225; for the full report, see DPRK Association for Human Rights Studies 2014). The government's external media apparatus echoed these themes. The obstructive/diffuse image management approach of the DPRK is clear: when faced with criticism, accuse the accusers and deny that any problems exist in North Korea.

This brief overview of North Korea's authoritarian image management efforts is by no means exhaustive. Yet clearly North Korea mixes propaganda and extraterritorial repression with attempting to get sympathetic foreigners to defend the DPRK abroad. This is all built on a foundation of denying access to information to outsiders. Two areas of North Korea's authoritarian image management will provide an opportunity to see in more detail how the state attempts to cultivate an appealing image and marginalize critics. The following sections will examine in detail North Korea's outreach to the Korean minority in Japan, as well as the global spread and activities of its sympathizer groups.

Chongryon and Authoritarian Image Management in Japan

Because Japan had colonized Korea, upon the empire's defeat in World War II there were about 2.4 million Koreans in Japan. In the first three and a half months after the war, about 800,000 returned to Korea. By the end of 1946, roughly 575,000 more returned (Mitchell 1967, 102–103). About 600,000 Koreans remained in Japan after 1948, many of whom had arrived in Japan several decades prior (Mitchell 1967, 104). During the time in which they had been in Japan, of course, Korea had been divided into two political entities which fought a war between 1950 and 1953, thus complicating the idea of returning to the peninsula.

Under the American occupation of Japan from 1945 to 1952, Koreans in Japan were denied citizenship and voting rights, and as registered aliens were fingerprinted and surveilled (Lie 2008, 37). Ultimately, Koreans in Japan were defined as foreigners and were presumed to be temporary residents

(Lie 2008, 37–38). Excluded from public sector jobs and from desirable private sector employment, many Koreans found themselves working in the informal sector or the black market (Lie 2008, 38). Stripped of their political rights, they had limited options to combat the widespread social discrimination they faced.

In this context, Koreans in Japan formed ethnic organizations to help advocate for changes and improve conditions for Koreans. One of the first postwar Korean organizations was the League of Koreans in Japan, or Choren, which formed in 1945 (Mitchell 1967, 104–107). Choren was left leaning, but not explicitly aligned with North Korea until 1948, and was eventually repressed by the American occupying forces and the Japanese government (Ryang 2016, 2–4). In 1946, a right-wing Korean group formed, which ultimately became the Community of Korean Residents in Japan, or Mindan (Mitchell 1967, 106–107). Mindan was sympathetic to South Korea and was anti-communist. Korean politics in Japan quickly became refracted through the emerging Cold War and the division of Korea (Lie 2008, 30–31).

Although Choren was repressed, a different pro–North Korea left-wing grouping reconstituted in May 1955 as the General Federation of Korean Residents in Japan, or Chongryon. Chongryon was founded "under the direct control of North Korea" (Shipper 2010, 60) with the aim of promoting "North Korea's position and securing mass support for the regime among Koreans in Japan" (Ryang 2016, 4). The choice to focus on attracting support for North Korea was accompanied by a reluctance to push too forcefully for change in Japan or to engage in Japanese domestic politics for fear of being repressed as Choren was in the 1940s (Lie 2008, 41). Instead, according to Ryang (2016, 6):

> Chongryun [sic] was able to redirect the passion of its followers away from their disenfranchised civil status in Japan and toward the utopic (and positive) future of re-joining a reunified Korea, the genuine homeland of all Koreans remaining in Japan.

The fact that Japan denied Koreans political rights and had no plans to incorporate them into society helped Chongryon's appeal in the early days, which pushed Koreans to align with home country co-ethnic organizations for support (Shipper 2010, 56). Of course, the notion of "home country" was not entirely clear for many Koreans in Japan. The vast majority had familial roots in the southern part of the peninsula, which was now the Republic of Korea. However, Mindan was a much weaker organization than Chongryon and received little support from the South Korean state until much later (Mitchell 1967, 125). According to Lie (2008, 39–40), "the South Korean government willfully neglected the South Korean diaspora in Japan until the 1970s."

Chongryon worked to fill this void with pro–North Korea political and so-cial activism designed to boost the image of North Korea among the Korean population in Japan. By 1957, it claimed about 90,000 members with a cen-tral headquarters, 440 branches throughout the country, a propaganda arm including a daily newspaper, and a network of booksellers and distributors (Mitchell 1967, 122–123). To a large extent, these efforts worked. Lie (2008, 42–43) sums up Chongryon and the DPRK's appeal:

> the legitimacy and even passion for North Korea was most robust in the 1950s and 1960s, a trend that owed in no small part to the [Japanese] Communist Party's support for Koreans before and after World War II; the Korean communists' impeccable credentials in resisting Japanese coloni-alism; the appeal of freedom, equality, and solidarity; and the ostensible economic successes of North Korea. . . . For many disappointed and disillu-sioned Zainichi in the 1950s and 1960s, North Korea, with its active propa-ganda, became a beacon of hope.[1]

The crown jewel in Chongryon's organizational structure was its education system, which North Korea supported financially (Mitchell 1967, 129; Ryang 2016, 6). By 1961 there were over 40,000 students in Chongryon's schools, which retained a special status separate from the Japanese education system (Ryang 1997, 24). The curriculum, especially before reforms in 1993, fea-tured North Korean political content and the Kim cult of personality explic-itly and frequently (Ryang 1997, 23–50). Much like in North Korean schools, textbooks and lessons for elementary schools featured the childhood biog-raphy of Kim Il Sung, while higher levels of education recounted Kim's rev-olutionary activities and political thought (Ryang 1997, 25). The medium of instruction is Korean, which is important given that most Koreans in Japan speak Japanese as a first language (Ryang 1997; Lie 2008, 107). These schools helped propagate the values and image of the North Korean government among the Korean population in Japan so that it would support the DPRK in its rivalry with South Korea.

---

[1] "Zainichi" means "resident in Japan." Sometimes Koreans in Japan are referred to as "Zainichi Koreans" or just "Zainichi."

At the apex of Chongryon's educational network stands Choson University in the suburbs of Tokyo.[2] Founded on April 10, 1956, with funding from the DPRK, the university was meant to produce an educated elite to work for Chongryon and its aims (Mitchell 1967, 123; Shipper 2010, 62). Ryang (1997, 37–43), herself a graduate of the institution, has provided an in-depth analysis of the university. She documents how over 10,000 students have graduated from the institution since its inception. The North Korean government appoints the university's professors and awards its degrees, which include several standard higher education subjects. The medium of instruction is Korean, and all students live on campus. The students go to North Korea as part of a graduation trip, and after completing their studies many go to work for Chongryon itself, either as teachers or somewhere in the organizational apparatus. Ryang, for example, was sent to work for Chongryon's daily newspaper, the *Choson Sinbo* (Ryang 1997, 17).

The most significant campaign in Chongryon's history was its effort to help "repatriate" about 90,000 Koreans (and Japanese spouses of Koreans) from Japan to North Korea between 1959 and 1984.[3] The Japanese government was a willing participant in this effort, as it wished to rid itself of Koreans, whom it perceived as pro-communist and/or criminal (Morris-Suzuki 2005). North Korea wished to attract more skilled labor and to score a propaganda "win" vis-à-vis South Korea (Morris-Suzuki 2005, 371).

In September 1958, Kim Il Sung announced that Koreans were welcome to come to North Korea from Japan to help build the new state (Mitchell 1967, 139–140). There is evidence that Kim was motivated at least in part to burnish the image of North Korea as a desirable destination. He told a Soviet diplomat in 1957 that North Korea would agree to help Koreans in Japan come study in the DPRK "because we don't want the Association of Korean Residents in Japan to regard the DPRK in a bad light" (quoted in Morris-Suzuki 2007, 176). Maintaining a positive image among Koreans in Japan and global public opinion more generally on the repatriation issue would "bring great political, as well as economic, benefits" to North Korea (quoted in Morris-Suzuki 2007, 181–182). In discussions with his Soviet counterpart in 1959, Kim's foreign minister Nam Il put this in the context of outmigration

---

[2] The name is sometimes translated as "Korea University," but here I will use the name Choson University both to avoid confusion with the Korea University in Seoul and to remain true to the Korean language name of the institution (조선대학교).

[3] "Repatriate" is in quotation marks because the vast majority of those sent to North Korea had never been there in the first place, either having been born in Japan or having come from the southern part of the Korean peninsula.

from South Korea, noting that "the emergence of the repatriation issue has brought political gains to the DPRK, while Syngman Rhee has lost out" (quoted in Morris-Suzuki 2007, 184).

Chongryon played a key role in the repatriation effort not only logistically, but also by actively propagating a positive image of North Korea so that Koreans in Japan would wish to move to the DPRK. Chongryon conducted an "emphatic propaganda campaign" to support repatriation to North Korea (Ryang 2016, 7). The organization "waged an all-out campaign for repatriation" that portrayed North Korea as a paradise and as the "true and only fatherland for all Koreans in Japan" (Ryang 1997, 114). Koreans in Japan "were given a glowing account of life in the northern half of the peninsula" (Mitchell 1967, 140), including the promise of good jobs, apartments, and education for their children. Chongryon's propaganda efforts "exploited the trope of a paradise on earth where every refrigerator was full of beef and pork and youths could study at Kim Il Sung University and possibly Moscow State University" (Lie 2008, 45). The Japanese press, with the urging of some in the Japanese government who wished to encourage Koreans to leave, and some on the Japanese left who wished to aid socialist causes, helped magnify positive messages about repatriation (Morris-Suzuki 2007, 161). Chongryon's school system spread the message to students and parents that "departure for the Fatherland was both their patriotic duty and their only chance of a brighter future" (Morris-Suzuki 2007, 167).

The juxtaposition with their conditions in Japan, with few employment prospects, limited political rights, and no significant support by the Japanese government, allowed the propaganda campaign to resonate. According to a 1959 survey by the Japanese Red Cross, about 75% of the registered returnees were unemployed (Mitchell 1967, 144; see also Ryang 1997, 113). The "pictures published by North Korea at the height of the repatriation movement contrasted the spotless new apartments promised to returnees with the squalor of their slum dwellings in Japan" (Morris-Suzuki 2005, 372). The organization's newspaper published letters from those who had returned, presenting enthusiastically positive accounts of life in North Korea as a "wonderful country full of opportunities" (Mitchell 1967, 154; Morris-Suzuki 2007, 163–164). The effort to support repatriation was multifaceted and reached deeply into the Korean community in Japan:

> In the years leading up to the mass emigration to North Korea, members of
> Chongryon disseminated North Korean propaganda at public events and

door to door in areas of Osaka and Tokyo that were home to Koreans. . . . Chongryon printed fliers and pamphlets urging Zainichi Koreans to return to the homeland, and Chongryon supporters drove around Korean areas of Osaka projecting greetings from Kim Il-sung and promising a better life across the sea. Constant messages from powerful sources fostered an imagining of North Korea as a place in which Zainichi Koreans would live free from the marginalizing practices in Japan. (Bell 2018, 8)

The 1959 DPRK pamphlet *On the Question of 600,000 Koreans in Japan* lays out the argument for migration to North Korea. It is a compilation of documents relevant to the Korean population in Japan, including government decisions and speeches by leaders. The foreword argues that Koreans ended up in Japan in the first place because of imperialism, and that once there they were subject to humiliating conditions. It goes on to argue that North Korea supported Koreans via educational funds and that many Koreans want to return to the DPRK. Observers are impressed that North Korea "has been turning into a happy land where the people, liberated from every kind of exploitation, enjoy a free life. And they tremble at the thought that South Korea has been turned into a living hell—a land of nonrights, poverty and death" (DPRK 1959, 3–4). Photos highlight the positive achievements of North Korea, including in education, farming, housing, and industry. They are juxtaposed with pictures of South Korean slums and of kids shining the boots of American soldiers. A February 15, 1959, editorial in the Korean Worker's Party newspaper, the *Rodong Sinmun*, makes essentially the same points: North Korea is progressing, South Korea is poor and repressive, and Koreans in Japan are suffering due to the policies of imperialists and their supporters (DPRK 1959, 132–137). While many of these claims are exaggerated, they retained enough truth that they held appeal for many Koreans in Japan at the time. Indeed, former Chongryon members old enough to recall the campaign acknowledge that it was persuasive.[4]

Most returnees—about 70,000—went in 1960 and 1961 (Morris-Suzuki 2005). Those who made the journey were quick to discover that conditions in North Korea were not as propitious as they had been led to believe (Morris-Suzuki 2005; Bell 2016, 2018). Although surveilled and monitored in North

---

[4] Interview, former Chongryon member, Tokyo, Japan August 10, 2019. The author conducted seven interviews in August 2019 with experts and former members of Chongryon in Tokyo. Snowball sampling was used.

Korea, returnees were able to stay in touch with their families in Japan to some extent and through coded language helped communicate the realities of North Korea (Bell 2018). For example, if a letter from a North Korean returnee said that the family in Japan should come visit North Korea when the former's young child got married, this would be taken as a sign not to come for a long time since any possible marriage would be many years down the road.[5] Particularly after family visits were allowed, "many Chongryon Koreans came to the realization that North Korea was a land of material shortage and political repression" (Ryang 2016, 8). However, repatriation also served another function, which was to attempt to keep returnees' family members returnees who remained in Japan loyal to Chongryon (Shipper 2010, 63). Indeed, some argue that the organization's remaining members are loyal primarily because they have family in North Korea and do not want to sever that link.[6]

Where does this leave Chongryon's efforts to portray North Korea positively today? The organization's support has eroded since the 1970s and stood at roughly 70,000 in 2016 according to the Japanese Public Security Intelligence Agency (Bell 2019, 32), although others put its active membership at closer to 30,000.[7] While there were about 40,000 pupils in Chongryon schools in the 1960s, there were only about 15,000 as of 2008 (Shipper 2010, 61–64). Chongryon's newspaper, the *Choson Sinbo*—in English rendered as *The People's Korea*—remains operational and is aimed directly at the Korean community in Japan, although the extent of its readership is unclear. Today it is only a website and not a physical newspaper, and it has Japanese- and Korean-language versions. There is virtually no enthusiasm for repatriation from Japan to North Korea. On the contrary, small numbers of previous repatriates to the DPRK have now returned to Japan, with about 200 to 300 in total returning between 2005 and 2015 (Bell 2016), although the Japanese government does not publish official detailed statistics on this matter.[8] Organizationally, a crackdown by the Japanese government starting in 2006 in response to North Korean nuclear tests had serious consequences for Chongryon (Hastings 2016, 65–66). Financial flows between the organization and North Korea became more difficult to

[5] Interview, journalist and researcher, August 5, 2019.
[6] Interview, former Chongryon member, August 10, 2019.
[7] Interview, civil society organization leader A, August 7, 2019; expert interview, civil society organization leader B, August 7, 2019.
[8] Interview, civil society organization leader A, August 7, 2019.

sustain, and ultimately Chongryon had to put its headquarters in Tokyo up for sale in 2012.

A major turning point in Chongryon's fortunes came in September 2002 when Kim Jong Il admitted to Japanese prime minister Junichiro Koizumi that North Korea had abducted more than a dozen Japanese citizens during the 1970s and 1980s. While North Korea's reputation in Japan had clearly been declining since before that time, this admission dealt a potentially fatal blow to Chongryon and North Korea's appeal among the Korean population in Japan. The arguments of some Japanese right-wing groups that had been claiming for years that North Korea had abducted citizens were suddenly vindicated. Some left-wing Japanese groups that had been casting doubt on such arguments suffered politically.[9]

Chongryon had been arguing that the kidnapping claims were just anti-DPRK propaganda prior to 2002. The admission by Kim Jong Il himself that the abductions indeed did occur put Chongryon in an almost impossible spot domestically. Many members were caught off guard, as they had assumed all along that the kidnapping story was too outlandish to be true.[10] After the confirmation, the argument shifted from denial to accusing the Japanese government of using the issue disingenuously. For example, the *Choson Sinbo* (2012, n.p.) argued that Japanese prime minister Shinzo Abe's approach to the kidnapping and remains issue was meant to create a pretext for aggression by exploiting Japan as a victim as much as possible and argued that Japan is abusing the issue to seek "impure political goals." The paper also criticized Abe for bringing the abduction issue to the United Nations on the grounds that it should be a bilateral issue (Choson Sinbo 2012).

Chongryon clearly had difficulty adapting to these new political realities (Ryang 2016, 9). Increasing numbers of Koreans in Japan applying for Japanese or South Korean citizenship sapped the strength of Chongryon. Changes in the 1990s to Japan's laws meant that Koreans faced fewer obstacles to applying for benefits and traveling abroad and were less susceptible to the threat of deportation (Ryang 1997, 125–126). South Korea as an economic and political success story from the 1990s onward, as compared to North Korea, has meant that the case Chongryon must make on behalf of the DPRK is more difficult. Generational change means that third- and

---

[9] Interview, journalist, August 10, 2019.
[10] Interview, civil society organization leader A, August 7, 2019; interview, former Chongryon member, August 10, 2019.

fourth-generation Koreans in Japan feel less attachment to the ideological struggles of the twentieth century than their parents or grandparents.

The adaptations that the organization did attempt have so far not been able to revive Chongryon or the DPRK's reputation among the broader Korean community in Japan. Economically, Chongryon adapted to changed international circumstances by engaging in smuggling and sanctions-busting activities to aid North Korea (Ryang 2016, 13). Starting in the late 1980s, Chongryon began to involve itself more in business ventures in Japan to support the North Korean government financially (Durand 2017, 103); however, with the tightening of the sanctions regime, many of these activities became more difficult or even impossible, even if they were not always technically illegal (Hastings 2016).

Educationally, Chongryon changed its school curriculum relatively quickly in the early 1990s to reflect changes in the broader political environment (Ryang 1997, 51–65). The educational committees overseeing Korean language and history instruction were still closely tied to the DPRK and the members visited North Korea annually, but the government appeared to loosen control over some other subjects (Ryang 1997, 58). Curricular reforms downplayed adoration of the Kims but continued to emphasize Korean nationalism and the greatness of the DPRK. The more overt elements of the personality cult were moved to instruction in Young Pioneers after-school activities and other venues, which meant that they were sometimes taken less seriously because they were not tied as closely to academic advancement (Ryang 1997, 61–62). The main rationale for the curricular reforms was so that graduates of Chongryon schools could be better prepared for Japanese university entrance exams. However, these reforms had ambiguous effects insofar as they may have loosened the ties students feel to the DPRK political system (Ryang 1997, 61–64). On top of these challenges, the Japanese government increased its pressure on Chongryon in general, and many Japanese prefectures stopped subsidizing its schools. In response, Chongryon has tried to make this a minority rights issue in international fora (Choson Sinbo 2018a, 2019).

Ideationally, Chongryon has tried to adjust its message over time, with varying degrees of success. It still sometimes highlights material progress and good living standards in North Korea (e.g., Choson Sinbo 2017a, 2017b). However, the "homeland orientation" of Korean nationalism in Japan has declined over time (Lie 2008). Chongryon attempts to cultivate "long-distance nationalism" for North Korea, which "entails a love for the imagined home country" (Shipper 2010, 58). However, as Koreans in Japan increasingly expect to live in Japan permanently and not "return" to North Korea, they tend more toward "diasporic nationalism" which "involves an idealized existence, independent from both homeland and the host society" (Shipper 2010, 58). North Korea is reimagined as a symbol of authentic Korean identity (Bell 2019, 38). This means that "members of Chongryon imagine themselves existing in a state of exile from the homeland, but without the attendant desire to return" (Bell 2019, 23). There is a simultaneous "longing" for North Korea paired with an understanding that return is unlikely (Bell 2019, 23–24).

Cultivating a long-distance nationalism and longing for North Korea is challenging given the ostensible decline in North Korea's appeal as generations overturn and political realities evolve. To overcome this challenge, Chongryon tries to emphasize the "debt" that Koreans in Japan owe to the organization and to the DPRK (Bell 2019, 35). It stresses that nobody supported Koreans in Japan for a long time except Chongryon and North Korea, so they should reciprocate by providing loyalty. The organization attempts to "reproduce the burden of this debt" (Bell 2019, 35). For example, Chongryon sometimes brings groups of school graduates or activists to North Korea to show them hospitality and political flattery. The expectation is that these trips induce a sense of indebted loyalty to the nation. They are reported in Chongryon's newspaper to magnify the impact of the trip beyond its direct participants (Choson Sinbo 2016, 2018c, 2018d). The organization's media furthermore continue to highlight discrimination faced by contemporary Koreans in Japan. In addition to the education issue mentioned earlier, the *Choson Sinbo* has highlighted hate speech faced by Koreans in Japan (Choson Sinbo 2015) and attacks on children wearing uniforms of Chongryon schools (Choson Sinbo 2018b). These stories are meant to position Chongryon as an advocate for Koreans in Japan, which in turn should be reciprocated with political loyalty.

It is noteworthy that Chongryon's obstructive image management techniques in Japan have for the most part not been directly coercive, at least as far as is publicly known. Aside from a few unconfirmed stories of physical intimidation between elite rivals for power within the organization, Chongryon by and large uses nonviolent image management techniques on behalf of its patron state.[11] Instead, it tries other methods to address criticism,

---

[11] Interview, journalist and researcher, August 5, 2019.

such as downplaying the Kim personality cult in Chongryon schools,[12] ignoring or isolating dissident former members of the organization,[13] and criticizing or attempting to discredit vocal critics as traitors.[14] The organization controls access to North Korea for Japan-based citizens and organizations, meaning that it is a gatekeeper for Japanese media wishing to report from North Korea. Some argue that it uses this position to punish organizations that have been recently critical of North Korea in the hopes of engendering self-censorship among Japanese media outlets so that they can protect access to lucrative reporting opportunities.[15]

The most sinister and coercive aspect of Chongryon's obstructive image management techniques stems from the reality that family members of Chongryon members in North Korea are potential hostages (Shipper 2010, 63). If Chongryon members become too critical, there may be repercussions for their family members in North Korea. Reliable information on this issue is difficult to obtain or verify; however, institutionally Chongryon is positioned to use family in North Korea to pressure members to remain loyal. It can influence communication between members and families in North Korea, as well as the flow of material goods between them. It can report to North Korean authorities on critics or dissidents in Japan. These are powerful incentives to remain at least outwardly loyal to Chongryon, but it seems that indirect suggestions are made, rather than direct threats of negative sanctions against Chongryon dissidents and their family members.[16] Indeed, if these sorts of punishments are carried out by Chongryon against organizational defectors, it does not seem to have been a powerful enough incentive to arrest the depletion of the organization's grassroots base.

Despite its waning power, Chongryon remains a part of North Korea's authoritarian image management portfolio, particularly as it pertains to feeding propaganda reports on the organization's activities back into North Korea. North Korea's official news agency, the Korean Central News Agency (KCNA), discusses Chongryon in two main ways: defending it from perceived attacks by the Japanese government and highlighting Chongryon events in Japan. These modes of discussing Chongryon highlight North Korea's goals of external security (signaling displeasure at the organization

---

[12] Interview, researcher on Chongryon schools, August 6, 2019; interview, journalist, August 10, 2019.

[13] Interview, journalist and researcher, August 5, 2019.

[14] Interview, civil society organization leader A, August 7, 2019.

[15] Interview, researcher, August 9, 2019.

[16] Interview, former Chongryon member, August 10, 2019.

being targeted by Japanese authorities in the hopes that policies will change) and internal security (showing that North Korean events are respected in Japan to a domestic audience in the hopes of generating legitimacy).

The former fits the narrative of Japan as a threat to North Korea and its interests. Most of the articles take the form of reporting on what other sympathetic organizations say about Japan's repression of Chongryon. This has the effect of simultaneously portraying Japan as menacing and unfair, while also magnifying the claim that North Korea has international sympathy. For example, a 1998 article reports on the Federation of Korean Nationals in China issuing a statement that "vehemently denounces the anti-DPRK, anti-Chongryon campaign of the Japanese authorities as a grave hostile act of trampling underfoot the national dignity and democratic national rights of Koreans in Japan and encroaching upon the sovereignty of the DPRK" (KCNA 1998, n.p.). The formulation was fundamentally unchanged nearly 20 years later as the KCNA emphasized in several articles how international groups condemned Japan's repression of Chongryon. It reported on support from sympathetic groups in, among others, Germany (KCNA 2014a), Brazil and India (KCNA 2014b), Kyrgyzstan (KCNA 2015a), Ethiopia (KCNA 2014c), and Pakistan and Bangladesh (KCNA 2015b). The aim is to create the impression that the international community supports Chongryon and North Korea's interests in Japan. It also serves to portray Japan, a perpetual enemy state for the DPRK, in a negative light, both of which are meant to enhance external security.

In addition to reporting on repression of Chongryon by the Japanese authorities, the KCNA portrays Chongryon and its events positively. This feeds back into domestic propaganda streams by showing that North Korea is seen as an attractive place by the Korean population in Japan. For example, in terms of events, the KCNA reported in September 2016 about a forum held in Osaka at the Korean Hall of Culture in which Chongryon officials gave speeches celebrating North Korean patriotism and commitment to Chongryon schools (KCNA 2016). The KCNA also highlights lectures about North Korea and Chongryon that the organization facilitates, such as one in 2006 in Tokyo marking the anniversary of Chongryon's founding (KCNA 2006). Another common type of article in this category are those that report on congratulatory messages from Chongryon organizations to the leader. For example, in 2013, KCNA (2013, n.p.) recounted how "Marshal Kim Jong Un received congratulatory messages and letters from organizations of the General Association of Korean Residents in Japan (Chongryon) on the 65th anniversary of the DPRK." It went on to list over 25 organizations that had sent messages to "wish Kim Jong Un good health for prosperity of the motherland and development of the movement of the Koreans in Japan." Articles like this are meant to portray the country's ruling system as respected among Koreans abroad, which is in turn meant to help legitimate it at home to enhance internal security.

Overall, the picture of Chongryon that emerges is of an organization well past its peak and seemingly heading for accelerated irrelevance in Japan. It still has an organizational and logistical role to play in North Korea's authoritarian image management, but as its declining membership in Japan and almost nonexistent appetite among its members to return to the DPRK both illustrate, its effectiveness has clear limits. However, it still has a function in the government's image management, as demonstrated by KCNA reports. Time will tell whether Chongryon's decline is ultimately terminal, but barring drastic changes to the political situation, the organization's slow adaptation, the limited appeal of its patron, and its hostile host environment all suggest that Chongryon will struggle to return to its glory days of the 1950s.

Friendship Groups and North Korea's Authoritarian Image Management

In contrast to the tightly organized, institutionalized, and geographically focused nature of Chongryon, a more diffuse network of North Korea sympathizers also exists around the world. Loosely styled after older Soviet versions of friendship associations, the Korea Friendship Association and various Juche Idea Study Groups support the DPRK and its perspectives abroad. The aim for the state is to show domestic and international audiences that North Korea has supporters around the world.

Getting foreigners to speak for North Korea has been a long-standing strategy. As Fahy (2019, 174) puts it, "North Korea operationalizes individuals from foreign nations" as part of its effort to project its desired image. Sometimes this effort consists of grim plans to hold foreigners in the country hostage while they are forced to issue laudatory statements about North Korea (Fahy 2019, 181–188). Another prong of this strategy, as discussed briefly earlier in this chapter, is to amplify the voices of sympathetic left-wing or self-styled anti-imperialist groups or to support the formation of such groups directly.

North Korea is not unique in being a communist-style regime that has friendship associations abroad. The Soviet Union pioneered this model in the 1920s by setting up variously named friendship societies in the West (David-Fox 2012, 38–40, 81–84; McNair 2015). The Union of Soviet Societies of Friendship and Cultural Relations with Foreign Countries and the related State Committee for Social Ties were meant to win new supporters abroad and showcase Soviet culture (Gould-Davies 2003, 205–206). China Friendship Societies have long been a feature of cultural exchange between China and foreign countries (Brady 2000, 953) and many remain active today.

During the 1960s and 1970s, North Korea was engaged in a diplomatic battle with South Korea for recognition, and earnestly reached out to many developing states for support (Young 2018, 367–368). As mentioned earlier, it cultivated ties with sympathetic left-wing groups and liberation movements (Fahy 2019, 177). A part of this effort was to set up friendship-type organizations to improve the image of the country among foreign publics. For example, the head of the Nigerian Committee for the Study of the Juche Idea recalls that the group was founded in the late 1970s (Byrne 2014). After an apparent lull in the 1990s as North Korea was preoccupied with the famine and its leadership transition, foreign friendship groups began to reappear in earnest from the early 2000s onward. The North Korean version of friendship societies go by various names: Juche Idea Study Groups, Society for the Study of Songun, and so on. While it appears that there is significant overlap in membership in these groups, the most prominent manifestation of this organizational complex today is the Korean Friendship Association (KFA). The KFA was founded in 2000 in Spain, and it runs the DPRK's external-facing website, http://www.korea-dpr.com/. According to its own explanation, the site has the "purpose of building international ties in the fields of culture, friendship, diplomacy and business between the Democratic People's Republic of Korea and other world nations." The KFA claims to have dozens of branches around the world.

The local groups themselves organize seminars, run websites and online forums, and maintain social media profiles. These efforts attempt to promote a positive image of the DPRK, correct perceived anti-North Korea bias in international media, and undermine what pro–North Korea groups see as American imperialism. For example, a summary of an October 2018 meeting in Belfast, Northern Ireland, reported on the website of the Korean Friendship Association Ireland, went as follows:

KFA Ireland held a successful meeting in Belfast, on Sunday October 28. Invited guest speaker was Dermot Hudson, Official Delegate of KFA UK. He gave an inspiring report back from his last visit to the Democratic People's Republic of Korea (DPRK), on the 70th anniversary of the foundation of the DPRK. Dr. Hudson also talked about the Down With Imperialism Union and the Workers' Party of Korea, both on the occasions for their anniversaries in October. Present at the meeting were KFA activists from different parts of Ireland, and many great discussions took place. (KFA Ireland 2018)

Photos from a similar meeting of KFA Ireland two years prior, this time in Dublin, indicate perhaps five or six audience members (KFA Ireland 2016).

These kinds of events, and the internet presence that captures them, has the appearance of a global spread. Appendix 3, gathered and updated as of November 2019, provides a snapshot of the web presence of KFA branches, Juche Idea Study Groups, and other fellow travelers such as the International Network for the Defence of Socialist Korea. There were likely many more, and more active, such groups during the Cold War, as communist solidarity had a readier audience and a more enabling international political environment. As noted previously, from the 1970s North Korea promoted Juche Idea Study Groups and other solidarity organizations. However, these groups are difficult to track systematically. Appendix 3 records all known groups that have been active in the post–Cold War era and which broadcast their activities online.

The data is imprecise and likely incomplete, but some patterns are still apparent. First, there is a high degree of overlap at the elite levels of the network. The same individuals routinely appear, particularly at KFA events. Twitter accounts regularly retweet or like one another's posts, which magnifies the content to a relatively tight network. This suggests that while the KFA network has the appearance of a global reach, the depth of its organization is questionable. Indeed, the founding personality behind the global KFA is a constant fixture. Alejandro Cao de Benós is a Spanish national who has been a long-time supporter of North Korea and is apparently recognized by the North Korean government. He founded the KFA in 2000 and since that time has overseen the proliferation of KFA branches. He is a strident defender of the DPRK and has appeared in several media outlets, documentaries, and pro-DPRK events. According to United Nations documents, he also acts as a financial go-between for North Korean firms (O'Carroll 2020), including apparently those selling drugs and weapons as the 2020 documentary

The Mole: Undercover in North Korea by Danish filmmaker Mads Brügger brought to light.

Second, the websites and social media accounts of these groups frequently link to or reproduce North Korean state media content directly. They sometimes feature their own content or perspectives, but often when they provide information about North Korea, it is reproduced or repurposed state propaganda, perhaps with an explanation or introduction. This means that the DPRK's external propaganda is amplified via multiple sources.

Third, there is some evidence of regional networking. For example, in November 2019, the Swedish Juche Study Group organized a European webinar to study Kim Jong Il's work "Socialism Is a Science" on the 25th anniversary of its publication. The virtual event featured contributions from Russia, Spain, Germany, Denmark, the United Kingdom, Ukraine, Italy, Germany, and Sweden, all extolling the wisdom of the piece and applying its lessons to today's context (Swedish Juche Study Group 2019). Likewise, pro-DPRK events in Ireland appear to frequently feature visitors from the United Kingdom and vice versa.

As to the effectiveness of these groups, it is unlikely that they are changing international discourse about North Korea in substantive ways. KFA members sometimes attend mainstream academic or policy conferences and distribute flyers and other materials containing their ideas, but it is not clear how effective this is. Elites from this network sometimes appear as commentators in mainstream Western media outlets, often introduced as supporters of North Korea. For example, in October 2017 the head of the United Kingdom's KFA, Dermot Hudson, appeared on the BBC television program *Daily Politics* to discuss North Korea (BBC 2017). Two years later, he explained the North Korean political concept of Juche to the *Associated Press* (Klug 2019). Cao de Benós sometimes gives commentary on North Korean issues, as when he spoke with *Channel 4 News* in June 2019 about the summitry between the United States and the DPRK (Channel 4 News 2019). There are also numerous profiles of him in Western media outlets. In general, however, the groups and their commentators appear to be seen by mainstream outlets as on the margins in terms of their credibility and are often presented as curiosities.

Domestically, the North Korean media reports regularly in positive terms about activities of sympathetic foreign groups. Perhaps for international audiences, reports about friendship groups and their pro-DPRK stances especially can be found during times when North Korea is facing international criticism, such as during tensions about missile launches or nuclear tests. However, the domestic legitimation functions of foreign supporter groups almost certainly outweigh their international functions in terms of image management. In domestic media, these reports are designed to show that foreigners take seriously the political ideologies of North Korea, revere the Kim family, and support North Korea's policies in the international sphere. Reporting of this sort is a routine feature of North Korean state media, and it helps to "create a sense of multiplicity and credibility by employing the perspective of international sources" (Fahy 2019, 202). The aim is to boost domestic legitimacy and thereby aid internal security.

Three brief recent examples give a flavor of this genre. A report on a regional solidarity meeting, similar to the Swedish webinar described earlier, discusses a Finnish event featuring "chiefs and delegates of organizations of friendship and solidarity with the Korean people in Europe" (KCNA 2019a, n.p.). In various speeches, the members "expressed the conviction that the Korean people who advance holding aloft the banner of Kimilsungism-Kimjongilism under the wise guidance of Supreme Leader Kim Jong Un would surely win a brilliant victory in socialist construction and national reunification" (KCNA 2019a, n.p.). Likewise, in an article titled "Seminars on Chairman Kim Jong Il's Exploits Held Abroad," the KCNA reported that "the representative of the German Branch of the Korean Friendship Association said that leader Kim Jong Il developed the Party, State and army on the basis of the Juche idea and laid the firm foundation for the building of a powerful socialist nation" (KCNA 2019b, n.p.). Finally, a report on a Korean art exhibition held in Bucharest, Romania, described how "on display at the venue of the exhibition were photos showing the revolutionary career and exploits of President Kim Il Sung and Chairman Kim Jong Il and the revolutionary activities of Supreme Leader Kim Jong Un" (KCNA 2019c, n.p.). The reporting on these kinds of events includes content from all over the world. The idea is to show a domestic audience that, in locations ranging from Venezuela to Nigeria to Syria to Nepal and everywhere in between, North Korea is looked to with respect and that its political model is worthy of adoration or perhaps even emulation.

KFA and related groups sometimes visit North Korea. When there, they are treated with more hospitality and attention than if they were visiting another country. In addition to having their activities reported in North Korean state media, the hospitality is likely designed to flatter them by making them feel important. A visual manifestation of this effort can be found on the

YouTube channel of *Koryo Media*, an apparently unofficial channel showing videos from North Korea's film production outfits.[17] Many of the videos are short and feature footage of foreign delegations, including friendship groups, arriving at Pyongyang airport and being greeted by guides and cameras. Footage of friendship groups arriving shows domestic audiences that the DPRK has friends abroad who wish to come visit North Korea, while simultaneously aiming to inflate the importance of the guests in their own minds so that they continue to support the DPRK.

North Korea continues to amplify the voices of its foreign friends as well as its steadfast diplomatic partners. Domestic media regularly feature reports of foreign persons praising North Korea's system and its leadership. North Korea sometimes succeeds in placing international supporters in front of mainstream foreign media audiences. In general, however, and leaving aside issues related to money laundering, smuggling, or other business ventures in which they may be involved, these groups appear to play more of a domestic legitimation function by showing the North Korean population that they are supported and respected abroad. Internationally, the network of North Korean supporters generally appears to be a fringe network not taken particularly seriously among most international audiences.

Conclusion: Slow Adaptation to Changing Circumstances

North Korea's authoritarian image management behavior is fundamentally defensive. If ever there was a well-developed desire to export the North Korean model, those dreams were dead by the 1990s. Gone too is active commitment to repatriating Chongryon Koreans to the DPRK. Instead, North Korea takes specific actions abroad designed mostly to serve its domestic legitimation efforts and achieve specific foreign policy goals to aid its internal and external security. Friendship association activities and Chongryon initiatives are reported back domestically to show that the country has supporters abroad. If the non-imperialist foreign gaze looks upon the DPRK positively, the logic seems to go, then North Koreans must be living under a government worthy of pride and loyalty.

---

[17] See https://www.youtube.com/channel/UCpn5wDAZkNflHb0zhop8T_g/featured (accessed September 2, 2020).

Clearly, it would have been easier for North Korea to present itself in a positive light abroad had Soviet communism not collapsed. The country would have had easier access to partners to help spread its messages and audiences to listen. Instead, North Korea has had to operate in a political environment with fewer natural supporters. If the global political environment were to turn and authoritarian powers like China or Russia were to embrace North Korea more emphatically, then this might improve the latter's ability to cultivate its image. Of course, North Korea has long been wary of relying too much on the support of these superpowers, so it is likely to continue its own strategy of authoritarian image management.

9

Conclusion

Looking Backward, Forward, and Inward

This book has argued that authoritarian states try to maintain a positive image abroad and to protect that image from reproach. They do so to enhance their internal and external regime security, or more colloquially, to make their world safe for dictatorship. To promote a positive image, they use tactics like externally facing propaganda and friendly relations with key opinion leaders. To protect that image, they try to expunge or distract from bad news about their states and attack—verbally or physically—the messengers of criticism about their regime. Authoritarian image management is a multidimensional concept reflecting the fact that authoritarian states use a suite of diverse tactics to control their image abroad. To describe and explain these efforts required a new concept and new ways of thinking about the relationships between constructs like soft power, public diplomacy, propaganda, public relations, transnational authoritarianism, and extraterritorial repression. The payoff is a new way to understand the external dimensions of authoritarian rule and its role in global politics. The argument was substantiated with an array of data, ranging from a database of extraterritorial repression to analysis of state media to PR contracts to fieldwork and interviews.

Rather than recapitulating the book's contributions here, I will leave it to readers to judge whether it has lived up to its aspirations. Instead, the remainder of this chapter will address three issues. First, it will complicate the models laid out in the book by considering temporal change, the proposed mechanisms in interaction with one another, and new opportunities afforded by technology. Second, it will consider the future of authoritarian image management. Third, it will ask what, if anything, democratic policymakers and publics should do.

Making the World Safe for Dictatorship, Alexander Dukalskis, Oxford University Press (2021). © Oxford University Press.
DOI: 10.1093/oso/9780197520130.003.0009

Dynamic Considerations: Complicating the Argument

The argument has been relatively simple: for security-seeking reasons, the leaders of authoritarian states care about how their political systems are viewed abroad, and they take steps to influence those perceptions. Four sets of mechanisms organize the image management efforts of authoritarian states. But as with all books, interesting avenues of inquiry had to be left unexplored due to space constraints. Here I suggest three considerations that might productively complicate the arguments put forward.

First is the issue of temporal change in tactics and patterns of authoritarian image management. Although my focus throughout this book has been mainly on the post–Cold War era, I sometimes invoked historical examples, such as the Soviet Union, Apartheid South Africa, and Maoist China, to illustrate my arguments. I also discussed some of North Korea's activities from the 1950s to the 1980s in more depth. These forays suggest an implicit point that should be made explicit: authoritarian image management is not only a post-1980s phenomenon. Historical analyses of how authoritarian states have sought to bolster their image could be an empirically rich way to build this concept. Historical perspective can tell us how states reacted to global contexts that looked different from the present or recent past, as well has how the effects of authoritarian image management have unfolded over time. Most of the cases examined in this book are truncated or "right censored" because the dictatorship in question survives, but historical analysis provides the advantage of temporal distance.

Attention to temporal dynamics can also give us clues about the future. Authoritarian regimes learn, adapt, and innovate (Hall and Ambrosio 2017; Morgenbesser 2020a). To be sure, sometimes they fail to learn the "correct" lessons that would entrench their power (Dukalskis and Raymond 2018), but in the aggregate, learning and diffusion can push authoritarian regimes toward greater sophistication (Morgenbesser 2020b). Paying attention to how authoritarian states innovate on the mechanisms described in this book and how their temporal and/or geographical diffusion unfolds could give clues to the future trajectory of authoritarian image management.

Second, this book has been relatively quiet on the role of technology. It did not categorize actions by their technological appearance; instead, it folded tactics into the mechanistic framework regardless of their technological mode. There is every reason to believe that authoritarian regimes will use new technologies available to them to bolster their image with the aim of enhancing their security. Just as dictatorships adapted to radio, television, and the internet, they will seize on artificial intelligence, virtual reality, digital currencies, "deep fake" video or audio methods, and other (and currently unforeseen) technologies to bolster their images, track dissidents, and try to make their world safe for dictatorship. They may not always be successful, and it may take time for them to learn to harness emerging technologies, but at minimum there is no reason to assume that emerging technologies are necessarily democratizing influences.

Social media is an instructive example (see, for example, Pearce and Kendzior 2012; Gunitsky 2015). In the early days, it seemed that platforms like Twitter and Facebook could link pro-democracy activists with each other and spread liberating information like never before. Indeed, social media did do some of those things, but authoritarian states and their supporters adapted. They used it to disseminate pro-regime propaganda, to track down and gather intelligence on dissidents, harass critics, sow distrust among activists, and distract public conversation. These tactics now appear with regularity in democracies, too. Aware of the importance of data, authoritarian states also created their own national versions of social networking sites, with servers held domestically, which gives them access to vast quantities of information about their citizens. How emerging and unforeseen technologies will influence authoritarian image management is unclear, but it is safe to assume that authoritarian states will attempt to use them wherever relevant to help them strive for internal and external security.

Third, the book elaborated four mechanisms of authoritarian image management and demonstrated their empirical validity, but it did not dwell on the interactions between the mechanisms. In general, the more multidimensional the authoritarian image management effort, the more successful it is likely to be, all else being equal. External propaganda alone is a weaker tactic than external propaganda combined with promoting friendly opinion leaders and minimizing criticism. Quantitative-minded scholars could index the strength of these tactics in combination and measure them against public opinion outcomes or policy changes to see if they have an additive or even multiplicative effect.

However, it is also worth considering that the four mechanisms may work at cross-purposes sometimes. Extraterritorial repression, if exposed, can undermine efforts at positive image building, or at least put more of a burden on it. The comments of supportive opinion leaders may sometimes contradict external propaganda. Regardless the fluid and dynamic nature of authoritarian image management means that the mechanisms bleed into one another and overlap in ways that the analytical model proffered here simplifies. There are advantages to simplification for theory-building as it allows processes to be seen more clearly, but adding complexity can reveal new insights as well. More detailed case studies of campaigns or foreign policy focal points could further illuminate dynamic interactions between the mechanisms.

How Safe Is the World for Dictatorship?

The question of how safe the world is for dictatorship can be answered in two ways. The first understanding is how safe the world is for the survival of authoritarianism. The answer to this question is unquestionably: very safe. There are debates about whether the world is becoming more autocratic or more democratic (see Lührmann and Lindberg 2019), but there are no serious defenders of the idea that democracy will decisively vanquish dictatorship. The organizing political principle of authoritarian rule is not going away. In the "internal security" sense, dictatorship writ large is safe, and authoritarian image management has contributed to that safety. Dictatorships will rise and fall, but dictatorship will remain, which means that authoritarian image management will also remain.

The second understanding queries how safe the world is for the expansion of dictatorship. As noted early in this book, there is no centralized authoritarian evangelist movement with traction that wishes to promote a specific brand of authoritarianism along the lines of the Comintern. However, there is a group of authoritarian states—with China and Russia the two most prominent in their own different ways—that wishes to undermine the liberal democratic model and to defend their own. If democracy does not look attractive as an alternative, then dictatorships like those in Beijing and Moscow can contend with a less potent ideological rival. Serious internal problems in the United States and divisions among European Union states help make the job of authoritarian image managers easier.

But probably the most important determinant of the foreseeable future of dictatorship will be the rise and intentions of China. Pre-reform China was ideologically expansive insofar as Mao posited China as a leader in the world communist revolution. Post-reform Chinese foreign policy has tended to tack more closely to Deng Xiaoping's advice that China should "bide its time, hide its brightness, not seek leadership, but do some things" (see Shambaugh 2013, 13–44), although Xi Jinping has taken a more aggressive tack. Analysis of China's "rise" or "development" indicates that Beijing understands that its international image and the ideas that underpin it require management at a global scale, given the size and scope of China's global activities (see Buzan 2014). Post-reform Chinese leaders have attempted to posit global concepts to characterize China's foreign policy orientations, such as Hu Jintao's "Harmonious World" and Xi's "Community of Shared Destiny for Mankind." While some may dismiss these formulations as window dressing, they are evidence that Beijing is thinking about its ideological concepts in global terms.

Needing to make its world safe for its own dictatorship necessitates undermining democracy and showcasing the successes of its own political model. The party's own internal documents, such as the well-known Document 9, verify that it sees liberal democracy as an existential threat (ChinaFile 2013). If China continues to be an economic success, it is only a matter of time before other states emulate it (see Gunitsky 2017). Indeed, there is already evidence of Beijing promoting "the China model" (see, e.g., Economy 2020), in part by promoting global norms friendly to its interests (e.g., Brazys and Dukalskis 2017; Rolland 2020). Barring an unforeseen collapse of the CCP, a rapid economic decline, and/or a war that it loses, it is likely that if China continues to rise on its current trajectory, then more countries will become more authoritarian. The open question then becomes whether Beijing will need to prop up the idea of dictatorship abroad with more than just authoritarian image management to make its own world safe for its own dictatorship. At the very least, China's authoritarian image management will continue to attempt to bolster the image of its authoritarianism which, along with some of its genuine successes and material power, will continue to make a potent force for the justification and perhaps even the expansion of dictatorship.

What Should Be Done?

Finally, I would like to offer some final remarks about what should be done about authoritarian image management. This book has aimed to be analytical and empirical, but clearly the subject matter raises normative and regulatory issues, not least because of the brutality of some extraterritorial repression and the human consequences of authoritarian rule. To the extent that policy recommendations flow from this book, these are it.

First, democracies should increase transparency about authoritarian image management. Initiatives like FARA in the United States or the European Union's Transparency Register are good starts. However, their filings are sometimes vague and are policed unevenly. Bolstering and expanding transparency laws pertaining to public relations and lobbying from foreign states could at least help us better understand the scope of authoritarian image management. Moves in the United States to make public the sources of funding to universities and think tanks could also help illuminate cases of authoritarian states and the supporters who are bolstering their image. The European Union's efforts to combat disinformation represents another intriguing model that combines a commitment to free expression with the need to understand and track speech that has the intent to undermine democracy. Efforts like this help researchers, journalists, and policymakers understand the scope and evolving tactics of authoritarian image management.

Second, states should improve the protections they offer to exiles from dictatorships who are critical of their home states. Obviously, this is a difficult and potentially resource-intensive undertaking for host states. However, it is worth it because exiled critics of authoritarian states are often powerful and knowledgeable voices for change. Better monitoring of threats and sensitization to the dangers that some exiles face could help reduce attacks. Improvement of Interpol's practices could reduce the ability of authoritarian states to target their exiled opponents with Red Notices (Cooley and Heathershaw 2017, 228–229; Lemon 2019). States should press dictatorships that attack or threaten exiles to stop and should consider nonviolent countermeasures where appropriate. Finding points of leverage may be challenging, particularly when the offending state is powerful, but if democracies work collectively, then they may be able to afford more protection for exiles. At the very least, they should not cooperate in extraterritorial repression.

Third, there needs to be more social awareness about the sources of authoritarian image management efforts in democracies. It should be known that journalists for *Xinhua* or RT, for example, are not editorially independent from their governments. In this sense, it is not accurate to equate these outlets with, for example, the BBC or NPR, the way that observers sometimes do. Independent public broadcasters like the BBC and NPR (the latter of which is mostly funded by non-government sources in any case) can report critically on their governments and present editorially independent news, whereas state-controlled media from authoritarian capitals generally have more of a propaganda mission. Labeling of these entities as affiliated with the relevant government, a step that YouTube and Twitter have taken, is a reasonable measure. However, the issue is muddied by the fact that public broadcasters in democracies are sometimes also labeled as such in these systems, even if they are legally and/or editorially independent of their governments. The YouTube distinction between "RT is funded in whole or in part by the Russian government" and "NPR is an American public broadcast service" is one that is probably lost on many viewers. However, it is a start, and the general point is that more awareness and media literacy can help readers and viewers filter information in more informed ways.

Fourth and finally, on a deeper level, democratic leaders need to stand up for the values of democracy. This book has been about authoritarian image management, but as of this writing, it seems that democracy's image is lacking. Doubts about the performance and leadership of some leading democracies degrade the image of democracy and help contribute to the sense that authoritarian practices are tolerable if they deliver prosperity or stability. Authoritarian practices by democratically elected leaders undermine the image and reality of democracy. Attacking or insulting the free press, denigrating minorities, glorifying repression, engaging in kleptocratic behavior, questioning without evidence the integrity of election results that do not go your way, and supporting nepotism all serve to relativize the offenses of authoritarian leaders. These actions do the job of authoritarian image managers for them. In a discouraging spiral, democratic shortcomings make the job of authoritarian image managers easier, which in turn may erode faith in democracy. Citizens of democracies should demand the best from their governments for a host of important reasons, a side effect of which is to make it harder to market authoritarianism. Democratically elected leaders should take seriously their responsibility to defend and safeguard the values of liberal democracy.

PR and Lobbying by Authoritarian States in the United States, 2018–2019

Foreign Principal	Country	Annual Contract Value (USD)	Date	Activities	Link
Embassy of Afghanistan	Afghanistan	420,000	2019	Lobbying	https://efile.fara.gov/docs/2244-Exhibit-AB-20190313-84.pdf
Transformation & Continuity	Afghanistan	1,200,000	2015 (ongoing)	PR, outreach to politicians and NGOs, media work	https://efile.fara.gov/docs/6065-Exhibit-AB-20140703-5.pdf
Islamic Republic of Afghanistan	Afghanistan	hourly	2018	Lobbying	https://efile.fara.gov/docs/2244-Exhibit-AB-20180926-83.pdf
Embassy of Afghanistan	Afghanistan	unspecified	2018	Lobbying	https://efile.fara.gov/docs/3712-Exhibit-AB-20180920-30.pdf
People's Democratic Republic of Algeria	Algeria	360,000	2018	Lobbying, "mobilize non-governmental organizational, public and media support for Algeria"; "enhance the image of Algeria in the United States of America"	https://efile.fara.gov/docs/6608-Exhibit-AB-20181106-1.pdf
Republic of Angola	Angola	4,100,000	2019	Technical services, lobbying, "enhance Angola's profile in the United States"	https://efile.fara.gov/2165-Exhibit-AB-20190625-73.pdf
Embassy of the Republic of Azerbaijan	Azerbaijan	180,000	2019	Lobbying, strategic guidance	https://efile.fara.gov/docs/6535-Exhibit-AB-20190429-4.pdf
Embassy of the Republic of Azerbaijan	Azerbaijan	240,000	2018	Lobbying, strategic guidance	https://efile.fara.gov/docs/6535-Exhibit-AB-20180305-1.pdf

(continued)

Foreign Principal	Country	Annual Contract Value (USD)	Date	Activities	Link
Embassy of the Republic of Azerbaijan	Azerbaijan	350,000	2018	Lobbying, consulting	https://efile.fara.gov/docs/6415-Exhibit-AB-20180424-10.pdf
Economic Development Board of the Kingdom of Bahrain	Bahrain	264,000	2019	Public relations	https://efile.fara.gov/docs/6582-Exhibit-AB-20191016-5.pdf
Embassy of the Kingdom of Bahrain	Bahrain	500,000	2018	Arranging meetings	https://efile.fara.gov/docs/6399-Exhibit-AB-20180227-16.pdf
Embassy of the Kingdom of Bahrain	Bahrain	780,000	2018	Strategic counsel, "assist in communicating priority issues regarding US-Bahrain relations to relevant U.S. audiences, including Congress, the executive branch, media and policy community. Registrant will also provide public relations assistance"	https://efile.fara.gov/docs/5430-Exhibit-AB-20180612-66.pdf
Concern Belneftekhim	Belarus	60,000	2019	Lobbying	https://efile.fara.gov/docs/6706-Exhibit-AB-20191101-2.pdf
Republic of Burundi	Burundi	unspecified	2015	Research and advice, "assist in communicating priority issues in the United States-Burundi bilateral relationship to relevant US audiences"	https://efile.fara.gov/docs/6305-Exhibit-AB-20150720-1.pdf
Kingdom of Cambodia	Cambodia	500,000	2019	Facilitating visits, lobbying, "arranging for visits by Cambodian officials to the US and visits by US officials to Cambodia to promote cultural exchanges and improved relations"	https://efile.fara.gov/docs/6655-Exhibit-AB-20190403-1.pdf

Principal	Country	Amount	Year	Description	URL
Royal Government of the Kingdom of Cambodia	Cambodia	720,000	2019	Lobbying, advice	https://efile.fara.gov/docs/5870-Exhibit-AB-20190410-14.pdf
Government of the Republic of Cameroon	Cameroon	400,000	2018	Unspecified	https://efile.fara.gov/docs/2165-Exhibit-AB-20180711-72.pdf
Republic of Cameroon	Cameroon	660,000	2019	"[P]romoting positive and favorable image"; "placing targeted opeds in conservative-oriented outlets in order to foster a robust and growing partnership narrative into the future"; "lay the foundation for longer term narrative growth in the United States"	https://efile.fara.gov/docs/6700-Exhibit-AB-20190722-2.pdf
US–China Transpacific Foundation	China	120,000	2019	Arrange travel for US Congressional members and staff to China	https://efile.fara.gov/docs/6328-Exhibit-AB-20190320-10.pdf
China–US Exchange Foundation	China	156,000	2018	Facilitate exchanges, arrange meetings with politicians	https://efile.fara.gov/docs/6584-Exhibit-AB-20180831-7.pdf
China–US Exchange Foundation	China	168,000	2019	Enable African American audiences to better understand China	https://efile.fara.gov/docs/6584-Exhibit-AB-20190201-9.pdf
China–US Exchange Foundation	China	180,000	2019	Lobbying, arranging meetings, strategic advice	https://efile.fara.gov/docs/6328-Exhibit-AB-20190115-8.pdf
Embassy of the PRC	China	288,000	2017	Public relations, training, crisis management	https://efile.fara.gov/docs/5875-Exhibit-AB-20170629-51.pdf
China–US Exchange Foundation	China	356,400	2017	Public relations, visits to China, maintenance of ChinaUSFocus.com	https://efile.fara.gov/docs/5875-Exhibit-AB-20170921-53.pdf
China–US Exchange Foundation	China	400,000	2019	Lobbying, government affairs	https://efile.fara.gov/docs/5430-Exhibit-AB-20190301-72.pdf
Embassy of the PRC	China	660,000	2019	Lobbying	https://efile.fara.gov/docs/2165-Exhibit-AB-20190828-74.pdf
China Daily Distribution Corporation	China	10,000,000	2019	Printing and distribution of China Daily	https://efile.fara.gov/docs/3457-Supplemental-Statement-20191115-31.pdf

(continued)

Foreign Principal	Country	Annual Contract Value (USD)	Date	Activities	Link
CGTN/CCTV	China	19,597,494	2019	Run CGTN America	https://efile.fara.gov/docs/6633-Registration-Statement-20190802-2.pdf
Charhar Institute	China	unspecified	2018	"[F]acilitate dialogues, negotiations and visits amongst public & government officials, think tanks, scholars and businessmen etc for trade and other bilateral disputes solving & consensus building between US and China"	https://efile.fara.gov/docs/6611-Exhibit-AB-20181203-1.pdf
Republic of Congo	Congo Brazzaville	2,000,000	2018	Lobbying, PR	https://efile.fara.gov/docs/6200-Exhibit-AB-20180724-7.pdf
Embassy of the Republic of Congo	Congo Brazzaville	96,0000	2017	Consulting, PR	https://efile.fara.gov/docs/6327-Exhibit-AB-20170508-2.pdf
Government of the Republic of Côte d'Ivoire	Côte d'Ivoire	unspecified	2019	Lobbying	https://efile.fara.gov/docs/5666-Exhibit-AB-20190905-51.pdf
Ambassador Serge Mombouli	DR Congo	36,000	2018	Speechwriting, consulting	https://efile.fara.gov/docs/6606-Exhibit-AB-20181105-1.pdf
DR Congo	DR Congo	1,250,000	2018	Lobbying, briefings of policymakers	https://efile.fara.gov/docs/6399-Exhibit-AB-20180717-22.pdf
Presidency of DRC	DR Congo	unspecified	2019	Strategic advice, outreach, etc.	https://efile.fara.gov/docs/6632-Exhibit-AB-20190128-1.pdf
Embassy of DR Congo	DR Congo	unspecified	2019	Lobbying	https://efile.fara.gov/docs/6649-Exhibit-AB-20190315-1.pdf
Office of the President Felix Tshisekedi of the Democratic Republic of Congo	DR Congo	90,000	2019	Consulting, PR for the president elect	https://efile.fara.gov/docs/6446-Exhibit-AB-20190123-7.pdf

Client	Country	Amount	Year	Services	Source
Egyptian Ministry of Investment & International Cooperation	Egypt	246,000	2017	Branding, PR	https://efile.fara.gov/docs/3301-Exhibit-AB-20171024-31.pdf
Republic of Equatorial Guinea	Equatorial Guinea	450,000	2018	PR, lobbying	https://efile.fara.gov/docs/5483-Exhibit-AB-20180706-45.pdf
Ministry of Justice	Kazakhstan	100,000	2019	Lobbying	https://efile.fara.gov/docs/6768-Exhibit-AB-20191212-2.pdf
Embassy of the Republic of Kazakhstan	Kazakhstan	140,000	2019	Public relations, social media advice	https://efile.fara.gov/docs/6064-Exhibit-AB-20190603-22.pdf
Ministry of Culture & Sports	Kazakhstan	360,000	2019	Arrange meetings w/ film and media executives	https://efile.fara.gov/docs/6540-Exhibit-AB-20190402-4.pdf
Embassy of the Republic of Kazakhstan	Kazakhstan	140,000	2018	Public relations, social media advice	https://efile.fara.gov/docs/6064-Exhibit-AB-20180606-14.pdf
Ministry of Justice	Kazakhstan	600,000	2019	Lobbying	https://efile.fara.gov/docs/6774-Exhibit-AB-20191220-1.pdf
Ministry of Justice	Kazakhstan	unspecified	2019	Strategic consulting	https://efile.fara.gov/docs/6628-Exhibit-AB-20190906-2.pdf
Ministry of Justice	Kazakhstan	2,000,000	2018	"Advice and counsel related to foreign relations issues, as well as educating the government and opinion leaders regarding the same"	https://efile.fara.gov/docs/5712-Exhibit-AB-20180523-36.pdf
Government of National Accord	Libya	1,500,000	2019	Lobbying; "the Registrant will highlight the Government of National Accord (GNA)'s contributions to combating terrorism; counsel GNA regarding outreach to U.S. and foreign think tanks; and prepare reports on Haffar's human rights violations and crimes against the Libyan people"	https://efile.fara.gov/docs/6728-Exhibit-AB-20190926-2.pdf

(continued)

Foreign Principal	Country	Annual Contract Value (USD)	Date	Activities	Link
Government of National Accord	Libya	1,800,000	2019	Lobbying, public relations	https://efile.fara.gov/docs/6170-Exhibit-AB-20190426-66.pdf
Libyan National Army	Libya	2,000,000	2019	Lobbying, "general public relations"	https://efile.fara.gov/docs/6682-Exhibit-AB-20190519-1.pdf
Ministry of Foreign Affairs	Morocco	240,000	2019	Lobbying, public relations	https://efile.fara.gov/docs/6723-Exhibit-AB-20190906-1.pdf
Ministry of Foreign Affairs	Morocco	240,000	2018	Lobbying, public relations	https://efile.fara.gov/docs/6497-Exhibit-AB-20180129-2.pdf
Embassy of Morocco	Morocco	480,000	2018	Outreach, PR, promote Morocco as golf/film destination	https://efile.fara.gov/docs/6540-Exhibit-AB-20180413-1.pdf
Ministry of Foreign Affairs	Morocco	900,000	2018	Lobbying, public relations	https://efile.fara.gov/docs/6505-Exhibit-AB-20180111-1.pdf
Embassy of Qatar	Qatar	15,000	2019	Promote Qatar to US cities and states, arrange delegations	https://efile.fara.gov/docs/6540-Exhibit-AB-20190122-2.pdf
Government Communications Office	Qatar	100,000	2018	Consulting, communications	https://efile.fara.gov/docs/6064-Exhibit-AB-20181031-17.pdf
Government Communications Office	Qatar	30,000	2019	Facilitate business contacts	https://efile.fara.gov/docs/6674-Exhibit-AB-20190508-1.pdf
Embassy of Qatar	Qatar	35,000	2019	Manage Qatar Harvey Fund	https://efile.fara.gov/docs/6777-Exhibit-AB-20191230-1.pdf
State of Qatar - Government Communications Office	Qatar	240,000	2019	Public relations	https://efile.fara.gov/docs/6064-Exhibit-AB-20191011-24.pdf
Embassy of Qatar	Qatar	300,000	2018	Lobbying	https://efile.fara.gov/docs/6517-Exhibit-AB-20180202-1.pdf
Embassy of State of Qatar	Qatar	360,000	2019	Research, advice, and engagement with NGO and academic audiences	https://efile.fara.gov/docs/6170-Exhibit-AB-20191210-72.pdf

Client	Country	Amount	Year	Activities	URL
Embassy of Qatar	Qatar	480,000	2019	Promote Qatar to US cities and states, arrange delegations	https://efile.fara.gov/docs/6540-Exhibit-AB-20190326-3.pdf
Embassy of Qatar	Qatar	600,000	2019	Lobbying, public relations	https://efile.fara.gov/docs/6723-Exhibit-AB-20190906-2.pdf
Embassy of Qatar	Qatar	600,000	2019	Lobbying, public relations	https://efile.fara.gov/docs/6627-Exhibit-AB-20190109-1.pdf
Embassy of State of Qatar	Qatar	1,380,000	2019	Lobbying, strategic guidance	https://efile.fara.gov/docs/6415-Exhibit-AB-20190723-16.pdf
State of Qatar	Qatar	2,760,000	2019	Lobbying, arranging meetings with business leaders	https://efile.fara.gov/docs/5928-Exhibit-AB-20190924-44.pdf
State of Qatar	Qatar	hourly	2018	"[E]ngage officials of the United States government with respect to the State of Qatar's dispute with the Kingdom of Saudi Arabia, the United Arab Emirates, Egypt and Bahrain, and in particular to advance legal and factual arguments in support of the State of Qatar's position in that dispute"	https://efile.fara.gov/docs/6560-Exhibit-AB-20180531-1.pdf
International Centre for Legal Protection	Russia	750,000	2019	Lobbying, public relations about sanctions	https://efile.fara.gov/docs/6713-Exhibit-AB-20190830-1.pdf
State Development Corporation	Russia	750,000	2019	Lobbying, public relations	https://efile.fara.gov/docs/6740-Exhibit-AB-20191009-1.pdf
RIA Global LLC	Russia	9,450,240	2019	Produce radio shows, web content, and news copy, including Sputnik	https://efile.fara.gov/docs/6524-Exhibit-AB-20190314-3.pdf
RIA Global LLC	Russia	9,436,900	2017	Produce radio shows, web content, and news copy, including Sputnik	https://efile.fara.gov/docs/6524-Exhibit-AB-20180216-2.pdf

(continued)

Foreign Principal	Country	Annual Contract Value (USD)	Date	Activities	Link
T&R Productions LLC	Russia	23,395,522	2019	Run RT	https://efile.fara.gov/docs/6485-Amendment-20190211-2.pdf
Rwanda Development Board	Rwanda	80,000	2018	Publicity for Rwanda: The Royal Tour	https://efile.fara.gov/docs/6170-Exhibit-AB-20180515-43.pdf
Royal Embassy of Saudi Arabia	Saudi Arabia	120,000	2019	Public relations	https://efile.fara.gov/docs/6761-Exhibit-AB-20191203-1.pdf
Royal Embassy of Saudi Arabia	Saudi Arabia	120,000	2019	Media outreach and engagement in Colorado	https://efile.fara.gov/docs/6760-Exhibit-AB-20191202-1.pdf
Muslim World League	Saudi Arabia	135,000	2018	Organize conference, arrange meeting with policymaker, promote image of Islam	https://efile.fara.gov/docs/6457-Exhibit-AB-20181012-5.pdf
Muslim World League	Saudi Arabia	38,000	2018	Consulting services, conference promotion.	https://efile.fara.gov/docs/6426-Exhibit-AB-20181229-4.pdf
Embassy of Saudi Arabia	Saudi Arabia	600,000	2018	Lobbying, government relations	https://efile.fara.gov/docs/6391-Exhibit-AB-20180820-5.pdf
Public Investment Fund	Saudi Arabia	1,440,000	2019	"[O]utreach and relationship-building to various stakeholders in business and the media"	https://efile.fara.gov/docs/6162-Exhibit-AB-20190225-3.pdf
Royal Embassy of Saudi Arabia	Saudi Arabia	1,518,000	2019	"[M]edia outreach and engagement efforts across select media markets throughout the U.S."; "inform the public, government officials and the media about the importance of fostering and promoting strong relations between the United States and the Kingdom of Saudi Arabia"	https://efile.fara.gov/docs/6749-Exhibit-AB-20191112-1.pdf
Ministry of Economy and Planning	Saudi Arabia	1,999,733	2017	Strategic consulting, communications	https://efile.fara.gov/docs/3301-Exhibit-AB-20180105-32.pdf
General Sports Authority	Saudi Arabia	264,000	2018	Consulting, lobbying, "attend quarterly events"	https://efile.fara.gov/docs/6519-Exhibit-AB-20180202-1.pdf
NEOM Company (government owned)	Saudi Arabia	2,100,000	2019	Strategic advice, narrative and messaging	https://efile.fara.gov/docs/6698-Exhibit-AB-20190708-1.pdf

Organization	Country	Amount	Year	Services	URL
Royal Embassy of Saudi Arabia	Saudi Arabia	2,100,000	2019	Lobbying	https://efile.fara.gov/docs/2244-Exhibit-AB-20191017-89.pdf
Royal Embassy of Saudi Arabia	Saudi Arabia	5,964,000	2019	Public relations, content development, event planning, research	https://efile.fara.gov/docs/5483-Exhibit-AB-20191030-69.pdf
Royal Embassy of Saudi Arabia	Saudi Arabia	5,151,500	2018	Public relations services, event planning	https://efile.fara.gov/docs/5483-Exhibit-AB-20190423-64.pdf
Government of the Republic of Singapore	Singapore	216,000	2018	"[S]trategic counsel, message and materials development, and media and public outreach support"	https://efile.fara.gov/docs/5867-Exhibit-AB-20180309-39.pdf
Singapore IMDA	Singapore	11,300	2019	"[S]trategic media counsel and recommendations"; media outreach and engagement	https://efile.fara.gov/docs/6064-Exhibit-AB-20190220-18.pdf
Government Technology Agency	Singapore	13,500	2018	"[T]o pitch and secure two phone interviews with principals in US on 18th Nov."	https://efile.fara.gov/docs/6227-Exhibit-AB-20181203-15.pdf
Singapore Economic Development Board	Singapore	1,481,763	2018	Marketing and communications	https://efile.fara.gov/docs/6387-Exhibit-AB-20170920-2.pdf
Federal Government of Somalia	Somalia	0	2019	Lobbying	https://efile.fara.gov/docs/6757-Exhibit-AB-20191127-1.pdf
Ministry of Finance	Somalia	420,000	2018	Lobbying, PR, improve relations between US and Somalia	https://efile.fara.gov/docs/5430-Exhibit-AB-20180501-65.pdf
Federal Government of Somalia	Somalia	1,200,000	2018	Lobbying	https://efile.fara.gov/docs/6399-Exhibit-AB-20180810-23.pdf
Transitional Council of Sudan	Sudan	6,000,000	2019	Lobbying, PR	https://efile.fara.gov/docs/6200-Exhibit-AB-20190617-8.pdf

(continued)

Foreign Principal	Country	Annual Contract Value (USD)	Date	Activities	Link
Embassy of Thailand, Office of Commercial Affairs	Thailand	16,500	2019	Lobbying	https://efile.fara.gov/docs/6699-Exhibit-AB-20190709-1.pdf
Embassy of Thailand, Office of Commercial Affairs	Thailand	hourly	2018	Consulting, lobbying.	https://efile.fara.gov/docs/3492-Exhibit-AB-20180718-53.pdf
Direct Media Sarl	Togo	hourly	2019	PR	https://efile.fara.gov/docs/6671-Exhibit-AB-20190507-1.pdf
Republic of Turkey	Turkey	270,000	2019	Lobbying	https://efile.fara.gov/docs/5931-Exhibit-AB-20190119-10.pdf
Republic of Turkey	Turkey	432,000	2019	Lobbying	https://efile.fara.gov/docs/6328-Exhibit-AB-20190212-9.pdf
Republic of Turkey	Turkey	1,700,000	2018	Consulting, lobbying	https://efile.fara.gov/docs/5712-Exhibit-AB-20180302-34.pdf
Embassy of Turkey	Turkey	866,666	2018/2019	PR; "public relations services, including strategic media outreach, influencer engagement, social media counsel, Consular support and grassroots engagement, and media monitoring"	https://efile.fara.gov/docs/6170-Exhibit-AB-20180504-41.pdf
Embassy of the United Arab Emirates	United Arab Emirates	80,000	2019	"[C]onduct targeted qualitative research (in-person focus groups) and nationwide quantitative research (online community discussions) regarding public attitudes"	https://efile.fara.gov/docs/5666-Exhibit-AB-20190730-50.pdf
Permanent Mission of the UAE to the UN	United Arab Emirates	400,000	2019	Strategic and communications counsel	https://efile.fara.gov/docs/5666-Exhibit-AB-20191121-54.pdf

Foreign Principal	Country	Amount	Year	Services	URL
United Arab Emirates	United Arab Emirates	540,000	2019	Strategic consulting, lobbying on defense matters	https://efile.fara.gov/docs/6567-Exhibit-AB-20190703-2.pdf
Embassy of the United Arab Emirates	United Arab Emirates	5,000,000	2018/2019	Strategic consulting, public opinion research, communications	https://efile.fara.gov/docs/5478-Exhibit-AB-20171222-28.pdf
Embassy of the UAE	United Arab Emirates	600,000	2018	Develop messages, talking points, strategic advice	https://efile.fara.gov/docs/6596-Exhibit-AB-20180927-1.pdf
Government of Ras Al Khaimah	United Arab Emirates	1,008,000	2019	PR, content creation, messaging	https://efile.fara.gov/docs/6227-Exhibit-AB-20190612-17.pdf
Expo 2020 Dubai	United Arab Emirates	1,044,000	2019	Public relations, "pitching international media and liaising with key stakeholders, including U.S. think tanks with an interest and research focus on the UAE and Middle Eastern affairs generally"	https://efile.fara.gov/docs/6530-Exhibit-AB-20190426-7.pdf
Embassy of the United Arab Emirates	United Arab Emirates	hourly	2019	Lobbying	https://efile.fara.gov/docs/6673-Exhibit-AB-20190429-1.pdf
Agency for Information and Mass Communication under the President of the Republic of Uzbekistan	Uzbekistan	10,000	2019	Invite Western journalists to Tashkent for 3-day press tour; "handle all communications with the media representatives, including ensuring that the journalists publish supportive and on-message articles following the trip"	https://efile.fara.gov/docs/6753-Exhibit-AB-20191120-1.pdf
Embassy of the Bolivarian Republic of Venezuela	Venezuela	0	2019	Lobbying, PR	https://efile.fara.gov/docs/5430-Exhibit-AB-20190417-75.pdf
Embassy of the Republic of Yemen	Yemen	720,000	2019	Public relations	https://efile.fara.gov/docs/5483-Exhibit-AB-20190408-63.pdf
Republic of Zimbabwe	Zimbabwe	1,080,000	2019	Consulting, PR	https://efile.fara.gov/docs/6446-Exhibit-AB-20190409-8.pdf
Minister of Foreign Affairs of the Republic of Zimbabwe	Zimbabwe	500,000	2019	Consulting	https://efile.fara.gov/docs/6415-Exhibit-AB-20190301-15.pdf

Authoritarian Actions Abroad Database (AAAD)—Codebook, Version 5 (September 2020)

Scope and Background

This database contains publicly available information regarding attempts by authoritarian states to repress exiles abroad from 1991 through 2019. This database contains information about cases in which authoritarian leaders try to silence their critics abroad. The database was inspired in part by the Exeter Central Asian Political Exiles Database (CAPE) (Heathershaw and Furstenberg 2020) as well as related work on political exiles featured in Cooley and Heathershaw (2017, 187–219) and the conceptual work found in Glasius (2018). This project differs from CAPE insofar as it moves beyond Central Asia to cast a global net and uses some different categories and definitions for each case.

Using strategic search terms and multiple sources, the events recorded in this database represent cases in which individuals, and sometimes groups, were targeted while abroad by their home state in some capacity. The countries included in the database are based on those defined as authoritarian in the Geddes, Wright, and Frantz (2014) "authoritarian spells" typology after 1991 and for the relevant years. Some adjustments were made for states that had become authoritarian after the GWF coding finished (e.g., Thailand in 2014; Turkey in 2014) or for cases omitted from the GWF data for other reasons, such as population size. Other regime data-gathering efforts were used as guidance in these cases (e.g., Wahman et al. 2013). Because authoritarian actions abroad of the sort tracked are usually secretive by nature, it is likely that for each case recorded there are many more that will never be publicly reported or verified.

The data are freely available here: https://alexdukalskis.wordpress.com/data. If you choose to use it, please credit it by citing this book (Alexander Dukalskis, *Making the World Safe for Dictatorship*, New York: Oxford University Press, 2021).

Search Process

Searching was done using a four-stage process.

First, where similar databases existed, their content was used. Most prominently, the CAPE database was drawn upon to categorize cases from Central Asian states, but other databases, such as the Front Line Defenders (2019) database and the Xinjiang Victims Database (2019), were also used given that researchers had already gathered the information and made it public.

Second, Google News and Google search terms were utilized to identify a population of news articles that contain information about the actions of authoritarian leaders against exiles abroad. A complete list of search terms can be found in in the "search procedure" section. For each search term, the first 10–20 Google pages were examined, and a population of relevant articles were gathered and then re-examined for data extraction. The search terms were designed to cast a wide net and therefore required readers to determine the relevance of each article.

Third, given the possibility of recency bias in Google News search terms, Lexis Advance UK was mined, with a focus on earlier years in the dataset, using similar search terms as those from the Google News and Google search procedures.

Fourth, after steps 1–3 were completed in English, searches were completed in Chinese, French, Arabic, Korean, Turkish, and Russian to find new cases and to re-evaluate cases for which more detail was available in non-English media.

Sourcing Criteria

Information from credible NGOs, international watchdog groups, and credible journalistic sources were sought. Where news articles were found, attempts to corroborate each incident were made. Often, multiple news sources report on the same event. Ultimately, if corroborated, the incident was included in the database. If the report was uncorroborated but the source is a credible organization, then the source was included in the database. Authoritarian actions abroad are often inherently secretive—indeed, they are usually designed as such—and so in cases where responsibility was not always clear, the coding team discussed the case and used its best judgment to determine whether the case should be included or excluded. The database was cross-checked and validated by the coding team to ensure inter-coder reliability.

List of Countries

Afghanistan 1992–
Algeria, 1992–
Angola, 1991–
Armenia, 1994–
Azerbaijan, 1991–
Belarus, 1991–
Burkina Faso, 1991–
Burundi, 1991–1993; 1996–2005
Cambodia, 1991–
Cameroon, 1991–
Central African Republic, 2003–
Chad, 1991–
China, 1991–
Congo–Brazzaville, 1997–
Congo, DRC, 1997–
Cuba, 1991–
Djibouti, 1991–
Egypt, 1991–
El Salvador, 1991–1994
Eritrea, 1993–
Ethiopia, 1991–2018

Gabon, 1991–
Gambia, 1991–
Georgia, 1991–2003
Ghana, 1991–1992
Guatemala, 1991–1995
Guinea, 1991–2010
Haiti, 1991–1994, 1999–2006
Indonesia, 1991–1999
Iran, 1991–
Iraq, 1991–2003
Ivory Coast, 1991–
Jordan, 1991–
Kazakhstan, 1991–
Kenya, 1991–2002
Kuwait, 1991
Kyrgyzstan, 1991–2010
Laos, 1991–
Lebanon, 1991–2005
Lesotho, 1991–1993
Liberia, 1991–2003
Libya, 1991–
Madagascar, 1991–
Malawi, 1991–1994
Malaysia, 1991–2018
Mauritania, 1991–
Mexico, 1991–2000
Mongolia, 1991–1993
Morocco, 1991–
Mozambique, 1991–
Myanmar, 1991–
Namibia, 1991–
Nepal, 2002–2006
Niger, 1996–1999
Nigeria, 1991–1999
North Korea, 1991–
Oman, 1991–
Pakistan, 1999–2008
Peru, 1992–2002
Qatar, 1991–
Russia, 1993–
Rwanda, 1991–
Saudi Arabia, 1991–
Senegal, 1991–2000
Serbia, 1992–2000
Sierra Leone, 1991–1998
Singapore, 1991–
Somalia, 1991–
South Africa, 1991–1994
Sri Lanka, 1991–1994
Sudan, 1991–

Swaziland, 1991–
Syria, 1991–
Tajikistan, 1991–
Tanzania, 1991–
Thailand, 2006–2007, 2014–
Togo, 1991–
Tunisia, 1991–2011
Turkey, 2014–
Turkmenistan, 1991–
UAE, 1991–
Uganda, 1991–
Uzbekistan, 1991–
Venezuela, 2005–
Vietnam, 1991–
Yemen, 1991–
Zambia, 1996–
Zimbabwe, 1991–

Coding Notes and Definitions

Column Name	Definition
ID	Placeholder for # of cases
Country	The source country of the action
Target Country	The country in which the incident occurred
Action	Type of action conducted by the source country. In some cases, attempts at repression are recorded. These cases contain an underscore and "attempt" to denote their distinction. For example, an assassination attempt is denoted by "assassination_attempt." In all cases the coding team made its best determination about the motivations for the action given available evidence.

Types of actions:

Threatened: Denotes an individual reporting being personally threatened by agents of their home state. Threats by online "trolls" were generally excluded because they are so ubiquitous and difficult to verify.

Family Threatened: Denotes an individual's family being coerced in the home state to target the exiled individual.

Arrested/detained: Denotes individuals who are arrested or detained in a foreign state on behalf of their state or are formally arrested or detained in foreign state by officials from the home state.

Column Name	Definition
	Attacked: Denotes an individual who was physically assaulted by the host state or its proxies while abroad.
	Extradited: Denotes individuals who were formally extradited to their home state while living in a foreign state or where there was an attempt to do so (denoted by "_attempt").
	Abducted: Denotes an individual who was kidnapped or where there was an attempt (denoted by "_attempt"), likely with the intent to extradite her/him back effectively informally to the home state.
	Assassinated: Denotes an individual who was killed or where there was an assassination attempt (denoted by "_attempt").
Target	Individuals or groups being targeted by their home state.
	Targets were disaggregated into the following categories:
	Journalist. Denotes an individual active in the media sector.
	Activist. Denotes an individual or group that criticizes the government and/or opposes it nonviolently.
	Opposition. Denotes a member of a political party opposed to the government. Where the opposition member is also former government official, the designation is made based on which category the individual is better known for.
	Former government official. Denotes someone who was a member of the regime and defected, or who was a member of the previous regime and is being targeted by the current regime. If members of the previous regime were arrested or extradited for violence or major human rights abuses associated with the previous regime, they are not included.
	Citizen. Denotes people who were not especially politically active abroad but who because of some aspect of their identity were seen as threatening to the source state's image.
Target_name	Name of target, if available.
Year	The year in which the incident occurred.
Month	When available, the month in which the incident occurred.
Persons_involved	In many cases, countries target groups involved in opposition or dissent. Where possible, these groups were separated into independent cases. However, some sources provide only generic information, so some cases involve more than one individual.
Source	Links that correspond with evidence that each event occurred. Where several links were available, one was chosen.

Detailed Search Procedures for Steps 2 and 3

To isolate specific cases in which authoritarian states target their own citizens abroad, use the following search terms and replace COUNTRY or NAME with the country in question or the leader's name (1991–2019).

Often variations of the verb render the same results, but sometimes a new case emerges. Omit additional verb-tense searches when necessary (i.e., if it is a smaller country and there are not many news articles, then just search one tense of the verb, but try a few before making this decision).

For larger countries, browse the first 10–20 pages of the Google search (if available). For smaller countries, browse through the first 5 pages, but if many results are found, then continue to 10–15 pages.

Gather all seemingly relevant articles first by browsing the headlines and key points. Once a country is completed, carefully read each relevant article again for potential data points.

Using Lexis Advance UK, use a restricted version of the initial search terms and target searches by year. Search for "COUNTRY and dissident and abroad and threat"; "COUNTRY and exile and abroad and assassin*"; and "COUNTRY and opposition and abroad and threat or assassin*." If new content emerges not captured by Google searches, then proceed to search more terms.

Initial Search Terms

COUNTRY silence *	COUNTRY targeted *	NAME repressed *
COUNTRY silences *	COUNTRY targeting *	NAME repressing *
COUNTRY silenced *	COUNTRY assassinate *	NAME repress *
COUNTRY silencing *	COUNTRY assassinated *	NAME intimidate *
COUNTRY censor *	COUNTRY assassinating *	NAME intimidated *
COUNTRY censored *	COUNTRY suppress *	NAME intimidates *
COUNTRY censorship *	COUNTRY suppressed *	NAME intimidating *
COUNTRY censors *	COUNTRY suppressing *	NAME threaten *
COUNTRY censoring *	COUNTRY repress *	NAME threatens *
COUNTRY intimidate *	COUNTRY repressing *	NAME threatened *
COUNTRY intimidated *	COUNTRY repressed *	NAME threatening *
COUNTRY intimidates *	COUNTRY disenfranchisement *	NAME murder *
COUNTRY intimidating *	COUNTRY disenfranchise *	NAME murders *
COUNTRY threaten *	COUNTRY disenfranchised *	NAME murdered *
COUNTRY threatens *	COUNTRY subpoena *	NAME murderer *
COUNTRY threatened *	COUNTRY subpoenaed *	NAME murdering *
COUNTRY threatening *	COUNTRY subpoenas *	NAME target *
COUNTRY murder *	NAME silence *	NAME targets *
COUNTRY murders *	NAME silences *	NAME targeted *
COUNTRY murdered *	NAME silenced *	NAME targeting *
COUNTRY murderer *	NAME silencing *	NAME assassinate *
COUNTRY murdering *	NAME censor *	NAME assassinated *
COUNTRY target *	NAME censored *	NAME subpoenaed *
COUNTRY targets *	NAME censorship *	NAME subpoenas *
	NAME censors *	NAME suppress *
	NAME censoring *	NAME suppressed *
	NAME disenfranchisement *	NAME suppression *
	NAME disenfranchise *	
	NAME disenfranchised *	
	NAME subpoena *	

Pro-DPRK Groups with Internet Presence (as of November 2019)

Name	Type	Location	Earliest year (founding, first evidence of activity)	Most recent evidence of activity	Website/Link	Twitter?	Facebook?
Asian Regional Institute of Juche Idea	JISG	India	1980	2017	www.ariji.website		
The Juche Idea Study Group of England	JISG	UK	1985	2019	http://juche007-anglo-peopleskoreafriendship.blogspot.com		X
Korean Friendship Association USA	KFA	USA	2000		https://www.kfausa.org	X	
KFA Serbia	KFA	Serbia	2000	2014	http://kfa-srbija.blogspot.com		
KFA Arabia	KFA	Middle East & North Africa	2000	2019	https://www.facebook.com/KFA.Arabia/		X
KFA Deutschland	KFA	Germany	2000	2019	https://www.facebook.com/KFAGermany/		X
KFA Peru	KFA	Peru	2008		http://institutoperuano-coreano.blogspot.com		X
Friends of Korea	KFA	UK	2009		https://friendsofkorea.blogspot.com		
Nigerian National Committee on the Study of Juche Idea	JISG	Nigeria	1970s	2019	http://nigeriajucheidea.blogspot.com		

(continued)

Name	Type	Location	Earliest year (founding, first evidence of activity)	Most recent evidence of activity	Website/Link	Twitter?	Facebook?
Association for the Study of Songun Politics UK	JISG	UK	2009	2019	https://web.archive.org/web/20180130023705/http://www.uk-songun.com:80/index.php		X
Juche Philosophy Study Group (Malta)	JISG	Malta	2009	2010	http://juchesongunmalta.blogspot.com/2010/04/juche-philosophy-and-songun-policy.html		
NJA For Studying Juche Idea & Songun Policy	JISG	Nepal	2010		http://www.juche-nepal.org		
Down with the south Korean puppet regime	Other		2010	2019	https://www.facebook.com/Down-with-the-south-Korean-puppet-regime-108799915854487/		X
KFA Makedonija	KFA	North Macedonia	2010	2019	https://www.facebook.com/KFA.MAKEDONIJA/		X
KFA Chile	KFA	Chile	2010	2019	http://www.kfachile.cl	X	X
KFA Espana	KFA	Spain	2011	2019	http://kfaspain.es	X	X
KFA–Brasil–Associação de Amizade com a Coreia	KFA	Brazil	2011	2019	https://www.facebook.com/KFA.Brasil/		X
Korean Friendship Association Valencia	KFA	Spain	2011	2019	https://www.facebook.com/KFAVALENCIA/	X	X
KFA Germany	KFA	Germany	2011	2019	https://www.facebook.com/groups/255807444479667/		X
KFA Italy	KFA	Italy	2012	2019	https://italiacoreapopolare.wordpress.com		X
KFA UK	KFA	UK	2012	2019	https://www.kfauk.com	X	X
KFA Euskal Herria	KFA	Basque Country	2012	2019	https://www.kfa-eh.org	X	X

Name	Type	Country	Year	Year	URL		
Korea Friendship Association (KFA) Thailand	KFA	Thailand	2012	2012	https://www.facebook.com/Korea-Friendship-Association-KFA-Thailand-271938859578526/		X
KFA Bangladesh	KFA	Bangladesh	2012	2012	https://www.facebook.com/KFAbd/		X
Korean Friendship Association Ireland	KFA	Ireland	2013	2017	https://jucheireland.wordpress.com	X	
Asociacion de Amistad Corea–Bolivia–KFA	KFA	Bolivia	2013	2019	http://kfa-bolivia.blogspot.com		
KFA Portugal	KFA	Portugal	2013	2013	http://infocoreia.blogspot.com	X	
KFA Scandinavia	KFA	Scandinavia (Denmark, Sweden, Norway, Finland)	2013	2017	https://www.facebook.com/kfa.denmark/		X
Oceania-DPRK Solidarity Committee	Other	Oceania	2013	2019	https://www.facebook.com/OceaniaDPRKSolidarityCommittee/		X
KFA Nicaragua	KFA	Nicaragua	2013	2019	https://twitter.com/KfaNicaragua	X	
KFA CANARIAS	KFA	Canary Islands	2013	2016	https://twitter.com/kfacanarias	X	
Juche Idea Study Group Uganda	JISG	Uganda	2013	2013	https://www.facebook.com/jucheideastudy.uganda/timeline?lst=10 0027209170606%3A10000648373863 6%3A1572951746		X
Ireland Juche-Songun Ideas Study Group	JISG	Ireland	2013	2014	https://antoinfletcher21.wordpress.com		
KFA Sweden	KFA	Sweden	2014	2013	http://kfa-sweden.blogspot.com		X
Thông Tin Triều Tiên–Korea News	Other	Vietnam	2014	2016	https://www.facebook.com/truekoreanews/		X
KFA-SGP	KFA	Singapore	2014	2019	https://kfasg.wordpress.com	X	

(continued)

Name	Type	Location	Earliest year (founding, first evidence of activity)	Most recent evidence of activity	Website/Link	Twitter?	Facebook?
KFA International	KFA		2014	2014	https://twitter.com/KFAinternatcom	X	
Spanish Juche Idea Study Group	JISG	Spain	2015	2019	https://ideajuchemadrid.com		
KFA Polska	KFA	Poland	2015	2016	http://kfapolska.org	X	
KFA Nederland	KFA	Netherlands	2016	2019	https://www.facebook.com/KFANL/		X
Juche Idea Study Group of Kentucky	JISG	USA	2016	2019	https://www.facebook.com/JucheKY/		X
Kimilsungism-Kimjongilism Study Group	Other		2016	2019	https://www.facebook.com/groups/1064704603639882/		X
Juche Idea Study Group	Other		2016	2019	https://www.facebook.com/groups/760620487408441/about/		X
Korean Friendship Association India	KFA	India	2017	2019	https://www.facebook.com/pg/Korean-Friendship-Association-India-1355130044609015/about/?ref=page_internal		X
KFA Mexico	KFA	Mexico	2017	2019	https://www.facebook.com/KFA.mx/		X
Anti-Imperialist National Democratic Front–South Korea	Other	South Korea	2017	2019	https://www.facebook.com/Anti-Imperialist-National-Democratic-Front-AINDF-of-south-Korea-103064310270186/		X
KFA Canada	KFA	Canada	2017	2019			X
Juche Songun Study	Other		2017	2019	https://www.facebook.com/groups/2078342996944943/		X
Comrades Socialism Juche Songun	Other		2017	2019	https://www.facebook.com/groups/1409225002505499/?ref=gysj		X

Name	Type	Country	Year	Year	URL		
KFA Slovenia	KFA	Slovenia	2017	2017	https://www.facebook.com/KFA-Slovenia-1745829925734351/		X
KFA Philippines	KFA	Philippines	2017	2018	https://www.facebook.com/KFAPhilippines/		X
Staffordshire Branch of the UK Korean Friendship Association	KFA	UK	2017	2019	https://www.facebook.com/Staffordshire-Branch-of-the-UK-Korean-Friendship-Association-426792611008845/		X
Centre For Study Of Juche Idea–India	JISG	India	2017	2019	https://www.facebook.com/CSJIIndia/		X
The Brazilian Centre for the Study of Songun Politics	Other	Brazil	2017	2019	https://cepsongunbr.wordpress.com		X
International Network for the Defence of Socialist Korea	Other		2018	2019	https://koreaisone.wordpress.com	X	X
Korean Friendship Association Greece	KFA	Greece	2018	2019	https://www.facebook.com/DPRKGREECE/	X	X
KFA Croatia	KFA	Croatia	2018	2019	https://www.facebook.com/KFA-Croatia-654761488256027/	X	X
KFA Romania	KFA	Romania	2018	2019	https://www.facebook.com/kfaromania/		X
KFA Turkey	KFA	Turkey	2018	2019	http://www.kfaturkey.org	X	X
Juche Idea Study Group Hong Kong	JISG	Hong Kong	2018	2019	https://www.facebook.com/香港主體思想研究証Juche-Idea-Study-Group-of-Hong-Kong-453792361723489/		X
Korean Friendship Association–Zimbabwe	KFA	Zimbabwe	2019	2019	https://www.facebook.com/zimjuchesongun/		X
East Midlands UK Korean Friendship Association	KFA	UK	2019	2019	https://www.facebook.com/East-Midlands-UK-Korean-Friendship-Association-2238668126388861/		X
Glasgow branch of the Juche Idea Study Group of Britain	JISG	UK	2019	2918	https://www.facebook.com/jisgbglasgow/		X

(continued)

Name	Type	Location	Earliest year (founding, first evidence of activity)	Most recent evidence of activity	Website/Link	Twitter?	Facebook?
Kimilsungism–Kimjongilism	Other		2019	2019	https://www.facebook.com/KimilsungismKimjongilism/		X
KFA Australia	KFA	Australia	2019	2019	https://www.facebook.com/KFA-Australia-2249646545309743/	X	X
KFA Indonesia	KFA	Indonesia	2019	2019	https://indonesia16.wixsite.com/kfaindonesia?fbclid=IwAR1e0N5yBDdF2Jo0gJfeRYdmJJsZXU3PezMv5zNYNtqWQzrK4_ZXMvwC11I	X	X
KFA Slovenia–Korean Friendship Association	KFA	Slovenia	2019	2019	https://www.facebook.com/kfaslovenia/?ref=py_c		X
KFA Argentina	KFA	Argentina	2012	2014	http://kfa-argentina.blogspot.com/2012/		
Russian Juche–Songun site	JISG	Russia		2019	http://juche-songun.ru		
Swedish Juche Study Group	JISG	Sweden		2019	https://svenskajuchegruppen.wordpress.com		
Songun Politics Study Group (USA)	Other	USA	2003	2008	http://www.songunpoliticsstudygroup.org		

References

Adamson, Fiona. 2019. "No Escape: Long-Distance Repression, Extraterritorial States and the Underworld of IR." Paper presented at the *2019 European Consortium of Political Research Joint Sessions of Workshops*, April 2019.

Adamson, Fiona. 2020. "Non-state Authoritarianism and Diaspora Politics." *Global Networks* 20 (1): 150–169.

Adler-Nissen, Rebecca. 2014. "Stigma Management in International Relations: Transgressive Identities, Norms, and Order in International Society." *International Organization* 68 (1): 143–176.

AFP. 2018. "No Place to Hide: Exiled Chinese Uighurs Feel State's Long Reach." *France 24*, August 17, 2018. Available at: https://www.france24.com/en/20180817-no-place-hide-exiled-chinese-uighurs-feel-states-long-reach (accessed April 9, 2020).

Allan, Bentley B., Srdjan Vucetic, and Ted Hopf. 2018. "The Distribution of Identity and the Future of International Order: China's Hegemonic Prospects." *International Organization* 72 (4): 839–869.

Allen-Ebrahimian, Bethany. 2019. "Exposed: China's Operating Manuals for Mass Internment and Arrest by Algorithm." *International Consortium of Investigative Journalists*, November 24, 2019. Available at: https://www.icij.org/investigations/china-cables/exposed-chinas-operating-manuals-for-mass-internment-and-arrest-by-algorithm/ (accessed April 9, 2020).

Ambrosio, Thomas. 2008. "Catching the 'Shanghai Spirit': How the Shanghai Cooperation Organization Promotes Authoritarian Norms in Central Asia." *Europe-Asia Studies* 60 (8): 1321–1344.

Ambrosio, Thomas. 2010. "Constructing a Framework of Authoritarian Diffusion: Concepts, Dynamics, and Future Research." *International Studies Perspectives* 11 (4): 375–392.

Amnesty International. 2011. *The Long Reach of the Mukhabaraat: Violence and Harassment against Syrians Abroad and Their Relatives Back Home*. London: Amnesty International, MDE 24/057/2011.

Amnesty International. 2013. "Repression Still Stalks Sudanese Activists Who Sought Safety in Egypt." *Amnesty International*, January 18, 2013. Available at: https://www.amnesty.org/en/latest/news/2013/01/repression-still-stalks-sudanese-activists-who-sought-safety-in-egypt/ (accessed January 7, 2020).

Amnesty International. 2019a. "Cambodia: Stop Pressuring Regional Neighbours to Harass Opposition Figures." *Amnesty International*, November 7, 2019. Available at: https://www.amnesty.org/en/latest/news/2019/11/cambodia-stop-pressuring-regional-neighbours-harass-opposition-figures/ (accessed January 7, 2020).

Amnesty International. 2019b. *Eritrea: Repression without Borders: Threats to Human Rights Defenders Abroad*. London: Amnesty International, AFR 64/0542/2019.

Archetti, Cristina. 2013. "Journalism in the Age of Global Media: The Evolving Practices of Foreign Correspondents in London." *Journalism* 14 (3): 419–436.

Art, David. 2012. "What Do We Know about Authoritarianism after Ten Years?" *Comparative Politics* 44 (3): 351–373.

Baddorf, Zack. 2017. "Rwanda President's Lopsided Re-election Is Seen as a Sign of Oppression." *New York Times*, August 6, 2017. Available at: https://www.nytimes.com/2017/08/06/world/africa/rwanda-elections-paul-kagame.html (accessed April 24, 2020).

Bader, Julia. 2015. "China, Autocratic Patron? An Empirical Investigation of China as a Factor in Autocratic Survival." *International Studies Quarterly* 59 (1): 23–33.

Bader, Julia, Jorn Grävingholt, and Antje Kästner. 2010. "Would Autocracies Promote Autocracy? A Political Economy Perspective on Regime-Type Export in Regional Neighborhoods." *Contemporary Politics* 16 (1): 81–100.

Bader, Max. 2017. "Coordination and Crisis Prevention: The Case of Post-Soviet Eurasia." In Johannes Gerschewski and Christoph H. Stefes, eds., *Crisis in Autocratic Regimes.* Boulder, CO: Lynne Reinner, pp. 135–153.

Bailard, Catie Snow. 2016. "China in Africa: An Analysis of the Effect of Chinese Media Expansion on African Public Opinion." *International Journal of Press/Politics* 21 (4): 446–471.

Bank, Andre. 2017. "The Study of Authoritarian Diffusion and Cooperation: Comparative Lessons on Interests Versus Ideology, Nowadays and in History." *Democratization* 24 (7): 1345–1357.

Bayulgen, Oksan, Ekim Arbatli, and Sercan Canbolat. 2018. "Elite Survival Strategies and Authoritarian Reversal in Turkey." *Polity* 50 (3): 333–365.

BBC. 2002. "China Admits Missing Dissident Arrested." *BBC News*, December 20, 2002. Available at: http://news.bbc.co.uk/2/hi/asia-pacific/2592965.stm (accessed April 9, 2020).

BBC. 2014. "Deadly China Blast at Xinjiang Railway Station." *BBC News*, April 30, 2014. Available at: https://www.bbc.com/news/world-asia-china-27225308 (accessed April 2, 2020).

BBC. 2017. "UK Activist Is Part of 'Korea Friendship Association.'" *BBC News*, October 17, 2017. Available at: https://www.bbc.com/news/av/uk-politics-41652650/uk-activist-is-part-of-korean-friendship-association (accessed November 25, 2019).

Behuria, Pritish. 2016. "Centralising Rents and Dispersing Power While Pursuing Development? Exploring the Strategic Uses of Military Firms in Rwanda." *Review of African Political Economy* 43 (150): 630–647.

Bell, Markus. 2016. "Making and Breaking Family: North Korea's Zainichi Returnees and 'the Gift.'" *Asian Anthropology* 15 (3): 260–276.

Bell, Markus. 2018. "Patriotic Revolutionaries and Imperial Sympathizers: Identity and Selfhood of Korean-Japanese Migrants from Japan to North Korea." *Cross-Currents* 27: 1–25.

Bell, Markus. 2019. "Reimagining the Homeland: Zainichi Koreans' Transnational Longing for North Korea." *Asia Pacific Journal of Anthropology* 20 (1): 22–41.

Beresford, Alexander, Marie E. Brady, and Laura Mann. 2018. "Liberation Movements and Stalled Democratic Transitions: Reproducing Power in Rwanda and South Africa through Productive Liminality." *Democratization* 25 (7): 1231–1250.

Betts, Alexander, and Will Jones. 2016. *Mobilising the Diaspora: How Refugees Challenge Authoritarianism.* New York: Cambridge University Press.

Bially Mattern, Janice. 2005. "Why 'Soft Power' Isn't So Soft: Representational Force and the Sociolinguistic Construction of Attraction in World Politics." *Millennium: Journal of International Studies* 33 (3): 583–612.

Blake, Heidi. 2019. *From Russia with Blood: Putin's Ruthless Killing Campaign and Secret War on the West*. London: William Collins.

Bob, Clifford. 2005. *The Marketing of Rebellion: Insurgents, Media, and International Activism*. Cambridge: Cambridge University Press.

Bogdanich, Walt, and Michael Forsythe. 2018. "How McKinsey Has Helped Raise the Stature of Authoritarian Governments." *New York Times*, December 15, 2018. Available at: https://www.nytimes.com/2018/12/15/world/asia/mckinsey-china-russia.html (accessed March 31, 2020).

Bovingdon, Gardner. 2010. *The Uyghurs: Strangers in Their Own Land*. New York: Columbia University Press.

Bozkurt, Abdullah. 2019. "Erdoğan's Thugs Plot to Kill Turkey Journalist in Denmark." *International Observatory of Human Rights*, January 29, 2019. Available at: https://observatoryihr.org/priority_posts/erdogans-thugs-plot-to-kill-turkish-journalist-in-denmark/ (accessed January 7, 2020).

Brady, Anne-Marie. 2000. "'Treat Insiders and Outsiders Differently': The Use and Control of Foreigners in the PRC." *China Quarterly* 164 (4): 943–964.

Brady, Anne-Marie. 2003. *Making the Foreign Serve China: Managing Foreigners in the People's Republic*. Lanham, MD: Rowman & Littlefield.

Brady, Anne-Marie. 2008. *Marketing Dictatorship: Propaganda and Thought Work in Contemporary China*. Lanham, MD: Rowman & Littlefield.

Brady, Anne-Marie. 2015. "China's Foreign Propaganda Machine." *Journal of Democracy* 26 (4): 51–59.

Brady, Anne-Marie. 2018. "China in Xi's 'New Era': New Zealand and the CCP's 'Magic Weapons.'" *Journal of Democracy* 29 (2): 68–75.

Brady, Henry E., and David Collier. 2010. *Rethinking Social Inquiry: Diverse Tools, Shared Standards*. Lanham, MD: Rowman & Littlefield.

Brancati, Dawn. 2014. "Democratic Authoritarianism: Origins and Effects." *Annual Review of Political Science* 17: 313–326.

Brazys, Samuel, and Alexander Dukalskis. 2017. "Canary in the Coal Mine? China, the UNGA, and the Changing World Order." *Review of International Studies* 43 (4): 742–764.

Brazys, Samuel, and Alexander Dukalskis. 2019. "Rising Powers and Grassroots Image Management: Confucius Institutes and China in the Media." *Chinese Journal of International Politics* 12 (4): 557–584.

Brazys, Samuel, and Alexander Dukalskis. 2020. "China's Message Machine." *Journal of Democracy* 31 (4): 59–73.

Brinks, Daniel, and Michael Coppedge. 2006. "Diffusion Is No Illusion: Neighbor Emulation in the Third Wave of Democracy." *Comparative Political Studies* 39 (4): 463–489.

Brown, Archie. 2009. *The Rise and Fall of Communism*. London: Vintage.

Brownlee, Jason. 2017. "The Limited Reach of Authoritarian Powers." *Democratization* 24 (7): 1326–1344.

Bueno de Mesquita, Bruce, and Alastair Smith. 2010. "Leader Survival, Revolutions, and the Nature of Government Finance." *American Journal of Political Science* 54 (4): 936–950.

Bueno De Mesquita, Bruce, Alastair Smith, James D. Morrow, and Randolph M. Siverson. 2005. *The Logic of Political Survival*. Cambridge, MA: MIT Press.

Bunge, Mario. 1997. Mechanism and Explanation. *Philosophy of the Social Sciences* 27 (4): 410–465.

Burgis, Tom. 2017. "Spies, Lies and the Oligarch: Inside London's Booming Secrets Industry." *Financial Times*, September 28, 2017. Available at: https://www.ft.com/content/1411b1a0-a310-11e7-9e4f-7f5e6a7c98a2 (accessed April 8, 2020).

Burnell, Peter, and Oliver Schlumberger. 2010. "Promoting Democracy—Promoting Autocracy? International Politics and National Political Regimes." *Contemporary Politics* 16 (1): 1–15.

Buzan, Barry. 2014. "The Logic and Contradictions of 'Peaceful Rise/Development' as China's Grand Strategy." *Chinese Journal of International Politics* 7 (4): 381–420.

Byler, Darren. 2018. "Violent Paternalism: On the Banality of Uyghur Unfreedom." *Asia Pacific Journal: Japan Focus* 16 (4): 1–15.

Byrne, Leo. 2014. "Interview: Thousands of North Korea Juche Supporters Exist in Nigeria." *NKNews.org*, June 17, 2014. Available at: https://www.nknews.org/2014/06/interview-thousands-of-north-korea-juche-supporters-exist-in-nigeria/ (accessed November 25, 2019).

Campbell, Charlie. 2015. "Thailand Defends Its Decision to Forcibly Return Uighur Migrants to China." *Time*, July 10, 2015. Available at: https://time.com/3952498/china-uighur-xinjiang-deportations-turkey-thailand-human-rights/ (accessed April 9, 2020).

CAPE. 2020. Odinaev, Ehson. Available at: https://excas.net/exile/odinaev-ehson/ (accessed January 7, 2020).

Cathcart, Adam, and Steven Denney. 2013. "North Korea's Cultural Diplomacy in the Early Kim Jong-un Era." *North Korean Review* 9 (2): 29–42.

CGTN America. 2016. "Chinese President Xi Jinping Visits with CCTV America via Video Call." *CGTN America*, February 19, 2016 (updated October 26, 2017). Available at: https://america.cgtn.com/2016/02/19/chinese-president-xi-jinping-visits-with-cctv-america-via-video-call (accessed November 11, 2019).

Cha, Victor. 2009. "A Theory of Sports and Politics." *International Journal of the History of Sport* 26 (11): 1581–1610.

Channel 4 News. 2019. "Alejandro Cao de Benós: Trump-Kim Meeting 'Good for the US, Good for the Whole World.'" *Channel 4 News*, June 30, 2019. Available at: https://www.channel4.com/news/alejandro-cao-de-benos-trump-kim-meeting-good-for-the-us-good-for-the-whole-world (accessed November 25, 2019).

Chapman, Hannah S., and Theodore P. Gerber. 2019. "Opinion-Formation and Issue-Framing Effects of Russian News in Kyrgyzstan." *International Studies Quarterly* 63 (3): 756–769.

Chemouni, Benjamin, and Assumpta Mugiraneza. 2020. "Ideology and Interests in the Rwandan Patriotic Front: Singing the Struggle in Pre-Genocide Rwanda." *African Affairs* 119 (474): 115–140.

Chen, Adrian. 2015. "The Agency." *New York Times Magazine*, June 2, 2015. Available at: https://www.nytimes.com/2015/06/07/magazine/the-agency.html?mcubz=0&module=inline (accessed November 13, 2020).

Chenoweth, Erica, Evan Perkoski, and Sooyeon Kang. 2017. "State Repression and Nonviolent Resistance." *Journal of Conflict Resolution* 61 (9): 1950–1969.

China Daily. 2007. "Full Text of Hu Jintao's Report at 17th Party Congress." *China Daily*, October 24, 2007. Available at: https://www.chinadaily.com.cn/china/2007-10/24/content_6204564.htm (accessed November 11, 2019).

China Daily. 2016. "'Red Star Over China' to Hit Chinese TV Screens." *China Daily*, October 19, 2016. Available at: https://www.chinadaily.com.cn/culture/2016-10/19/content_27108352.htm (accessed May 13, 2020).

ChinaFile. 2013. "Document 9: A ChinaFile Translation." *ChinaFile*, August 11, 2013. Available at: https://www.chinafile.com/document-9-chinafile-translation (accessed September 10, 2020).

Choson Sinbo. 2012. "[시론]일본은 평양선언의 정신으로 돌아가야 한다 [Japan Should Return to the Spirit of the Pyongyang Declaration]." *Choson Sinbo*, September 14, 2012. Available at: http://chosonsinbo.com/2012/09/sinbo-k_120919-2/ (accessed March 16, 2020).

Choson Sinbo. 2015. "《재일조선인에 대한 헤이트스피치는 인권침해》, 일본정부가 첫 권고 [Hate Speech to Korean Residents in Japan Is a Violation of Human Rights, First Recommended by the Japanese Government." *Choson Sinbo*, December 24, 2015. Available at: http://chosonsinbo.com/2015/12/20151224suk/ (accessed March 16, 2020).

Choson Sinbo. 2016. "김정은시대 조선청년된 존엄과 긍지 / 김일성사회주의청년동맹 제9차 대회에 참가한 재일본조선청년동맹대표단 [The Dignity and Pride of Young Koreans during the Kim Jong Un Era / Delegation of the Young Men's Alliance of Korean People in Japan to Participate in the 9th Session of the Kim Il Sung Socialist Youth League." *Choson Sinbo*, November 16, 2016. Available at: http://chosonsinbo.com/2016/11/16suk-2/ (accessed March 16, 2020).

Choson Sinbo. 2017a. "려명거리가 훌륭히 완공 / 불굴의 정신력, 자력자강의 창조물 [Ryomyong Street has been Successfully Completed / The Indomitable Spirit, the Self-Strengthening Creation]." *Choson Sinbo*, April 19, 2017. Available at: http://chosonsinbo.com/2017/04/yr0419-1/ (accessed March 16, 2020).

Choson Sinbo. 2017b. "년로자들에게 보람을 안겨주는 사회적시책 [A Rewarding Social Policy for the Elderly]." *Choson Sinbo*, October 10, 2017. Available at: http://chosonsinbo.com/2017/10/10suk-8/ (accessed March 16, 2020).

Choson Sinbo. 2018a. "총련에서 유엔 마이노리티포럼에 처음으로 참가 / 조선학교 차별, 재일조선청년들의 반대투쟁을 보고 [Chongryon Participates in the U.N. Minority Forum for the First Time / Reporting Discrimination against Choson Schools and the Korean Youth against the Japanese]." *Choson Sinbo*, March 29, 2018. Available at: http://chosonsinbo.com/2018/03/sinbo-k_180409-4/ (accessed March 16, 2020).

Choson Sinbo. 2018b. "원아들까지 폭행하는 나라가 무슨 《법치국가》인가 / 조선중앙통신사 론평 [What Kind of Country Is It That Attacks Kindergarteners? / Commentary on the Korean Central News Agency]." *Choson Sinbo*, July 24, 2018. Available at: http://chosonsinbo.com/2018/07/kcna_180724-2/ (accessed March 16, 2020).

Choson Sinbo. 2018c. "효고일군대표단, 력사적시기에 조국을 방문 / 상상을 초월하는 발전모습에 감탄 [A Delegation of Hyogo Workers to Visit their Homeland in Historical Times / Admiring the Extraordinary Form of Development]." *Choson Sinbo*, May 12, 2018. Available at: http://chosonsinbo.com/2018/05/11suk-22/ (accessed March 16, 2020).

Choson Sinbo. 2018d. "조국에서 도꾜중고 6, 7기생들과의 상봉모임 / 민족교육의 《맏아들학교》의 긍지와 자부심 새겨 [Meeting with 6th and 7th Graders of Tokyo Middle School in My Home Country / Pride and Dignity of Son of National Education]." *Choson Sinbo*, July 18, 2018. Available at: http://chosonsinbo.com/2018/07/il-1771/ (accessed March 16, 2020).

Choson Sinbo. 2019. "부당한 차별적조치의 철회를 / 조선유치반의 제외를 노리는 일본당국 [The Withdrawal of Unjust Discriminatory Measures / The Japanese Authorities Seeking to Exclude Joseon Kindergartens]." *Choson Sinbo*, September

2, 2019. Available at: http://chosonsinbo.com/2019/09/hj190902/ (accessed March 16, 2020).

Chou, Mark, Chengxin Pan, and Avery Poole. 2017. "The Threat of Autocracy Diffusion in Consolidated Democracies? The Case of China, Singapore and Australia." *Contemporary Politics* 23 (2): 175–194.

Clifford, Stephanie. 2008. "Tibet Backers Show China Value of P.R." *New York Times*, April 14, 2008. Available at: https://www.nytimes.com/2008/04/14/business/media/14adco.html (accessed November 11, 2019).

Clunan, Anne L. 2014. "Why Status Matters in World Politics." In T.V. Paul, Deborah Welch Larson, and William C. Wohlforth, eds., *Status in World Politics*. Cambridge: Cambridge University Press, pp. 273–296.

Cohen, Stanley. 2000. *States of Denial: Knowing about Atrocities and Suffering*. London: Polity Press.

Collyer, Michael, and Russell King. 2015. "Producing Transnational Space: International Migration and the Extra-territorial Reach of State Power." *Progress in Human Geography* 39 (2): 185–204.

Cooley, Alexander. 2015. "Countering Democratic Norms." *Journal of Democracy* 26 (3): 49–63.

Cooley, Alexander, and John Heathershaw. 2017. *Dictators without Borders: Power and Money in Central Asia*. New Haven, CT: Yale University Press.

Cooley, Alexander, John Heathershaw, and J. C. Sharman. 2018. "Laundering Cash, Whitewashing Reputations." *Journal of Democracy* 29 (1): 39–53.

Corporate Europe Observatory. 2015. "Spin Doctors to the Autocrats: How European PR Firms Whitewash Repressive Regimes." Available at: https://corporateeurope.org/sites/default/files/20150120_spindoctors_mr.pdf

Cox, Michael, G. John Ikenberry, and Takashi Inoguchi, eds. 2000. *American Democracy Promotion: Impulses, Strategies, and Impacts*. Oxford: Oxford University Press.

Cozma, Raluca, and Kuan-Ju Chen. 2013. "What's in a Tweet? Foreign Correspondents' Use of Social Media." *Journalism Practice* 7 (1): 33–46.

Cumings, Bruce. 2005. *Korea's Place in the Sun: A Modern History*. New York: W.W. Norton.

Cumings, Bruce. 1996. "South Korea's Academic Lobby." *JPRI Occasional* Paper No. 7. Oakland, CA: Japan Policy Research Institute.

Custer, Samantha, Brooke Russell, Matthew DiKorenzo, Mengfan Cheng, Siddhartha Ghose, Harsh Desai, Jacob Sims, and Jennifer Turner. 2018. *Ties That Bind: Quantifying China's Public Diplomacy and Its "Good Neighbor" Effect*. Williamsburg, VA: AidData at William & Mary.

d'Hooghe, Ingrid. 2005. "Public Diplomacy in the People's Republic of China." In Jan Melissen, ed., *The New Public Diplomacy: Soft Power in International Relations*. London: Palgrave, pp. 88–105.

Daily Nation. 2011. "Exiled Former Rwandan Top Officials Handed Jail Terms." *Daily Nation*, January 14, 2011. Available at: https://www.nation.co.ke/News/africa/-/1066/1089824/-/123micg/-/ (accessed April 17, 2020).

Dalmasso, Emanuela, Adele Del Sordi, Marlies Glasius, Nicole Hirt, Marcus Michaelsen, Abdulkader S. Mohammad, and Dana Moss. 2018. "Intervention: Extraterritorial Authoritarian Power." *Political Geography* 64: 95–104.

Daniszewski, John. 2012. "AP Opens Full News Bureau in North Korea." *Associated Press*, January 16, 2012. Available at: https://www.ap.org/ap-in-the-news/2012/ap-opens-full-news-bureau-in-north-korea (accessed November 19, 12018).

Davenport, Christian. 2007. "State Repression and Political Order." *Annual Review of Political Science* 10: 1–23.

David-Fox, Michael. 2012. *Showcasing the Great Experiment: Cultural Diplomacy and Western Visitors to the Soviet Union, 1921–1941.* New York: Oxford University Press.

Davis, David R., Amanda Murdie, and Coty Garnett Steinmetz. 2012. "Makers and Shapers: Human Rights INGOs and Public Opinion." *Human Rights Quarterly* 34 (1): 199–224.

de la Torre, Carlos. 2017. "Hugo Chavez and the Diffusion of Bolivarianism." *Democratization* 24 (7): 1271–1288.

Del Sordi, Adele, and Emanuela Dalmasso. 2018. "The Relation between External and Internal Legitimation: The Religious Foreign Policy of Morocco and Kazakhstan." *Taiwan Journal of Democracy* 14 (1): 95–116.

Demick, Barbara. 2014. "96 Died in Recent Clashes in Uighur Region, China Reports." *Los Angeles Times*, August 2, 2014. Available at: https://www.latimes.com/world/asia/la-fg-china-uighur-deaths-20140802-story.html (accessed April 2, 2020).

Department of Justice. 2020a. "Foreign Agents Registration Act." Available at: https://www.justice.gov/nsd-fara (accessed January 2, 2020).

Department of Justice. 2020b. "FARA Forms." Available at: https://www.justice.gov/nsd-fara/fara-forms (accessed January 2, 2020).

Des Forges, Alison. 1999. "Leave None to Tell the Story: Genocide in Rwanda." *Human Rights Watch*. Available at: https://www.hrw.org/reports/1999/rwanda/ (accessed April 18, 2020).

Desrosiers, Marie-Eve, and Haley J. Swedlund. 2019. "Rwanda's Post-Genocide Foreign Aid Relations: Revisiting Notions of Exceptionalism." *African Affairs* 118 (472): 435–462.

Desrosiers, Marie-Eve, and Susan Thomson. 2011. "Rhetorical Legacies of Leadership: Projections of 'Benevolent Leadership' in Pre- and Post-Genocide Rwanda." *Journal of Modern African Studies* 49 (3): 429–453.

Ding, Sheng. 2010. "Analyzing Rising Power from the Perspective of Soft Power: A New Look at China's Rise to the Status Quo Power." *Journal of Contemporary China* 19 (64): 255–272.

DPRK. 1959. *On the Question of 600,000 Koreans in Japan.* Pyongyang: Foreign Languages.

DPRK Association for Human Rights Studies. 2014. "Report of the DPRK Association for Human Rights Studies." Available at: https://www.ncnk.org/resources/publications/Report_of_the_DPRK_Association_for_Human_Rights_Studies.pdf (accessed March 16, 2020).

Dukalskis, Alexander. 2017. *The Authoritarian Public Sphere: Legitimation and Autocratic Power in North Korea, Burma, and China.* New York: Routledge.

Dukalskis, Alexander, and Johannes Gerschewski. 2017. "What Autocracies Say (and What Citizens Hear): Proposing Four Mechanisms of Autocratic Legitimation." *Contemporary Politics* 23 (3): 251–268.

Dukalskis, Alexander, and Johannes Gerschewski. 2020. "Adapting or Freezing? Ideological Reactions of Communist Regimes to a Post-Communist World." *Government & Opposition* 55 (3): 511–532.

Dukalskis, Alexander, and Zachary Hooker. 2011. "Legitimating Totalitarianism: Melodrama and Mass Politics in North Korean Film." *Communist and Post-Communist Studies* 44 (1): 53–62.

Dukalskis, Alexander, and Hyung-Min Joo. 2020. "Everyday Authoritarianism in North Korea." *Europe-Asia Studies*, early view. doi: https://doi.org/10.1080/09668136.2020.1840517.

Dukalskis, Alexander, and Junhyoung Lee. 2020. "Everyday Nationalism and Authoritarian Rule: A Case Study of North Korea." *Nationalities Papers* 48 (6): 1052–1068.

Dukalskis, Alexander, and Christopher Patane. 2019. "Justifying Power: When Autocracies Talk about Themselves and Their Opponents." *Contemporary Politics* 25 (4): 457–478.

Dukalskis, Alexander, and Christopher Raymond. 2018. "Failure of Authoritarian Learning: Explaining Burma/Myanmar's Electoral System." *Democratization* 25 (3): 545–563.

Durand, James F. 2017. "Japan, Chongryon, and Sanctions." *International Journal of Korean Studies* 11 (1): 95–118.

DW. 2004. "Germany and Iran Embroiled in Diplomatic Spat." *DW*, April 28, 2004. Available at: https://www.dw.com/en/germany-and-iran-embroiled-in-diplomatic-spat/a-1184162 (accessed January 7, 2020).

DW. 2016. "Turkish Newspaper 'Zaman' Shuts Down in Germany Amid 'Threats.'" *DW*, September 9, 2016. Available at: https://www.dw.com/en/turkish-newspaper-zaman-shuts-down-in-germany-amid-threats/a-19540340 (accessed January 7, 2020).

Eagleton, Terry. 2007. *Ideology: An Introduction*. London: Verso.

Economy, Elizabeth. 2018. *The Third Revolution: Xi Jinping and the New Chinese State*. New York: Oxford University Press.

Economy, Elizabeth. 2020. "Exporting the China Model." Testimony before the U.S.-China Economic and Security Review Commission, Hearing on the "China Model." *Council on Foreign Relations*, March 13, 2020. Available at: https://www.uscc.gov/sites/default/files/testimonies/USCCTestimony3-13-20%20(Elizabeth%20Economy)_justified.pdf (accessed June 3, 2020).

Edel, Mirjam, and Maria Josua. 2018. "How Authoritarian Rulers Seek to Legitimize Repression: Framing and Mass Killings in Egypt and Uzbekistan." *Democratization* 25 (5): 882–900.Edney, Kingsley. 2012. "Soft Power and the Chinese Propaganda System." *Journal of Contemporary China* 21 (78): 899–914.

Edney, Kingsley. 2014. *The Globalization of Chinese Propaganda: International Power and Domestic Political Cohesion*. New York: Palgrave MacMillan.

Edney, Kingsley, Stanley Rosen, and Ying Zhu, eds. 2020. *Soft Power with Chinese Characteristics: China's Campaign for Hearts and Minds*. New York: Routledge.

Embassy of the People's Republic of China in the Kingdom of Sweden. 2018. "Chinese Embassy Spokesperson's Remarks on *Expressen*'s Article about China." Available at: http://www.chinaembassy.se/eng/sgxw/t1573515.htm (accessed December 15, 2018).

Erlanger, Steven. 2017. "What Is RT?" *New York Times*, March 8, 2017. Available at: https://www.nytimes.com/2017/03/08/world/europe/what-is-rt.html (accessed November 13, 2020).

Escriba-Folch, Abel, and Joseph Wright. 2015. *Foreign Pressure and the Politics of Autocratic Survival*. Oxford: Oxford University Press.

Fahy, Sandra. 2015. *Marching Through Suffering: Loss and Survival in North Korea*. New York: Columbia University Press.

Fahy, Sandra. 2019. *Dying for Rights: Putting North Korea's Human Rights Abuses on the Record*. New York: Columbia University Press.

Farhi, Paul. 2015. "Eric Talmadge Is the Only Western Reporter Regularly in North Korea. Here's What It's Like." *Washington Post*, January 18, 2015. Available at: https://www.washingtonpost.com/lifestyle/style/eric-talmadge-is-the-only-western-reporter-regularly-in-north-korea-heres-what-its-like/2015/01/18/2a01808e-9a9f-11e4-96cc-e858eba91ced_story.html?noredirect=on&utm_term=.b3440530746b (accessed November 19, 2018).

FCCC. 2018. "Access Denied: Surveillance, Harassment, and Intimidation as Reporting Conditions in China Deteriorate: A Foreign Correspondents' Club of China Report on Working Conditions in 2017." Available at: https://www.dropbox.com/s/95ghn59rl93ceu9/Access%20Denied-FCCC%20report%202017.pdf?dl=0 (accessed January 14, 2019).

FCCC. 2020. "Control, Halt, Delete: Reporting in China under Threat of Expulsion: FCCC Report on Media Freedoms in 2019." Available at: https://www.dropbox.com/s/gky8352xue74kuh/control-halt-delete.pdf?dl=0 (accessed November 9, 2020).

Fifield, Anna. 2019. *The Great Successor: The Divinely Perfect Destiny of Brilliant Comrade Kim Jong Un*. New York: Hachette.

Finnemore, Martha. 2009. "Legitimacy, Hypocrisy, and the Social Structure of Unipolarity: Why Being a Unipole Isn't All It's Cracked Up to Be." *World Politics* 61 (1): 58–85.

Fordham, Benjamin O., and Victor Asal. 2007. "Billiard Balls or Snowflakes? Major Power Prestige and the International Diffusion of Institutions and Practices." *International Studies Quarterly* 51 (1): 31–52.

Freeden, Michael. 1996. *Ideologies and Political Theory: A Conceptual Approach*. Oxford: Clarendon Press.

Freedom House. 2019. "Freedom in the World 2019: Democracy in Retreat." Available at: https://freedomhouse.org/sites/default/files/Feb2019_FH_FITW_2019_Report_ForWeb-compressed.pdf.

Front Line Defenders. 2019. "Location." Available at: https://www.frontlinedefenders.org/en/location (accessed January 3, 2020).

Front Line Defenders. 2020. "Case History: Jiang Yefei." *Front Line Defenders*. Available at: https://www.frontlinedefenders.org/en/case/case-history-jiang-yefei (accessed April 9, 2020).

Gall, Carlotta. 2018. "U.S. Is 'Working on' Extraditing Gulen, Top Turkish Official Says." *New York Times*, December 16, 2018. Available at: https://www.nytimes.com/2018/12/16/world/europe/fethullah-gulen-turkey-extradite.html (accessed March 18, 2020).

Gandhi, Jennifer, and Ellen Lust-Okar. 2009. "Elections under Authoritarianism." *Annual Review of Political Science* 12: 403–422.

Gauthier, Brandon K. 2014. "'Bring All the Troops Home Now!' The American-Korean Friendship and Information Center and North Korean Public Diplomacy, 1971–1976." *Yonsei Journal of International Studies* 5 (3): 147–158.

Geddes, Barbara, Joseph Wright, and Erica Frantz. 2014b. "Autocratic Breakdown and Regime Transitions: A New Data Set." *Perspectives on Politics* 12 (2): 313–331.

Gerring, John. 1997. "Ideology: A Definitional Analysis." *Political Research Quarterly* 50 (4): 957–994.

Gerring, John. 2007. *Case Study Research: Principles and Practices*. Cambridge: Cambridge University Press.

Gerschewski, Johannes. 2013. "The Three Pillars of Stability: Legitimation, Repression, and Co-optation in Autocratic Regimes." *Democratization* 20 (1): 13–38.

Ghodes, Anita R., and Sabine C. Carey. 2017. "Canaries in a Coal-Mine? What the Killings of Journalists Tell Us about Future Repression." *Journal of Peace Research* 54 (2): 157–174.

Glasius, Marlies. 2018a. "What Authoritarianism Is . . . and Is Not: A Practice Perspective." *International Affairs* 94 (3): 515–533.

Glasius, Marlies. 2018b. "Extraterritorial Authoritarian Practices: A Framework." *Globalizations* 15 (2): 179–197.

Glasius, Marlies, Jelmer Schalk, and Meta De Lange. 2020. "Illiberal Norm Diffusion: How Do Governments Learn to Restrict Nongovernmental Organizations?" *International Studies Quarterly* 64 (2): 453–468.

Global Times. 2015. "'L'Obs' China Articles Biased, Unprofessional." *Global Times*, December 26, 2015. Available at: http://www.globaltimes.cn/content/960651.shtml (accessed January 14, 2019).

Global Times. 2018. "Western Hysteria over Journalist Visa Rejection Reveals a Thirst for the Negative." *Global Times*, August 24, 2018. Available at: http://www.globaltimes.cn/content/1116840.shtml (accessed January 14, 2019).

Gould-Davies, Nigel. 1999. "Rethinking the Role of Ideology in International Politics during the Cold War." *Journal of Cold War Studies* 1 (1): 90–109.

Gould-Davies, Nigel. 2003. "The Logic of Soviet Cultural Diplomacy." *Diplomatic History* 27 (2): 193–214.

Graham-Harrison, Emma. 2018a. "China 'Ejects' US Journalist Known for Reporting on Xinjiang Repression." *The Guardian*, August 22, 2018. Available at: https://www.theguardian.com/world/2018/aug/22/china-ejects-us-journalist-known-for-reporting-on-xinjiang-repression (accessed January 14, 2019).

Graham-Harrison, Emma. 2018b. "Critics of Saudi Regime Are at Risk—Wherever They May Be." *The Guardian*, October 10, 2018. https://www.theguardian.com/world/2018/oct/10/critics-of-saudi-regime-are-at-risk-wherever-they-may-be

Grauvogel, Julia, and Christian Von Soest. 2014. "Claims to Legitimacy Count: Why Sanctions Fail to Instigate Democratisation in Authoritarian Regimes." *European Journal of Political Research* 53 (4): 635–653.

Gready, Paul. 2010. "'You're Either with Us or against Us': Civil Society and Policy Making in Post-Genocide Rwanda." *African Affairs* 109 (437): 637–657.

Green, Emma. 2013. "When Western Journalists Loved China's Communists." *The Atlantic*, October 24, 2013. Available at: https://www.theatlantic.com/china/archive/2013/10/when-western-journalists-loved-chinas-communists/280814/.

Greitens, Sheena Chestnut, Myunghee Lee, and Emir Yazici. 2020. "Counterterrorism and Preventive Repression: China's Changing Strategy in Xinjiang." *International Security* 44 (3): 9–47.

Gunitsky, Seva. 2015. "Corrupting the Cyber-Commons: Social Media as a Tool of Autocratic Stability." *Perspectives on Politics* 13 (1): 42–54.

Gunitsky, Seva. 2017. *Aftershocks: Great Powers and Domestic Reforms in the Twentieth Century*. Princeton, NJ: Princeton University Press.

Haas, Mark L. 2014. "Ideological Polarity and Balancing in Great Power Politics." *Security Studies* 23 (4): 715–753.

Hafner-Burton, Emilie M. 2008. "Sticks and Stones: Naming and Shaming the Human Rights Enforcement Problem." *International Organization* 62 (4): 689–716.

Haggard, Stephan, and Marcus Noland. 2007. *Famine in North Korea: Markets, Aid and Reform*. New York: Columbia University Press.

Hall, Richard. 2019. "The Kingdom of Spin: Saudi Arabia's PR Machine and the Murder of Jamal Khashoggi." *The Independent*, October 2, 2019. Available at: https://www.independent.co.uk/news/world/middle-east/saudi-arabia-mohammad-bin-salman-khashoggi-public-relations-a9129386.html (accessed April 3, 2020).

Hall, Stephen G. F., and Thomas Ambrosio. 2017. "Authoritarian Learning: A Conceptual Overview." *East European Politics* 33 (2): 143–161.

Hamilton, Clive, and Mareike Ohlberg. 2020. *Hidden Hand: Exposing How the Chinese Communist Party is Reshaping the World*. London: OneWorld.

Hamilton, John M., and Eric Jenner. 2004. "Redefining Foreign Correspondence." *Journalism* 5 (3): 301–321.

Hannerz, Ulf. 2004. *Foreign News: Exploring the World of Foreign Correspondents*. Chicago: University of Chicago Press.

Harlan, Chico. 2012. "In Authoritarian North Korea, Hints of Reform." *Washington Post*, September 3, 2012. Available at: https://www.washingtonpost.com/world/asia_pacific/in-authoritarian-north-korea-hints-of-reform/2012/09/03/bb5d95ce-f275-11e1-adc6-87dfa8eff430_story.html?utm_term=.ddf4cd1469fc (accessed June 24, 2019).

Hartig, Falk. 2016. "How China Understands Public Diplomacy: The Importance of National Image for National Interests." *International Studies Review* 18 (4): 655–680.

Hastings, Justin V. 2016. *A Most Enterprising Country: North Korea in the Global Economy*. Ithaca, NY: Cornell University Press.

Hayman, Rachel. 2011. "Funding Fraud? Donors and Democracy in Rwanda." In Scott Strauss and Lars Waldorf, eds., *Remaking Rwanda: State Building and Human Rights after Mass Violence*. Madison: University of Wisconsin Press, pp. 118–131.

Haynes, Deborah. 2018. "Russian Troll Threats and Techniques Revealed." *The Times*, April 2, 2018. Available at: https://www.thetimes.co.uk/article/troll-threats-and-techniques-revealed-7hhn3xrqs.

Heathershaw, John, and Saipira Furstenberg. 2020. "Central Asian Political Exiles Database (CAPE), Parameters and Definitions." Available at: https://excas.net/projects/political-exiles/ (accessed January 3, 2020).

Hedstrom, Peter, and Richard Swedberg. 1998. "Social Mechanisms: An Introductory Essay." In Peter Hedstrom and Richard Swedberg, eds. *Social Mechanisms: An Analytical Approach to Social Theory*. Cambridge: Cambridge University Press, pp. 1–31.

Heilmann, Sebastian, and Dirk H. Schmidt. 2014. *China's Foreign Political and Economic Relations: An Unconventional Global Power*. Lanham, MD: Rowman & Littlefield.

Hendrix, Cullen S., and Wendy H. Wong. 2013. "When Is the Pen Truly Mighty? Regime Type and the Efficacy of Naming and Shaming in Curbing Human Rights Abuses." *British Journal of Political Science* 43 (3): 651–672.

Hoffmann, Bert. 2015. "The International Dimension of Authoritarian Regime Legitimation: Insights from the Cuban Case." *Journal of International Relations and Development* 18 (4): 556–574.

Holbig, Heike. 2011. "International Dimensions of Legitimacy: Reflections on Western Theories and the Chinese Experience." *Journal of Chinese Political Science* 16 (2): 161–181.

Holbig, Heike. 2013. "Ideology after the End of Ideology: China and the Quest for Autocratic Legitimation." *Democratization* 20 (1): 61–81.

Holmes, Oliver. 2015. "Thailand Forcibly Sends Nearly 100 Uighur Muslims Back to China." *The Guardian*, July 9, 2015. Available at: https://www.theguardian.com/world/

2015/jul/09/thailand-forcibly-sends-nearly-100-uighur-muslims-back-to-china (accessed January 3, 2020).

Howell, Edward. 2020. "The Juche H-Bomb? North Korea, Nuclear Weapons and Regime-State Survival." *International Affairs* 96 (4): 1051–1068.

Human Rights Watch. 1995. "Rwanda: The Crisis Continues." Available at: https://www.hrw.org/report/1995/04/01/rwanda/crisis-continues (accessed April 17, 2020).

Human Rights Watch. 2014. "Rwanda: Repression across Borders." *Human Rights Watch*, January 28, 2014. Available at: https://www.hrw.org/news/2014/01/28/rwanda-repression-across-borders# (accessed April 17, 2020).

Human Rights Watch. 2016. "Boxed In: Women and Saudi Arabia's Male Guardianship System." Available at: https://www.hrw.org/report/2016/07/16/boxed/women-and-saudi-arabias-male-guardianship-system.

Human Rights Watch. 2019a. "UAE: Unrelenting Harassment of Dissidents' Families." *Human Rights Watch*, December 22, 2019. Available at: https://www.hrw.org/news/2019/12/22/uae-unrelenting-harassment-dissidents-families (accessed January 3, 2020).

Human Rights Watch. 2019b. "Egypt: Families of Dissidents Targeted." *Human Rights Watch*, November 19, 2019. Available at: https://www.hrw.org/news/2019/11/19/egypt-families-dissidents-targeted (accessed January 7, 2020).

Hunerven, Adam. 2019. "Spirit Breaking: Capitalism and Terror in Northwest China." *Chuang* 2. Available at: http://chuangcn.org/journal/two/spirit-breaking/ (accessed April 2, 2020).

Ikenberry, G. John. 2001. "American Power and the Empire of Capitalist Democracy." *Review of International Studies* 27 (5): 191–212.

Ikenberry, G. John, and Charles A. Kupchan. 1990. "Socialization and Hegemonic Power." *International Organization* 44 (3): 283–315.

Jaafari, Shirin. 2019. "International Community Has 'Failed' in the Aftermath of Khashoggi's Death." *Public Radio International*, October 2, 2019. Available at: https://www.pri.org/stories/2019-10-02/international-community-has-failed-aftermath-khashoggis-death.

Jackson, Nicole J. 2010. "The Role of External Factors in Advancing Non-Liberal Democratic Forms of Political Rule: A Case Study of Russia's Influence on Central Asian Regimes." *Contemporary Politics* 16 (1): 101–118.

Jones, Will. 2012. "Between Pyongyang and Singapore: The Rwandan State, Its Rulers, and the Military." In Maddalena Campioni and Patrick Noack, eds., *Rwanda Fast Forward: Social, Economic, Military and Reconciliation Prospects*. London: Palgrave Macmillan, pp. 228–248.

Jones, Will. 2016. "Victoire in Kigali, or: Why Rwandan Elections Are Not Won Transnationally." *Journal of Eastern African Studies* 10 (2): 343–365.

Jost, John T. 2006. "The End of the End of Ideology." *American Psychologist* 61 (7): 651–670.

Josua, Maria. 2020. "Causing and Communicating Bad News: How Autocrats Legitimize Repression." Paper presented at the 2020 European Consortium for Political Research annual convention, August 24–28, 2020.

Jourde, Cedric. 2007. "The International Relations of Small Neoauthoritarian States: Islamism, Warlordism, and the Framing of Stability." *International Studies Quarterly* 51 (2): 481–503.

Kailitz, Steffen. 2013. "Classifying Political Regimes Revisited: Legitimacy and Durability." *Democratization* 20 (1): 39–60.

Kailitz, Steffen, and Daniel Stockemer. 2017. "Regime Legitimation, Elite Cohesion and the Durability of Autocratic Regime Types." *International Political Science Review* 38 (3): 332–348.

Kaphle, Anup. 2015. "The Foreign Desk in Transition." *Columbia Journalism Review* 53 (6): 15. March–April. Available at: https://www.cjr.org/analysis/the_foreign_desk_in_transition.php (accessed November 23, 2018).

KCNA. 1998. "Stop to Anti-Chongryon Campaign Called For." *KCNA Watch*, November 11, 1998. Available at: https://kcnawatch.org/newstream/1452000190-109074235/stop-to-anti-chongryon-campaign-called-for/ (accessed July 16, 2019).

KCNA. 2006. "Lecture Given in Tokyo to Mark Anniversary of Chongryon." *KCNA Watch*, May 27, 2006. Available at: https://kcnawatch.org/newstream/1451884286-711569778/lecture-given-in-tokyo-to-mark-anniversary-of-chongryon/ (accessed July 16, 2019).

KCNA. 2013. "Congratulations to Kim Jong Un from Chongryon Organizations." *KCNA Watch*, September 9, 2013. Available at: https://kcnawatch.org/newstream/1451900911-924804592/congratulations-to-kim-jong-un-from-chongryon-organizations/ (accessed July 16, 2019).

KCNA. 2014a. "Japan's Suppression of Chongryon Denounced in Germany." *KCNA Watch*, April 15, 2014. Available at: https://kcnawatch.org/newstream/1451896271-280544603/japans-suppression-of-chongryon-denounced-in-germany/ (accessed July 16, 2019).

KCNA. 2014b. "Japanese Authorities' Crackdown upon Chongryon Condemned by Brazilian Political Party, Indian Organization." *KCNA Watch*, April 18, 2014. Available at: https://kcnawatch.org/newstream/1451903827-759859179/japanese-authorities-crackdown-upon-chongryon-condemned-by-brazilian-political-party-indian-organization/ (accessed July 16, 2019).

KCNA. 2014c. "Pakistani, Ethiopian Bodies Condemn Japan's Anti-Chongryon Campaign." *KCNA Watch*, April 18, 2014. Available at: https://kcnawatch.org/newstream/1451896714-876451554/pakistani-ethiopian-bodies-condemn-japans-anti-chongryon-campaign/ (accessed July 16, 2019).

KCNA. 2015a. "Japanese Authorities' Crackdown upon Officials of Chongryon Flayed by Koreans in Kyrgyzstan." *KCNA Watch*, April 15, 2014. Available at: https://kcnawatch.org/newstream/1451904184-357869489/japanese-authorities-crackdown-upon-officials-of-chongryon-flayed-by-koreans-in-kyrgyzstan/ (accessed July 16, 2019).

KCNA. 2015b. "Pakistani, Bangladeshi Organizations Term Suppression of Chongryon Human Rights Abuse." *KCNA Watch*, April 7, 2015. Available at: https://kcnawatch.org/newstream/1451904750-943568805/pakistani-bangladeshi-organizations-terms-suppression-of-chongryon-human-rights-abuse/ (accessed July 16, 2019).

KCNA. 2016. "'Our National Forum 2016' Held in Osaka, Japan." *KCNA Watch*, September 19, 2016. Available at: https://kcnawatch.org/newstream/263508/our-national-forum-2016-held-in-osaka-japan/ (accessed July 16, 2019).

KCNA. 2019a. "European Regional Solidarity Meeting Held." *KCNA Watch*, July 14, 2019. Available at: https://kcnawatch.org/newstream/1563085953-474849274/european-regional-solidarity-meeting-held/ (accessed November 11, 2019).

KCNA. 2019b. "Seminars on Chairman Kim Jong Il's Exploits Held Abroad." *KCNA Watch*, June 27, 2019. Available at: https://kcnawatch.org/newstream/1561606246-990812762/seminars-on-chairman-kim-jong-ils-exploits-held-abroad/ (accessed November 11, 2019).

KCNA. 2019c. "Korean Book, Photo and Art Exhibition Takes Place in Romania." *KCNA Watch*, November 6, 2019. Available at: https://kcnawatch.org/newstream/1573021869-141890916/korean-book-photo-and-art-exhibition-takes-place-in-romania/ (accessed November 11, 2019).

Keck, Margaret E., and Kathryn Sikkink. 1998. *Activists beyond Borders: Advocacy Networks in International Politics*. Ithaca, NY: Cornell University Press.

Kerr, Simeon. 2017. "Saudi Arabia to Launch Global PR Offensive to Counter Negative Press." *Financial Times*, December 12, 2017. Available at: https://www.ft.com/content/c7d57f8e-96ca-11e7-a652-cde3f882dd7b (accessed March 8, 2019).

Kertzer, Joshua D., and Thomas Zeitzoff. 2017. "A Bottom-Up Theory of Public Opinion about Foreign Policy." *American Journal of Political Science* 61 (3): 543–558.

Kester, Bernadette. 2010. "The Art of Balancing: Foreign Correspondents in Non-Democratic Countries: The Russian Case." *International Communication Gazette* 72 (1): 51–69.

KFA Ireland. 2016. "Public KFA-Meeting Successfully Held in Dublin." *Korea Friendship Association Ireland*, February 22, 2016. Available at: https://jucheireland.wordpress.com/2016/02/22/public-kfa-meeting-successfully-held-in-dublin/ (accessed November 11, 2019).

KFA Ireland. 2018. "Public Meeting Held in Belfast." *Korea Friendship Association Ireland*, November 1, 2018. Available at: https://jucheireland.wordpress.com/2018/11/01/public-meeting-held-in-belfast/ (accessed November 11, 2019).

Kim, Byung-Kook, and Ezra F. Vogel, eds. 2011. *The Park Chung Hee Era: The Transformation of South Korea*. Cambridge, MA: Harvard University Press.

King, Gary, Jennifer Pan, and Margaret E. Roberts. 2013. "How Censorship in China Allows Government Criticism but Silences Collective Expression." *American Political Science Review* 107 (2): 326–343.

Klug, Foster. 2019. "Juche Rules North Korean Propaganda, but What Does It Mean?" *Associated Press*, September 30, 2019. Available at: https://apnews.com/d63d00ce9de042dc88b9df2c40be53ee (accessed November 25, 2019).

Kneuer, Marianne, and Thomas Demmelhuber. 2016. "Gravity Centres of Authoritarian Rule: A Conceptual Approach." *Democratization* 23 (5): 775–796.

Knight, Kathleen. 2006. "Transformations of the Concept of Ideology in the Twentieth Century." *American Political Science Review* 100 (4): 619–626.

Koh Gui Qing and John Shiffman. 2015. "Beijing's Covert Radio Network Airs China-Friendly News across Washington, and the World." *Reuters*, November 2, 2015. Available at: https://www.reuters.com/investigates/special-report/china-radio/ (accessed November 11, 2019).

Krishnan, Ananth. 2018. "China Is Buying Good Press across the World, One Paid Journalist at a Time." *ThePrint*, November 24, 2018. Available at: https://theprint.in/opinion/china-is-paying-foreign-journalists-including-from-india-to-report-from-beijing/154013/ (accessed February 18, 2019).

Kunczik, Michael. 1997. *Images of Nations and International Public Relations*. Mahwah, NJ: Lawrence Erlbaum Associates.

Kuo, Lily. 2018. "From Denial to Pride: How China Changed Its Language on Xinjiang's Camps." *The Guardian*, October 22, 2018. Available at: https://www.theguardian.com/world/2018/oct/22/from-denial-to-pride-how-china-changed-its-language-on-xinjiangs-camps (accessed November 20, 2018).

Kuran, Timur. 1995. *Private Truths, Public Lies: The Social Consequences of Preference Falsification*. Cambridge, MA: Harvard University Press.

Kwon, Heonik, and Byung-Ho Chung. 2012. *North Korea: Beyond Charismatic Politics*. Lanham, MD: Rowman & Littlefield.

Lamb, Kate. 2019. "Thai Government Pressed over Missing Lao Activist Od Sayavong." *The Guardian*, September 7, 2019. Available at: https://www.theguardian.com/world/ 2019/sep/07/thai-government-pressed-over-missing-lao-activist-od-sayavong (accessed January 7, 2020).

Lankina, Tomila, Alexander Libman, and Anastassia Obydenkova. 2016. "Authoritarian and Democratic Diffusion in Post-Communist Regions." *Comparative Political Studies* 49 (12): 1599–1629.

Lankov, Andrei. 2002. "Kim Takes Control: The 'Great Purge' in North Korea, 1956–1960." *Korean Studies* 26 (1): 87–119.

Larson, Deborah Welch, and Alexei Shevchenko. 2010. "Status Seekers: Chinese and Russian Responses to U.S. Primacy." *International Security* 34 (4): 63–95.

Larson, Deborah Welch, T. V. Paul, and William C. Wohlforth. 2014. "Status and World Order." In T. V. Paul, Deborah Welch Larson, and William C. Wohlforth, eds., *Status in World Politics*. Cambridge: Cambridge University Press, pp. 3–29.

Leibold, James. 2020. "Surveillance in China's Xinjiang Region: Ethnic Sorting, Coercion, and Inducement." *Journal of Contemporary China*, 29 (121): 46–60.

Lemon, Edward. 2019. "Weaponizing Interpol." *Journal of Democracy* 30 (2): 15–29.

Levitsky, Steven, and Lucan A. Way. 2006. "Linkage versus Leverage: Rethinking the International Dimension of Regime Change." *Comparative Politics* 38 (4): 379–400.

Lewis, David. 2015. "'Illiberal Spaces': Uzbekistan's Extraterritorial Security Practices and the Spatial Politics of Contemporary Authoritarianism." *Nationalities Papers* 43 (1): 140–159.

Lie, John. 2008. *Zainichi (Koreans in Japan): Diasporic Nationalism and Postcolonial Identity*. Berkeley: University of California Press.

Lillis, Joanna. 2019. "Kazakhstan: Nazarbayev Takes Back Control." *Eurasianet*, October 21, 2019. Available at: https://eurasianet.org/kazakhstan-nazarbayev-takes-back-control (accessed October 29, 2019).

Lim, Louisa, and Julia Bergin. 2018. "Inside China's Audacious Global Propaganda Campaign." *The Guardian*, December 7, 2018. Available at: https://www.theguardian. com/news/2018/dec/07/china-plan-for-global-media-dominance-propaganda-xi-jinping (accessed December 17, 2019).

Lipton, Eric, Brooke Williams, and Nicholas Confessore. 2014. "Foreign Powers Buy Influence at Think Tanks." *New York Times*, September 6, 2014. Available at: https:// www.nytimes.com/2014/09/07/us/politics/foreign-powers-buy-influence-at-think-tanks.html (accessed April 8, 2020).

Liu, Hailong. 2020. *Propaganda: Ideas, Discourses and Its Legitimization*. New York: Routledge.

Longman, Timothy. 2011. "Limitations to Political Reform: The Undemocratic Nature of Transition in Rwanda." In Scott Strauss and Lars Waldorf, eds., *Remaking Rwanda: State Building and Human Rights after Mass Violence*. Madison: University of Wisconsin Press, pp. 25–47.

Longman, Timothy. 2017. *Memory and Justice in Post-Genocide Rwanda*. New York: Cambridge University Press.

Lorentzen, Peter L., and Xi Lu. 2018. "Personal Ties, Meritocracy, and China's Anti-Corruption Campaign." Working Paper. Available at SSRN: https://dx.doi.org/10.2139/ssrn.2835841 (accessed April 4, 2020).

Lorenz, Andreas. 2012. "Kim Jong Un Sends Cautious Signals of Reform." *Spiegel Online*, July 12, 2012. Available at: https://www.spiegel.de/international/world/kim-jong-un-sends-cautious-signs-of-reform-in-north-korea-a-844061.html (accessed June 24, 2019).

Lovell, Julia. 2019. *Maoism: A Global History*. London: Bodley Head, Penguin Random House.

Loyle, Cyanne E. 2018. "Transitional Justice and Political Order in Rwanda." *Ethnic and Racial Studies* 41 (4): 663–680.

Lührmann, Anna, and Staffan I. Lindberg. 2019. "A Third Wave of Autocratization Is Here: What Is New about It?" *Democratization* 26 (7): 1095–1113.

Maerz, Seraphine M. 2016. "The Electronic Face of Authoritarianism: E-government as a Tool for Gaining Legitimacy in Competitive and Non-competitive Regimes." *Government Information Quarterly* 33 (4): 727–735.

Maerz, Seraphine F. 2018. "Ma'naviyat in Uzbekistan: An Ideological Extrication from Its Soviet Past?" *Journal of Political Ideologies* 23 (2): 205–222.

Maerz, Seraphine F. 2019. "Simulating Pluralism: The Language of Democracy in Hegemonic Authoritarianism." *Political Research Exchange* 1 (1): 1–23.

Magaloni, Beatriz, and Ruth Kricheli. 2010. "Political Order and One-Party Rule." *Annual Review of Political Science* 13: 123–143.

Martin, Quinn. 2019. "Uzbekistan Reforms Aim to Build Domestic Capital Market." *EmergingMarkets.me*, November 17, 2019. Available at: http://emergingmarkets.me/uzbekistan-reforms-aim-to-build-domestic-capital-market/ (accessed May 12, 2020).

Matfess, Hilary. 2015. "Rwanda and Ethiopia: Developmental Authoritarianism and the New Politics of African Strong Men." *African Studies Review* 58 (2): 181–204.

Maynard, Jonathan. 2013. "A Map of the Field of Ideological Analysis." *Journal of Political Ideologies* 18 (3): 299–327.

McAdams, A. James. 2017. *Vanguard of the Revolution: The Global Idea of the Communist Party*. Princeton, NJ: Princeton University Press.

McCombs, Maxwell. 2005. "A Look at Agenda-Setting: Past, Present and Future." *Journalism Studies* 6 (4): 543–557.

McCormick, Andrew. 2019. "'Even if You Don't Think You Have a Relationship with China, China Has a Big Relationship with You': An Oral History of China's Foreign Press Training Programs." *Columbia Journalism Review*, June 20, 2019. Available at: https://www.cjr.org/special_report/china-foreign-journalists-oral-history.php (accessed January 15, 2020).

McNair, John. 2015. "Winning Friends, Influencing People: Soviet Cultural Diplomacy in Australia, 1928–1968." *Australian Journal of Politics and History* 61 (4): 515–529.

Meldrum, Andrew. 2011. "Rwanda Journalists under Threat." *Public Radio International*, December 30, 2011. Available at: https://www.pri.org/stories/2011-12-30/rwanda-journalists-under-threat (accessed April 28, 2020).

Melissen, Jan. 2005. "The New Public Diplomacy: Between Theory and Practice." In Jan Melissen, ed., *The New Public Diplomacy: Soft Power in International Relations*. London: Palgrave, pp. 3–27.

Melnykovska, Inna, Hedwig Plamper, and Rainer Schweickert. 2012. "Do Russia and China Promote Autocracy in Central Asia?" *Asia Europe Journal* 10 (1): 75–89.

Michaelsen, Marcus. 2018. "Exit and Voice in a Digital Age: Iran's Exiled Activists and the Authoritarian State." *Globalizations* 15 (2): 248–264.

Michaelsen, Marcus, and Marlies Glasius. 2018. "Authoritarian Practices in the Digital Age." *International Journal of Communication* 12: 3788–3794.

Michaelson, Ruth. 2019. "'What They Did to Me Was So Horrific': Brutal Silencing of a Saudi Feminist." *The Guardian*, May 24, 2019. Availale at: https://www.theguardian.com/global-development/2019/may/24/what-they-did-to-me-was-so-horrific-brutal-silencing-of-a-saudi-feminist-loujain-al-hathloul.

Miskimmon, Alister, Ben O' Loughlin, and Laura Roselle. 2013. *Strategic Narratives: Communication Power and the New World Order*. New York: Routledge.

Mitchell, Richard H. 1967. *The Korean Minority in Japan*. Berkeley: University of California Press.

Møller, Jørgen, and Svend-Erik Skaaning. 2013. "Autocracies, Democracies, and the Violation of Civil Liberties." *Democratization* 20 (1): 82–106.

Møller, Jorgen, Svend-Erik Skaaning, and Jakob Tolstrup. 2017. "International Influences and Democratic Regression in Interwar Europe: Disentangling the Impact of Power Politics and Demonstration Effects." *Government and Opposition* 52 (4): 559–586.

Moravcsik, Andrew. 2000. "The Origins of Human Rights Regimes: Democratic Delegation in Postwar Europe." *International Organization* 54 (2): 217–252.

Morgenbesser, Lee. 2017. "The Autocratic Mandate: Elections, Legitimacy and Regime Stability in Singapore." *The Pacific Review* 30 (2): 205–231.

Morgenbesser, Lee. 2019. "Cambodia's Transition to Hegemonic Authoritarianism." *Journal of Democracy* 30 (1): 158–171.

Morgenbesser, Lee. 2020a. "The Menu of Autocratic Innovation." *Democratization* 27 (6): 1053–1072.

Morgenbesser, Lee. 2020b. *The Rise of Sophisticated Authoritarianism in Southeast Asia*. Cambridge: Cambridge University Press.

Morris-Suzuki, Tessa. 2005. "A Dream Betrayed: Cold War Politics and the Repatriation of Koreans from Japan to North Korea." *Asian Studies Review* 29 (4): 357–381.

Morris-Suzuki, Tessa. 2007. *Exodus to North Korea: Shadows from Japan's Cold War*. Lanham, MD: Rowman & Littlefield.

Moss, Dana M. 2016. "Transnational Repression, Diaspora Mobilization, and the Case of the Arab Spring." *Social Problems* 63 (4): 480–498.

Moss, Dana M. 2018. "The Ties That Bind: Internet Communication Technologies, Networked Authoritarianism, and 'Voice' in the Syrian Diaspora." *Globalizations* 15 (2): 265–282.

Mozur, Paul. 2019. "Being Tracked While Reporting in China, Where 'There Are No Whys.'" *New York Times*, April 16, 2019. Available at: https://www.nytimes.com/2019/04/16/insider/china-xinjiang-reporting-surveillance-uighur.html (accessed November 13, 2020).

Mozur, Paul. 2020. "China Post-Coronavirus: Signs of Life, Censorship and Paranoia." *New York Times*, April 16, 2020. Available at: https://www.nytimes.com/2020/04/16/business/china-coronavirus-censorship.html (accessed November 13, 2020).

Mutethya, Edith. 2018. "2018 Seminar for Kenyan Journalists Kicks off in Beijing." *China Daily*, August 9, 2018. Available at: http://www.chinadaily.com.cn/a/201808/09/WS5b6c48aca310add14f384f17.html (accessed November 20, 2018).

Nathan, Andrew. 2015. "China's Challenge." *Journal of Democracy* 26 (1): 156–170.

Nathan, Andrew J., and Andrew Scobell. 2012. *China's Search for Security*. New York: Columbia University Press.

Nebehay, Stephanie. 2018. "U.N. Says It Has Credible Reports That China Holds Million Uighurs in Secret Camps." *Reuters*, August 10, 2018. Available at: https://www.reuters.com/article/us-china-rights-un/u-n-says-it-has-credible-reports-that-china-holds-million-uighurs-in-secret-camps-idUSKBN1KV1SU (accessed April 2, 2020).

Ngabonziza, Dan. 2019. "Rwanda Screens 'The Royal Tour' Documentary to Global Tour Operators in London." *KT Press*, November 6, 2019. Available at: https://www.ktpress.rw/2019/11/rwanda-screens-the-royal-tour-documentary-to-global-tour-operators-in-london/ (accessed April 30, 2020).

Nixon, Ron. 2016. *Selling Apartheid: South Africa's Global Propaganda War*. London: Pluto Books.

Norkus, Zenonas. 2005. "Mechanisms as Miracle Makers? The Rise and Inconsistencies of the 'Mechanismic Approach' in Social Science and History." *History and Theory* 44 (3): 348–372.

Nyamwasa, Kayumba, Patrick Karegaya, Theogene Rudasingwa, and Gerald Gahima. 2010. *Rwanda Briefing*. Copy on file with author.

Nye, Joseph. 1990. "Soft Power." *Foreign Policy* 80: 153–171.

Nye, Joseph. 2008. "Public Diplomacy and Soft Power." *Annals of the American Academy of Political and Social Science* 616 (1): 94–109.

O'Carroll, Chad. 2020. "Spanish Aristocrat behind a North Korea Sympathizer Group Violated UN Sanctions." *NKNews.org*, August 10, 2020. Available at: https://www.nknews.org/2020/08/spanish-aristocrat-behind-a-north-korea-sympathizer-group-violated-un-sanctions/ (accessed September 2, 2020).

Ohlberg, Mareike. 2019. "Propaganda beyond the Great Firewall: Chinese Party-State Media on Facebook, Twitter, and YouTube." *Mercator Institute for China Studies*. Available at: https://www.merics.org/en/china-mapping/propaganda-beyond-the-great-firewall (accessed January 15, 2020).

Öhman, Daniel, and Besir Kavak. 2018. "Secret Police Intervention Following Suspicion of Turkish Murder-Plot in Denmark." *Sverige Radio*, June 13, 2018. Available at: https://sverigesradio.se/sida/artikel.aspx?programid=83&artikel=6975341 (accessed January 7, 2020).

Omelicheva, Mariya Y. 2016. "Authoritarian Legitimation: Assessing Discourses of Legitimacy in Kazakhstan and Uzbekistan." *Central Asian Survey* 35 (4): 481–500.

Ong, Lynette H. 2018. "'Thugs-for-Hire': Subcontracting of State Coercion and State Capacity in China." *Perspectives on Politics* 16 (3): 680–695.

Orttung, Robert W., and Elizabeth Nelson. 2019. "Russia Today's Strategy and Effectiveness on YouTube." *Post-Soviet Affairs* 35 (2): 77–92.

Owen, John M., IV. 2010. *The Clash of Ideas in World Politics: Transnational Networks, States, and Regime Change, 1510–2010*. Princeton, NJ: Princeton University Press.

Öztürk, Ahmet Erdi, and Semiha Sözeri. 2018. "Diyanet as a Turkey Foreign Policy Tool: Evidence from the Netherlands and Bulgaria." *Politics and Religion* 11 (3): 624–648.

Pak, Jung H. 2020. *Becoming Kim Jong Un: A Former CIA Officer's Insights into North Korea's Enigmatic Young Dictator*. New York: Ballantine.

Parker, Jason C. 2016. *Hearts, Minds, Voices: US Cold War Public Diplomacy and the Formation of the Third World*. New York: Oxford University Press.

Paul, T. V., Deborah Welch Larson, and William C. Wohlforth, eds. 2014. *Status in World Politics*. Cambridge: Cambridge University Press.

Pearce, Katy E., and Sarah Kendzior. 2012. "Networked Authoritarianism and Social Media in Azerbaijan." *Journal of Communication* 62 (2): 283–298.

Peisakhin, Leonid, and Arturas Rozenas. 2018. "Electoral Effects of Biased Media: Russian Television in Ukraine." *American Journal of Political Science* 62 (3): 535–550.

Peskin, Victor. 2011. "Victor's Justice Revisited: Rwandan Patriotic Front Crimes and the Prosecutorial Endgame at the ICTR." In Scott Strauss and Lars Waldorf, eds., *Remaking Rwanda: State Building and Human Rights after Mass Violence.* Madison: University of Wisconsin Press, pp. 173–183.

Phillips, Tom, and Oliver Holmes. 2016. "Activist Who Vanished in Thailand Is Being Held in China, Says Wife." *The Guardian*, February 3, 2016. Available at: https://www. theguardian.com/world/2016/feb/03/activist-li-xin-vanished-in-thailand--held-in-china-says-wife (accessed April 9, 2020).

Pomerantsev, Peter. 2019. *This Is Not Propaganda: Adventures in the War against Reality.* London: Faber & Faber.

Pottier, Johan. 2002. *Re-Imagining Rwanda: Conflict, Survival and Disinformation in the Late Twentieth Century.* New York: Cambridge University Press.

Primiano, Christopher B. 2013. "China under Stress: The Xinjiang Question." *International Politics* 50 (3): 455–473.

Prunier, Gerard. 2009. *Africa's World War: Congo, the Rwandan Genocide, and the Making of a Continental Catastrophe.* New York: Oxford University Press.

Pu, Xiaoyu, and Randall L. Schweller. 2014. "Status Signaling, Multiple Audiences, and China's Blue-Water Naval Ambition." In T. V. Paul, Deborah Welch Larson, and William C. Wohlforth, eds., *Status in World Politics.* Cambridge: Cambridge University Press, pp. 141–162.

Pu, Xiaoyu. 2012. "Socialisation as a Two-way Process: Emerging Powers and the Diffusion of International Norms." *Chinese Journal of International Politics* 5 (4): 341–367.

Pu, Xiaoyu. 2019. *Rebranding China: Contested Status Signaling in the Changing Global Order.* Stanford, CA: Stanford University Press.

Purdekova, Andrea. 2011. "'Even if I Am Not Here, There Are So Many Eyes': Surveillance and State Reach in Rwanda." *Journal of Modern African Studies* 49 (3): 475–497.

Purdekova, Andrea, Filip Reyntjens, and Nina Wilen. 2018. "Militarization of Governance after Conflict: Beyond the Rebel-to-Ruler Frame—the Case of Rwanda." *Third World Quarterly* 39 (1): 158–174.

Putz, Catherine. 2019. "Turkey Seeks Extradition of 2 Gulen School Employees from Kyrgyzstan." *The Diplomat*, December 31, 2019. Available at: https://thediplomat.com/2019/12/turkey-seeks-extradition-of-2-gulen-school-employees-from-kyrgyzstan/ (accessed January 7, 2019).

Radchenko, Sergey. 2014. "1956." In Stephen A. Smith, ed., *The Oxford Handbook of The History of Communism.* Oxford: Oxford University press, pp. 140–155.

Ramzy, Austin, and Chris Buckley. 2019. "'Absolutely No Mercy': Leaked Files Expose How China Organized Mass Detentions of Muslims." *New York Times*, November 16, 2019. Available at: https://www.nytimes.com/interactive/2019/11/16/world/asia/china-xinjiang-documents.html (accessed April 22, 2020).

Rauhala, Emily. 2015. "China Expels French Journalist for Terrorism Coverage." *Washington Post*, December 26, 2015. Available at: https://www.washingtonpost.com/news/worldviews/wp/2015/12/26/china-expels-french-journalist-for-terrorism-coverage/?utm_term=.aeb179c26db2 (accessed January 14, 2019).

Rawnsley, Gary D. 2015. "To Know Us Is to Love Us: Public Diplomacy and International Broadcasting in Contemporary Russia and China." *Politics* 35 (3–4): 273–286.

Repnikova, Maria. 2017. *Media Politics in China: Improvising Power under Authoritarianism*. Cambridge: Cambridge University Press.

Reporters Without Borders. 2019. "China's Pursuit of a New World Media Order." Available at: https://rsf.org/sites/default/files/en_rapport_chine_web_final.pdf (accessed March 25, 2019).

Reuters. 2017. "Turkey Promises to Eliminate Anti-China Media Reports." *Reuters*, August 3, 2017. Available at: https://www.reuters.com/article/us-china-turkey/turkey-promises-to-eliminate-anti-china-media-reports-idUSKBN1AJ1BV (accessed May 12, 2020).

Reuters. 2020. "Exclusive: Iranian Diplomats Instigated Killing of Dissident in Istanbul, Turkish Officials Say." *Reuters*, March 27, 2020. Available at: https://www.reuters.com/article/us-turkey-iran-killing-exclusive/exclusive-iranian-diplomats-instigated-killing-of-dissident-in-istanbul-turkish-officials-say-idUSKBN21E3FU (accessed September 2, 2020).

Reyntjens, Filip. 2011. "Constructing the Truth, Dealing with Dissent, Domesticating the World: Governance in Post-Genocide Rwanda." *African Affairs* 110 (438): 1–34.

Reyntjens, Filip. 2013. *Political Governance in Post-Genocide Rwanda*. New York: Cambridge University Press.

Reyntjens, Filip. 2015. "The Struggle over Truth: Rwanda and the BBC." *African Affairs* 114 (457): 637–648.

Reyntjens, Filip. 2016. "(Re-)imagining a Reluctant Post-Genocide Society: The Rwandan Patriotic Front's Ideology and Practice." *Journal of Genocide Research* 18 (1): 61–81.

Riding, Alan. 1991. "Iran's Premier in Stormy Time Found Slain Near Paris." *New York Times*, August 9, 1991, Section A, p. 6. Available at: https://www.nytimes.com/1991/08/09/world/iran-s-premier-in-stormy-time-found-slain-near-paris.html (accessed January 3, 2020).

Risse, Thomas, Stephen C. Ropp, and Kathryn Sikkink. 1999. *The Power of Human Rights: International Norms and Domestic Change*. Cambridge: Cambridge University Press.

Roberts, Margaret E. 2018. *Censored: Distraction and Diversion inside China's Great Firewall*. Princeton, NJ: Princeton University Press.

Roberts, Sean R. 2012. "Imaginary Terrorism? The Global War on Terror and the Narrative of the Uyghur Terrorist Threat." *Institute for European, Russian and Eurasian Studies Working Paper*. Available at: http://www.ponarseurasia.org/sites/default/files/Roberts_WorkingPaper_March2012.pdf (accessed April 2, 2020).

Roberts, Sean R. 2018. "The Biopolitics of China's 'War on Terror' and the Exclusion of the Uyghurs." *Critical Asian Studies* 50 (2): 232–258.

Roberts, Sean R. 2020. *The War on the Uyghurs: China's Campaign Against Xinjiang's Muslims*. Manchester: Manchester University Press.

Rolland, Nadège. 2020. "China's Vision for a New World Order." *The National Bureau of Asian Research*, Special Report #83.

Ron, James, and David Crow. 2015. "Who Trusts Local Human Rights Organizations: Evidence from Three World Regions." *Human Rights Quarterly* 37 (1): 188–239.

Ron, James, Howard Ramos, and Kathleen Rodgers. 2005. "Transnational Information Politics: NGO Human Rights Reporting, 1986–2000." *International Studies Quarterly* 49 (3): 557–588.

Roselle, Laura, Alister Miskimmon, and Ben O'Loughlin. 2014. "Strategic Narrative: A New Means to Understand Soft Power." *Media, War & Conflict* 7 (1): 70–84.

Rothschild, Jacob E., and Richard M. Shafranek. 2017. "Advances and Opportunities in the Study of Political Communication, Foreign Policy, and Public Opinion." *Political Communication* 34 (4): 634–643.

Russell, Jago. 2018. "Turkey's War on Dissent Goes Global." *Foreign Policy*, May 1, 2018. Available at: https://foreignpolicy.com/2018/05/01/turkeys-war-on-dissent-goes-global/ (accessed January 7, 2020).

Rutatina, Richard, and Jill Rutaremara. 2010. *Response to Allegations by Four Renegades.* Copy on file with author.

Ryang, Sonia. 1997. *North Koreans in Japan: Language, Ideology, and Identity.* Boulder, CO: Westview Press.

Ryang, Sonia. 2016. "The Rise and Fall of Chongryun: From Chosenjin to Zainichi and Beyond." *The Asia-Pacific Journal: Japan Focus* 14 (15): 1–16.

Scalapino, Robert A., and Chong-sik Lee. 1972. *Communism in Korea, Part 1: The Movement.* Berkeley: University of California Press.

Schatz, Edward. 2008. "Transnational Image Making and Soft Authoritarianism in Kazakhstan." *Slavic Review* 67 (1): 50–62.

Schatz, Edward, and Renan Levine. 2010. "Framing, Public Diplomacy, and Anti-Americanism in Central Asia." *International Studies Quarterly* 54 (3): 855–869.

Schatz, Edward and Elena Maltseva. 2012. "Kazakhstan's Authoritarian 'Persuasion.'" *Post-Soviet Affairs* 28 (1): 45–65.

Schedler, Andreas. 2002. "Elections without Democracy: The Menu of Manipulation." *Journal of Democracy* 13 (2): 36–50.

Schedler, Andreas, and Bert Hoffmann. 2016. "Communicating Authoritarian Elite Cohesion." *Democratization* 23 (1): 93–117.

Schenkkan, Nate. 2018. "The Remarkable Scale of Turkey's 'Global Purge.'" *Foreign Affairs*, January 29, 2018. Available at: https://www.foreignaffairs.com/articles/turkey/2018-01-29/remarkable-scale-turkeys-global-purge (accessed May 12, 2020).

Schlumberger, Oliver, and Andre Bank. 2001. "Succession, Legitimacy, and Regime Stability in Jordan." *Arab Studies Journal* 9–10 (1–2): 50–72.

Segal, David. 2018. "How Bell Pottinger, P.R. Firm for Despots and Rogues, Met Its End in South Africa." *New York Times*, February 4, 2018. Available at: https://www.nytimes.com/2018/02/04/business/bell-pottinger-guptas-zuma-south-africa.html (accessed April 8, 2020).

Shambaugh, David. 2013. *China Goes Global: The Partial Power.* New York: Oxford University Press.

Shambaugh, David. 2015. "China's Soft-Power Push: The Search for Respect." *Foreign Affairs* 94: 99–107.

Shao, Heng. 2014. "Explosion Hits Urumqi Right after President Xi Jinping's Visit." *Forbes*, April 30, 2014. Available at: https://www.forbes.com/sites/hengshao/2014/04/30/explosion-hits-urumqi-right-after-president-xi-jinpings-visit/#21ccd7613c45 (accessed April 2, 2020).

Sharp, Paul. 2005. "Revolutionary States, Outlaw Regimes and the Techniques of Public Diplomacy." In Jan Melissen, ed., *The New Public Diplomacy: Soft Power in International Relations.* London: Palgrave, pp. 106–123.

Sheffield, Hazel. 2012. "The AP's North Korea Bureau." *Columbia Journalism Review* 2, August 2012. Available at: https://archives.cjr.org/behind_the_news/the_aps_north_korea_bureau.php (accessed November 19, 2018).

Shim, David, and Dirk Nabers. 2013. "Imaging North Korea: Exploring Its Visual Representation in International Politics." *International Studies Perspectives* 14 (3): 289–306.

Shin, Gi-Wook. 2006. *Ethnic Nationalism in Korea: Genealogy, Politics, and Legacy.* Stanford, CA: Stanford University Press.

Shipper, Apichai W. 2010. "Nationalisms of and against Zainichi Koreans in Japan." *Asian Politics & Policy* 2 (1): 55–75.

Shirk, Susan. 2018. "The Return to Personalistic Rule." *Journal of Democracy* 29 (2): 22–36.

Silverstein, Ken. 2012. "Buckraking around the World With Tony Blair." *The New Republic*, September 12, 2012. Available at: https://newrepublic.com/article/107248/buckraking-around-the-world-tony-blair.

Smith, Hazel. 2015. *North Korea: Markets and Military Rule.* Cambridge: Cambridge University Press.

Smith-Finley, Joanne. 2019. "Securitization, Insecurity and Conflict in Contemporary Xinjiang: Has PRC Counter-Terrorism Evolved into State Terror?" *Central Asian Survey* 38 (1): 1–26.

State Council. 1990. "Regulations Concerning Foreign Journalists and Permanent Offices of Foreign News Agencies." Available at: https://en.wikisource.org/wiki/Regulations_Concerning_Foreign_Journalists_and_Permanent_Offices_of_Foreign_News_Agencies (accessed December 10, 2018).

State Council. 2008. "Regulations of the People's Republic of China on News Coverage by Permanent Offices of Foreign Media Organizations and Foreign Journalists." Available at: http://www.china-embassy.org/eng/ywzn/mtyw/press_1/t944225.htm (accessed December 10, 2018).

Stier, Sebastian. 2015. "Democracy, Autocracy and the News: The Impact of Regime Type on Media Freedom." *Democratization* 22 (7): 1273–1295.

Stone Fish, Isaac. 2014. "The Controversy over Pyongyang's Associated Press Bureau." *Foreign Policy*, December 24, 2014. Available at: https://foreignpolicy.com/2014/12/24/pyongyang-associated-press/ (accessed November 19, 2018).

Storey, Andy. 2012. "Structural Violence and the Struggle for State Power in Rwanda: What Arusha Got Wrong." *African Journal on Conflict Resolution* 12 (3): 7–31.

Straits Times. 2019. "China's Police State Goes Global, Leaving Refugees in Fear." *Straits Times*, July 23, 2019. Available at: https://www.straitstimes.com/asia/australianz/chinas-police-state-goes-global-leaving-refugees-in-fear (accessed April 9, 2020).

Straus, Scott, and Lars Waldorf. 2011. "Introduction: Seeing like a Post-Conflict State." In Scott Strauss and Lars Waldorf, eds., *Remaking Rwanda: State Building and Human Rights after Mass Violence.* Madison: University of Wisconsin Press, pp. 3–21.

Suh, Dae-Sook. 2002. "Military-First Politics of Kim Jong Il." *Asian Perspective* 26 (3): 145–167.

Swedish Juche Study Group. 2019. "North European Juche Seminar." Available at: https://svenskajuchegruppen.wordpress.com/nyheter/ (accessed November 11, 2019).

Tansey, Oisin. 2007. "Process Tracing and Elite Interviewing: A Case for Non-Probability Sampling." *PS: Political Science and Politics* 40 (4): 765–772.

Tansey, Oisin. 2016a. *The International Politics of Authoritarian Rule.* Oxford: Oxford University Press.

Tansey, Oisin. 2016b. "The Problem with Autocracy Promotion." *Democratization* 21 (1): 141–163.

Taylor, Philip M. 2003. *Munitions of the Mind: A History of Propaganda from the Ancient World to the Present Day*. Manchester: Manchester University Press.

Thomson, Susan. 2018. *Rwanda: From Genocide to Precarious Peace*. New Haven, CT: Yale University Press.

Thyen, Kressen, and Johannes Gerschewski. 2018. "Legitimacy and Protest under Authoritarianism: Explaining Student Mobilization in Egypt and Morocco during the Arab Uprisings." *Democratization* 25 (1): 38–57.

Tilly, Charles. 2001. "Mechanisms in Political Processes." *Annual Review of Political Science* 4: 24–41.

Tobin, David. 2020. "A 'Struggle of Life or Death': Han and Uyghur Insecurities on China's North-West Frontier." *China Quarterly* 242: 301–323.

Tracy, Marc, Edward Wong, and Lara Jakes. 2020. "China Announces That It Will Expel American Journalists." *New York Times*, March 17, 2020. Available at: https://www.nytimes.com/2020/03/17/business/media/china-expels-american-journalists.html (accessed April 8, 2020).

Tredaniel, Marie, and Pak K. Lee. 2018. "Explaining the Chinese Framing of the 'Terrorist' Violence in Xinjiang: Insights from Securitization Theory." *Nationalities Papers* 46 (1): 177–195.

Tsai, Wen-Hsuan. 2017. "Enabling China's Voice to Be Heard by the World: Ideas and Operations of the Chinese Communist Party's External Propaganda System." *Problems of Post-Communism* 64 (3–4): 203–213.

Tsourapas, Gerasimos. 2020. "Global Autocracies: Strategies of Transnational Repression, Legitimation, and Co-optation in World Politics. *International Studies Review*, early view. doi: https://doi.org/10.1093/isr/viaa061.

Turner, Simon. 2013. "Staging the Rwandan Diaspora: The Politics of Performance." *African Studies* 72 (2): 265–284.

Tynan, Deirdre. 2012. "Kazakhstan: Top-Notch PR Firms Help Brighten Astana's Image." *Eurasianet*, January 18, 2012. https://eurasianet.org/kazakhstan-top-notch-pr-firms-help-brighten-astanas-image.

UNHCR. 2014. "Report of the Detailed Findings of the Commission of Inquiry on Human Rights in the Democratic People's Republic of Korea." A/HRC/25/CRP.1. Available at: https://www.ohchr.org/en/hrbodies/hrc/coidprk/pages/commissioninquiryonhrindprk.aspx.

van Ham, Peter. 2001. "The Rise of the Brand State: The Postmodern Politics of Image and Reputation." *Foreign Affairs* 80 (5): 2–6.

van Ham, Peter. 2002. "Branding Territory: Inside the Wonderful Worlds of PR and IR Theory." *Millennium: Journal of International Studies* 31 (2): 249–269.

Vanderhill, Rachel. 2013. *Promoting Authoritarianism Abroad*. Boulder, CO: Lynne Reinner.

Vanderklippe, Nathan. 2018. "The Globe's Nathan VanderKlippe Recounts Surveillance, Threats of Arrest, Destruction of Photos While Reporting in Xinjiang." *Globe and Mail*, November 4, 2018. Available at: https://www.theglobeandmail.com/world/article-the-globes-nathan-vanderklippe-recounts-surveillance-threats-of/ (accessed December 14, 2018).

Vatlin, Alexander, and Stephen A. Smith. 2014. "The Evolution of the Comintern, 1919–1943. In Stephen A. Smith, ed., *The Oxford Handbook of the History of Communism*. Oxford: Oxford University Press, pp. 187–202.

von Soest, Christian. 2015. "Democracy Prevention: The International Collaboration of Authoritarian Regimes." *European Journal of Political Research* 54 (4): 623–638.

von Soest, Christian, and Julia Grauvogel. 2017. "Identity, Procedures and Performance: Systematically Assessing Authoritarian Regimes' Claims to Legitimacy." *Contemporary Politics* 23 (3): 287–305.

Wahman, Michael, Jan Teorell, and Axel Hadenius. 2013. "Authoritarian Regime Types Revisited: Updated Data in Comparative Perspective." *Contemporary Politics* 19 (1): 19–34.

Waldorf, Lars. 2011. "Instrumentalizing Genocide: The RPF's Campaign against 'Genocide Ideology.'" In Scott Strauss and Lars Waldorf, eds., *Remaking Rwanda: State Building and Human Rights after Mass Violence*. Madison: University of Wisconsin Press, pp. 48–66.

Walker, Christopher. 2018. "What Is 'Sharp Power'?" *Journal of Democracy* 29 (3): 9–23.

Wang, Hongying. 2003. "National Image Building and Chinese Foreign Policy." *China: An International Journal* 1 (1): 46–72.

Wang, Yiwei. 2008. "Public Diplomacy and the Rise of Chinese Soft Power." *The ANNALS of the American Academy of Political and Social Science* 616 (1): 257–273.

Wang, Zheng. 2012. *Never Forget National Humiliation: Historical Memory in Chinese Politics and Foreign Relations*. New York: Columbia University Press.

Wang, Zheng. 2014. "The China Dream: Concept and Context." *Journal of Chinese Political Science* 19 (1): 1–13.

Wanta, Wayne, and Yu-Wei Hu. 1993. "The Agenda-Setting Effects of International News Coverage: An Examination of Differing News Frames." *International Journal of Public Opinion Research* 5 (3): 250–264.

Way, Lucan A. 2015. "The Limits of Autocracy Promotion: The Case of Russia in the 'Near Abroad.'" *European Journal of Political Research* 54 (4): 691–706.

Weiss, Jessica Chen, and Allan Dafoe. 2019. "Authoritarian Audiences, Rhetoric, and Propaganda in International Crises: Evidence from China." *International Studies Quarterly* 63 (4): 963–973.

Wemple, Erik. 2014. "New York Times Editor on China Visa Problem: 'We're a Little Bit Hostages.'" *Washington Post*, November 12, 2014. Available at: https://www.washingtonpost.com/blogs/erik-wemple/wp/2014/11/12/new-york-times-editor-on-china-visa-problem-were-a-little-bit-hostages/?noredirect=on&utm_term=.bc5690f66adc (accessed March 24, 2019).

Wen, Philip, Michael Martina, and Ben Blanchard. 2018. "Exclusive: In Rare Coordinated Move, Western Envoys Seek Meeting on Xinjiang Concerns." *Reuters*, November 15, 2018. Available at: https://www.reuters.com/article/us-china-xinjiang-exclusive/exclusive-in-rare-coordinated-move-western-envoys-seek-meeting-on-xinjiang-concerns-idUSKCN1NK0H0 (accessed May 14, 2020).

Weyland, Kurt. 2017a. "Autocratic Diffusion and Cooperation: The Impact of Interests vs. Ideology." *Democratization* 24 (7): 1235–1252.

Weyland, Kurt. 2017b. "Fascism's Missionary Ideology and the Autocratic Wave of the Interwar Years." *Democratization* 24 (7): 1253–1270.

Whang, Taehee, Michael Lammbrau, and Hyung-min Joo. 2017. "Talking to Whom? The Changing Audience of North Korean Nuclear Tests." *Social Science Quarterly* 98 (3): 976–992.

White, Duncan. 2019. *Cold Warriors: Writers Who Waged the Literary Cold War*. London: Little, Brown.

Whitehead, Laurence. 2014. "Antidemocracy Promotion: Four Strategies in Search of a Framework." *Taiwan Journal of Democracy* 10 (2): 1–24.

Wickham, Dorothy. 2019. "The Lesson from My Trip to China? Solomon Islands Is Not Ready to Deal with This Giant." *The Guardian*, December 22, 2019. https://www.theguardian.com/world/commentisfree/2019/dec/23/the-lesson-from-my-trip-to-china-solomon-islands-is-not-ready-to-deal-with-this-giant (accessed April 4, 2020).

Wilson, Jeanne L. 2015. "Russia and China Respond to Soft Power: Interpretation and Readaptation of a Western Concept." *Politics* 35 (3–4): 287–300.

Wong, Edward. 2013. "Bloomberg News Is Said to Curb Articles That Might Anger China." *New York Times*, November 8, 2013. Available at: https://www.nytimes.com/2013/11/09/world/asia/bloomberg-news-is-said-to-curb-articles-that-might-anger-china.html?pagewanted=all (accessed March 24, 2019).

Wong, Edward. 2016. "Xi Jinping's News Alert: Chinese Media Must Serve the Party." *New York Times*, February 22, 2016. Available at: https://www.nytimes.com/2016/02/23/world/asia/china-media-policy-xi-jinping.html (accessed November 11, 2019).

Wrong, Michela. 2019. "Rwanda's Khashoggi: Who Killed the Exiled Spy Chief?" *The Guardian*, January 15, 2019. Available at: https://www.theguardian.com/news/2019/jan/15/rwanda-who-killed-patrick-karegeya-exiled-spy-chief (accessed April 17, 2020).

Xinjiang Victims Database. 2019. "Xinjiang Victims Database." Available at: https://shahit.biz/eng/ (accessed January 3, 2020).

Xu, Jian, and Yongrong Cao. 2019. "The Image of Beijing in Europe: Findings from *The Times, Le Figaro, Der Spiegel* from 2000 to 2015." *Place Branding and Public Diplomacy* 15 (3): 185–197.

Yablokov, Ilya. 2015. "Conspiracy Theories as a Russian Public Diplomacy Tool: The Case of Russia Today (RT)." *Politics* 35 (3–4): 301–315.

Yakouchyk, Katsiaryna. 2019. "Beyond Autocracy Promotion: A Review." *Political Studies Review* 17 (2): 147–160.

Yang, Jisheng. 2013. *Tombstone: The Great Chinese Famine, 1958–1962*. New York: Farrar Straus Giroux.

Yeh, Emily. 2012. "On 'Terrorism' and the Politics of Naming." *Hot Spots, Fieldsights*, April 8, 2012. Available at: https://culanth.org/fieldsights/on-terrorism-and-the-politics-of-naming (accessed April 9, 2020).

Yeo, Andrew, and Danielle Chubb. 2018. *North Korean Human Rights: Activists and Networks*. New York: Cambridge University Press.

York, Geoffrey. 2012. "How a U.S. Agency Cleaned Up Rwanda's Genocide-Stained Image." *Globe & Mail*, January 31, 2012. Available at: https://www.theglobeandmail.com/news/world/how-a-us-agency-cleaned-up-rwandas-genocide-stained-image/article542612/ (accessed April 4, 2019).

York, Geoffrey. 2019. "Suspects in Murder of Rwandan Dissident Patrick Karegeya Are 'Directly Linked' to Paul Kagame's Government, Police Say." *Globe & Mail*, April 18, 2019. Available at: https://www.theglobeandmail.com/world/article-suspects-in-murder-of-rwandan-dissident-patrick-karegeya-are-directly/ (accessed April 17, 2020).

Young, Benjamin R. 2015. "Hammer, Sickle, and the Shamrock: North Korea's Relations with the Worker's Party of Ireland." *Journal of Northeast Asian History* 12 (2): 105–130.

Young, Benjamin R. 2018. "Not There for the Nutmeg: North Korean Advisors in Grenada and Pyongyang's Internationalism, 1979–1983." *Cross-Currents: East Asian History and Culture Review* 7 (2): 364–387.

Young, Benjamin R. 2020. "Cultural Diplomacy with North Korean Characteristics: Pyongyang's Exportation of the Mass Games to the Third World, 1972–1996." *International History Review* 42 (3): 543–555.

Young, Joseph K., and Steve Shellman. 2019. "Protestors, Terrorists, or Something Else? How to Think about Dissident Groups." *Conflict Management and Peace Science* 36 (6): 645–660.

Youssef, Nour. 2017. "Egyptian Police Detain Uighurs and Deport Them to China." *New York Times*, July 6, 2017. Available at: https://www.nytimes.com/2017/07/06/world/asia/egypt-muslims-uighurs-deportations-xinjiang-china.html (accessed April 9, 2020).

Zakaria, Fareed. 1994. "Culture Is Destiny: A Conversation with Lee Kuan Yew." *Foreign Affairs* 73 (2): 109–126.

Zand, Bernhard. 2018. "A Surveillance State Unlike Any the World Has Ever Seen." *Spiegel Online*, July 26, 2018. Available at: http://www.spiegel.de/international/world/china-s-xinjiang-province-a-surveillance-state-unlike-any-the-world-has-ever-seen-a-1220174.html (accessed December 14, 2018).

Zenz, Adrian. 2019. "'Thoroughly Reforming Them Towards a Healthy Heart Attitude': China's Political Re-education Campaign in Xinjiang." *Central Asian Survey* 38 (1): 102–128.

Zhao, Kejin. 2015. "The Motivation behind China's Public Diplomacy." *Chinese Journal of International Politics* 8 (2): 167–196.

Zhao, Kejin. 2016. "China's Rise and Its Discursive Power Strategy." *Chinese Political Science Review* 1 (3): 539–564.

Zhong, Raymond, Aaron Krolik, Paul Mozur, Ronen Bergman, and Edward Wong. 2020. "Behind China's Twitter Campaign, a Murky Supporting Chorus." *New York Times*, June 8, 2020. Available at: https://www.nytimes.com/2020/06/08/technology/china-twitter-disinformation.html (accessed November 13, 2020).

Zorbas, Eugenia. 2011. "Aid Dependence and Policy Independence: Explaining the Rwandan Paradox." In Scott Strauss and Lars Waldorf, eds., *Remaking Rwanda: State Building and Human Rights after Mass Violence*. Madison: University of Wisconsin Press, pp. 103–117.

Index

Tables and Figures are indicated by *t* and *f* following the page number.